5-04

IN PURSUIT OF
HAPPINESS

Other books by Frank Minirth

Christian Psychiatry
Love Is a Choice
Happiness Is a Choice
100 Ways to Overcome Depression

IN PURSUIT OF HAPPINESS

CHOICES THAT CAN CHANGE YOUR LIFE

FRANK MINIRTH, M.D.

Fleming H. Revell
A Division of Baker Book House Co
Grand Rapids, Michigan 49516

Published by Fleming H. Revell
a division of Baker Book House Company
P.O. Box 6287, Grand Rapids, MI 49516-6287
www.bakerbooks.com

Printed in the United States of America

Library of Congress Cataloging-in-Publication Data
Minirth, Frank B.
    In pursuit of happiness : choices that can change your life / Frank Minirth.
        p.   cm.
    Includes bibliographical references.
    ISBN 0-8007-1851-8 (cloth)
    1. Christian life. 2. Emotions—Religious aspects—Christianity. 3. Decision making—Religious aspects—Christianity. I. Title.
BV4501.3.M56 2004
248.8'6—dc22   2003021642

Some of the information in this book is medical. This book is not intended as a specific medical guide for any individual, in any regard, for any disease. It is not intended for the purpose of diagnosing, treating, curing, or preventing any disease. It is not intended as a specific medical guide for those helping others. It is the author's belief that every person needs a personal physician regarding any health decision.

Contents

Preface 9

Introduction: Choices—the Hinges of Destiny 11

1. Discouragement: Pursuing Hope 13
2. Depression: Pursuing Well-Being 24
3. Anger: Pursuing Forgiveness 47
4. Anxiety: Pursuing Peace 52
5. Worry: Pursuing Calm 62
6. Stress: Pursuing Rest 68
7. Loss and Grief: Pursuing Comfort 84
8. Trials: Pursuing Victory 91
9. Loneliness: Pursuing Relationships 106
10. Drug Abuse: Pursuing Freedom 116
11. Marriage: Pursuing Unity 123
12. Teens: Pursuing Basic Needs 129
13. Troubled Teens: Pursuing Help 134
14. The Mature Years: Pursuing Fulfillment 142
15. Reviving Hope 153
16. Changing Your Life Forever 157

Appendixes 166

A Scriptures for Encouragement 167
B Depression and Grace 186
C Should a Christian Use Psychiatric Medications? 187

D   The Brain under Stress: Neuroimaging of the Brain   189
E   Data on Major Depressive Disorder (MDD)   197
F   Major Depressive Disorder Differential   198
G   The Synapses, Neurotransmitters, and Chemicals
     within the Nerve Cell   201
H   Stress, Genetics, and Choice   207
I   The Chemistry of Depression   209
J   The Antidepressants   211
K   Medications and Herbs: Past, Present, Future   213
L   Common Medications and Herbs for Anxiety   226
M   Troubled Teens and Medication   230
N   Medications and Herbs for Dementia   232
O   Medications for Seniors   234
P   Drugs with Possible Antidepressant Effects   237
Q   Possible Antidepressants of the Future   240
R   Genetic Factors in Psychiatric Disorders   241
S   Psychiatric Medications by Categories of Use   243

Notes   253
Glossary   254
Bibliography   275

Preface

It was 1978—President Jimmy Carter was sharing the gospel; Billy Graham was leading thousands to Christ; Bill Bright was pursuing his goal of spreading the good news to every nation; Bill Gothard was lecturing to thousands on the subject of basic youth conflicts; Wycliff Translators were continuing their goal of translating the Bible in every language; James Dobson was establishing Focus on the Family; some churches were drifting liberal, while others stood firm; Rev. Jim Jones alarmed the world by ordering the mass suicide of more than nine hundred followers; a 7.7 earthquake in Iran killed more than twenty-five thousand people; the minimum wage was $2.65 and a new car cost $5,405—when *Happiness Is a Choice* hit a nerve and was destined to become the number one Christian book on depression of all time.

Now we live in a different world—medical knowledge has doubled every five years, Life 101 has become an ever challenging course, and my knowledge of the Scripture has greatly increased in scope. Our times demand a new and more comprehensive book to complement *Happiness Is a Choice. In Pursuit of Happiness* does just that—dealing not only with choices for overcoming depression but also with choices for overcoming anger, discouragement, anxiety, worry, stress, loss, grief, trials, loneliness, and drug abuse and dealing with healthy choices for marriage, teens, and seniors. In short, this is a book that shows the way to pursue happiness through our medical, behavioral, and, most important of all, spiritual choices. Even the appendixes and glossary are filled with practical details.

9

It was 1978—Mary Alice and I celebrated our tenth anniversary, we had our second daughter, and God blessed far beyond our dreams the ministry he had entrusted to us.

My prayer, as you read this book, is that you will learn how to pursue happiness in every area of your life.

Choices—the Hinges of Destiny

> Two roads diverged in a wood, and I—
> I took the one less traveled by,
> And that has made all the difference.
>
> Robert Frost

Is happiness a choice? Are choices the very hinges of destiny? Do we make choices or are we just a product of our genes, as some scientists say? Are we just a product of our past, as some psychologists say? Are we just a product of God's sovereignty, as some theologians say? Indeed, do we have a free will? Do we chart our own course in life, or are we just on autopilot?

I believe we can make choices in life that will produce health and will help us overcome emotional problems (addictions, anxiety, anger, discouragement, depression, despair, burnout, grief, guilt, loneliness, and worry). We can learn about choices and how to make the ones that will give us hope and happiness.

Webster's *New World Thesaurus* provides the following synonyms for the word *choice:* selection, preference, alternative, election, substitute, favorite, pick, a good bet. It is my premise that choices or alternatives or preferences are the hinges of destiny. The closing lines of Robert Frost's classic poem illustrate this:

Two roads diverged in a wood, and I—
I took the one less traveled by,
And that has made all the difference.

While I was growing up, my family attended a small evangelical church where, I recall, there was a tremendous emphasis on choice. In my memory I can still see the little white church in a grove of trees in the country, and my mind still reverberates with the hymns we sang that focused on will: "Why do you wait, dear brother, O why do you tarry so long? . . . Why not accept His salvation?" "Renounce at once thy stubborn will, be saved, O tonight." "'Almost persuaded,' now to believe; 'almost persuaded,' Christ to receive."[1]

Many years later I attended a seminary that emphasized the sovereignty of God. A few of my colleagues did not even believe in free will. They felt we didn't really have a choice in anything. They agreed with a Calvinist who, when he fell over a log accidentally, said, "Thank God that's over." Ironically, during this same time period, I wrote two best-selling books on choice: *Happiness Is a Choice* and *Love Is a Choice*.

Do our free will and God's sovereignty exist only as a paradox? The Bible teaches both. They do not negate one another. The Bible certainly teaches the sovereignty of God, but it also teaches the concept of choice.

The best-known verse on choice is Joshua 24:15: "Choose for yourselves this day whom you will serve. . . . But as for me and my house, we will serve the LORD." Another interesting verse on choice is found in the New Testament: "But one thing is needed, and Mary has chosen that good part, which will not be taken away from her" (Luke 10:42). A third great verse on choice is found in Deuteronomy 30:19: "I call heaven and earth as witness today against you, that I have set before you life and death, blessing and cursing; therefore choose life, that both you and your descendants may live."

I still believe in the sovereignty of God. He is omnipotent, ubiquitous, immutable, and in complete control; and yet the Bible also teaches the importance of our individual choice. It is our responsibility to choose to follow him and to choose the ways that lead to health and happiness.

1

Discouragement

Pursuing Hope

If you would have some worthwhile plans
You've got to watch your can'ts and can's.

Walter B. Knight

Have you ever felt discouraged? Life does have a way of discouraging most of us from time to time, and we begin to feel that we don't have what it takes to get the job done. The stresses of life can easily bring us down into despair, ready to give up. There are many people, now considered famous, who at one time felt like we do. They were common, ordinary people who did not give up when discouragement struck. Instead, they tried just one more time, they made the necessary new choices, and they achieved success.

As a kid, I used to entertain the fantasy that there was buried treasure in the woods behind my house. I spent many a day looking for that pot of gold. Needless to say, I never found a treasure in my backyard, but since then I have found something more valuable than gold. I have discovered that the right choices can bring me the most treasured commodity in the world—happiness. There may be buried treasure in your own backyard. The choices you make can lead you to it.

In this chapter there are choices that will help you overcome the discouragement you face when you feel ordinary or when other

13

stresses of life weigh on your shoulders. Remember that often God uses ordinary people, whose potential may not be obvious, for extraordinary purposes.

Many years ago Basil Miller wrote a book that included a story with encouragement that still rings true today. He retold a Persian legend about a wealthy landowner who was one day visited by a traveler. This visitor showed the Persian nobleman a huge piece of gold, which the Persian offered to buy. When his offer was refused, the nobleman determined to do whatever was necessary to find for himself a piece of gold as large and beautiful as the one he had seen. He sold his extensive estate and began wandering around the world in search of his treasure.

Years later a ragged, tired traveler stopped at the same wealthy estate. While there, he saw several pieces of gold as beautiful as the one he had coveted. On inquiring where they had come from, he was told that they had been buried in the bed of the crystal stream running at the rear of one of the stables.

This traveler was he who had once owned the estate. He had searched the world for gold, but all the while it was buried near his back door, beneath the grass, within easy reach![1]

You too may have gold within reach, but your sense of discouragement keeps you from seeing it. Under your discouragement, there may be hope. Hidden in your feeling of being ordinary, there may be an extraordinary purpose. In your struggle, there may be victory. Within a passing opportunity, there may be success.

By choosing not to give in to discouragement, you can go from ordinary to extraordinary. You can go from defeat to victory. You can go from failure to success. Here are twelve choices for overcoming discouragement.

■ Overcoming Discouragement

1. Don't Stop Short of the Gold

During the California Gold Rush, there was a man who sold all he had and bought a mine. He worked for many months and found nothing. Finally, in frustration he gave up and sold it to people in the East. Several years later, the new owners decided to check the mine for gold. They found the rusted pick where the old miner had abandoned it and the lantern where it had sat when it went out. They started to dig, and before long they found gold. They had dug only six inches—the old miner had been six inches short of the gold!

So often in our own lives we stop too soon. We give up at the first sign of failure. We get discouraged. I believe God is fervently searching: "For the eyes of the LORD run to and fro throughout the whole earth, to show Himself strong on behalf of those whose heart is loyal to Him" (2 Chron. 16:9). God is looking: "I sought for a man among them who would make a wall, and stand in the gap" (Ezek. 22:30). God is looking for men and women so he can find the gold in their lives through Christ. Don't stop short of realizing your potential in Christ—don't stop short of the gold.

2. Ride Out Your Storm

There are many people who have not realized their potential because they are so beaten down by the storms of life. A friend once asked Stradivarius, who perfected the violin, how long it took to make a violin. Stradivarius said, "A thousand years." He went on to say that a violin can be made only from a tree that is tempered by the wind, beaten by sleet, scorched by summer, and blasted by the ice of winter—a thousand years. In other words, it takes a very strong, weather-worn tree to make a violin. A protected tree would never do.

Likewise, it's often the people who have experienced failure who can realize the gold in their life. Failure may seem like an enemy, but if we respond to it with renewed determination to persevere, it can be beneficial. Handel said, "Our antagonist is our greatest helper." Only those who have learned how to bear their burdens and keep going can help lift the burdens of others.

John Bunyan wrote *Pilgrim's Progress,* one of the best-sellers of all time, a truly great Christian book, in the New Bedford jail. Milton wrote his sweetest poems while in total blindness. When I wrote *Christian Psychiatry,* I sent it to seven different publishers; I received six responses with the words, "Returned with thanks." The seventh one accepted it. That book, to some degree, set the pace for Christian psychiatry around the globe. I remember how I felt at age twelve when I was diagnosed with diabetes. Yet, if there had not been diabetes, there would be no clinic today; there would be no books; there would be no radio program for Christ.

The disappointments and failures of life may very well move us toward Christ and spur us on to do things for him. This is illustrated in Scripture, especially in the life of one of my favorite characters in the Bible, the apostle Paul. In his second letter to the Corinthians, Paul writes:

> And He said to me, "My grace is sufficient for you, for My strength is made perfect in weakness." Therefore most gladly I will rather boast in my infirmities, that the power of Christ may rest upon me. Therefore I take pleasure in infirmities, in reproaches, in needs, in persecutions, in distresses, for Christ's sake. For when I am weak, then I am strong.
>
> 2 Corinthians 12:9–10

3. Realize God Uses Ordinary People

You say, "But I'm just ordinary." I say, "Congratulations! You're God's kind of person. God uses ordinary people just like you." Paul states it like this:

> For you see your calling, brethren, that not many wise according to the flesh, not many mighty, not many noble, are called. But God has chosen the foolish things of the world to put to shame the wise, and God has chosen the weak things of the world to shame the things which are mighty.
>
> 1 Corinthians 1:26–27

God chooses ordinary people. When I think about this, I always think of Gideon. When God's chosen nation of Israel fell into sin and trouble, God chose an unlikely source to lead them out. Gideon was the least member of his family. His family was the least family in the tribe. So when God got ready, he chose one of the least of the least. "He said to Him, 'O my Lord, how can I save Israel? Indeed my clan is the weakest in Manasseh, and I am the least in my father's house.' And the LORD said to him, 'Surely I will be with you'" (Judges 6:15–16). God uses ordinary people just like you and me.

In Hebrews 11, God's hall of fame, we are reminded that God chose liars, drunkards, adulterers, manipulators, those who had been irreverent, and a harlot. He even chose a shepherd boy. God chooses people with flaws, ordinary people just like us.

4. Dream Your Dreams

Envision what you can do for Christ, and then let him make your dream a reality in your life. Let him reveal the gold in you.

Livingston had a vision of going to Africa. He did it for Jesus Christ. Moody was told that the world has yet to see what God can do with a man totally dedicated to him. Moody came as close as anyone to being that man. Beethoven said, "There are not any erected barriers which can say to aspiring talent, 'Thus far and no farther.'"

I remember many years ago when I was in medical school, Mary Alice and I came across Habakkuk 1:5, and we said to Christ, "We're not gifted, but we love you. We both pray that you will make that verse come true in our lives, that we will work a work for you in our days through Christ." Mary Alice and I committed ourselves to basing our lives on that verse. We were willing to give everything we had in life to accomplish a dream for Christ.

This is what God wants us to do. Dream the dream for Christ and then take advantage of the opportunities he provides to chart the unknown, set a new course, or blaze a new trail. It will take a lifetime of devotion to accomplish all that God wants to do through us.

Many years ago a lady spoke at a commencement and said that she believed God was looking for someone to have a great ministry for him, maybe another Spurgeon, maybe another Dwight L. Moody. In that group sat the young Billy Graham who went on to become the greatest evangelist the world has ever known.

If Edison, then you; if Lincoln, then you; if Billy Graham, then you; if Dwight L. Moody, then you; if Wesley, then you. It's through the determination of fulfilling your dream for Christ that you are strengthened to fight the fight, scale the peaks, and overcome the enemy. First Corinthians 9:26 says, "Therefore I run thus: not with uncertainty. Thus I fight: not as one who beats the air." Dream the dream, whether big or small, for Jesus Christ.

5. Don't Let the Negatives Defeat You

Don't let negative words that others speak defeat you, keep you from realizing your potential, and prevent you from finding gold in your life through Christ. I'm sure you have heard things like: "You won't succeed." "You can't be happy." "You have nothing to offer." "You'll never amount to anything." Though the person was wrong to say such things, still, they were said. It's up to you to refuse to let them defeat you. Focus on what you know to be true. Go on for Christ.

6. Realize That You Are Special

A few years ago I made an amazing discovery. I'm the best in the world at doing what I do. I may not be the best at exegesis or the best at surgery or the best at many things, but as a whole package, I'm God's best—and you are too. You are God's best in the whole world at the ministry he has for you. You are very special.

I remember when Rachel, our oldest daughter, was born. Mary Alice and I had been married for seven years and had prayed many years for a special child. We had lost several babies trying to have Rachel. We claimed Genesis 29:20, "So Jacob served seven years for Rachel, and they seemed but a few days to him because of the love he had for her." We wanted Rachel to know that she was something special. We claimed it for her. There is a song by Bill Gaither that I used to sing to Rachel: "You're something special. You're the only one of your kind."

7. Focus on Behavior

Most of us struggle with certain behaviors we'd like to change or with certain goals we'd like to achieve. You may feel that it's impossible to change and move in the direction you would like to go, but there are steps you can take to turn things around.

Start with behavior. People often feel so bad that they think they will never feel like doing anything; but if they wait until they *feel* better, they may be right. You have no control over how you feel. You can't say to yourself, *Hey, I feel bad and I'm going to feel good,* and, presto, you feel good. It's as though feelings have a mind of their own. What we can control, however, is what we do. We can control what time we get up, whether we exercise, and whether we memorize Scripture. We can control whether we call a friend who can cheer us up. We are in control of what we do.

Be creative. Brainstorm. Name your problems and write them down. Then list at least one hundred options for fixing them. Don't evaluate the ideas as you write, because you will stifle your creativity. List every option that flows through that creative mind of yours, no matter how outlandish it may seem. When you get to about one hundred, go back and pick out five to ten of the good options. You may be surprised. Sometimes the options that sounded crazy turn out to have potential later.

Be specific. People usually don't follow through because they're not specific about what they want to do. Be specific, making detailed plans.

Start small. For example, to begin with, do just ten push-ups per day for exercise. Memorize just one verse per month for spiritual growth. Talk to just one person per week for encouragement. Start small.

Use your time wisely. Abraham Lincoln went from a cabin to the White House by using what he called "two spare minutes a day." Lincoln would tear pages from books and paste them to a plow. As he plowed, he would read those pages. Making good use of spare moments can reap great benefits. Many years ago, Dr. Elliott, president of Harvard, said if a person used fifteen minutes a day reading the classics, then in ten years, he or she would have a better education than anyone who finished Harvard. Fifteen minutes a day can make a huge difference.

Be committed. If you fail, don't get discouraged. If you fail, make a new plan, set small goals, and commit yourself anew. Allow *no* excuses.

Start with what you have. You have Christ, and he wants to help you overcome negative behaviors and reach your goals.

8. Count the Cost

An extremely interesting verse is tucked away in Luke 14:28: "For which of you, intending to build a tower, does not sit down first and count the cost?" One summer we were high in the mountains of Montana, and we took an evening horseback ride. As we followed the trail, we started up a little mountain and went higher and higher and higher. I got to thinking, one misstep by our horses would send us plunging hundreds and hundreds of feet down below. I became more and more concerned and began to wish we had not attempted the trail. As it turned out, we finished the ride safely, and at the end we saw an unbelievably beautiful sunset.

There's an old story of the Amazon about a young man taken by a guide high into the Andes. They went higher and higher. The mountains were jagged and steep. There were deep valleys and gorges below. Finally, they went between two mountains that were so close together that the sun shone there hardly more than an hour or two a day. They went into a cave near the source of the Amazon. Inside, there were obvious signs of gold just beneath the soil in a crystal clear stream that flowed in the back. The guide said, "This is yours for mining if you want to do it." The young man said, "I think the cost is too high."

The guide later brought another young man to the place and asked, "What do you think? Is the cost too high?" This young man said, "I've counted the cost, and I think there are nuggets galore. There are veins of gold. I'm going for the gold just beneath the surface."

My prayer for you is that you count the cost and then go for the gold in your life. To do this, you must recognize that reaching the gold is worth the struggle. The gold may result from giving up some sin for peace with God. The gold may result from giving up financial dishonesty for peace of mind. The gold may result from giving up an affair for a wonderful wife and children. Reaching the gold is always worth the cost.

9. Overcome the Most Common "I Can'ts"

A great orator once said, "They can, because they think they can." To that I would add, "We can, because we think we can through Christ." Our success is always through Christ.

For many years, Henry Ford told engineers working for him to build an eight-cylinder motor. They kept saying it couldn't be done. He said to do it anyway, and eventually they did.

My mother always said, "*Can't* never could do anything." Many people never reach their potential because they think they are incapable. The reality is that we can do whatever Christ wants us to do. He doesn't want all of us to do the same thing, but there is something uniquely suited to each person's skills that he or she can accomplish. It's important to discover what we are suited for so we're not pursuing an unrealistic goal. God will help us fulfill our potential and go from the "I can't" to the "I can through Christ."

Here are the "I can'ts" I hear most often:

"I can't do it because I'm not smart enough." Daniel Webster was considered slow in learning. Isaac Newton was never a leader of his class. Albert Einstein, with one of the greatest intellects of all time, had a lot of trouble in school. Adam Clark, a well-known Bible commentator, was a school dunce as a boy. Thomas Edison, *Time Life*'s selection as the greatest contributor to humanity in the last hundred years, flunked out of school because of his inability to pay attention (perhaps he had attention-deficit/hyperactivity disorder, or ADHD). Edison's parents were told to take him home, that he didn't belong in school. Do you know how many times Babe Ruth struck out on his way to more than seven hundred home runs? Thousands of times.

All of these men caught the vision that they were special and could do what needed to be done. In any area of life, there will be times of failure. You'll hit some home runs, and you will fail at times. That doesn't mean you can't get the job done. You can get it done through Christ.

"I can't because I'm too poor." Gifford, the great mathematician, wrote his first book on scraps of leather while working as a shop apprentice. Ritenhouse calculated eclipses on a plow handle. Emerson said of the great Galileo, "Galileo discovered more splendid signs of celestial phenomenon with an opera glass than anyone since with a great telescope." These men may have been poor, but they didn't let that stop them from accomplishing great things.

The same principle applies to us. It's not how rich we are in material goods that matters. It is how rich we are in Christ. Let him supply all you need to accomplish all he wants you to do. And use what he gives you.

"I can't because my parents told me I couldn't." Parents need to be aware of the powerful influence their prophecies concerning their children can have. And children must remember that the most powerful influence in their life is not parents (good and bad) but Christ. He often helps people do what seemed impossible.

10. Be Persistent

Jesus told an interesting story:

"There was a widow in that city, and she kept coming to [the judge], saying, 'Give me legal protection from my opponent.' For a while he was unwilling; but afterward he said to himself, 'Even though I do not fear God nor respect man, yet because this widow bothers me, I will give her legal protection, otherwise by continually coming she will wear me out.'"

Luke 18:3–5 NASB

The widow knew her only hope was in the judge's protection, so she was persistent in her request until she got what she needed.

You too must be persistent. It is one of the most important factors in your reaching your potential.

11. Dwell with Christ

The key to reaching your potential doesn't lie within you. Christ expects you to be responsible, but your potential dwells in him. The key to reaching your potential is to let Christ do it through you. It has to be Christ. There's no way we can compare with his power. There is a Persian fable about a piece of clay that had an uncommonly sweet fragrance. The clay was questioned as to its true identity. It was thought that it had to be something other than common clay:

> "Nay, I am but a piece of clay."
> "Then whence this wondrous sweetness, pray?"
> "Friend, if the secret I disclose,
>   I have been dwelling with a rose."

In the same way we must dwell with Christ, making our relationship with him the most important part of our life. As we become more like him, he will be able to use us for his glory.

Many years ago, Mary Alice and I claimed 1 Chronicles 4:10: "And Jabez called on the God of Israel, saying, 'Oh, that You would bless me indeed, and enlarge my territory, that Your hand would be with me, and that You would keep me from evil, that I may not cause pain!' So God granted him what he requested."

If God's hand is with you, then you will reach your potential, for he will help you do it.

12. Actualize the Impossible

The Pyrenees Mountains rise between France and Spain. When Napoleon was planning to conquer Spain, people asked him how he could do it with all those mountains in the way. He said, "Mountains? There are no mountains." What he was doing was actualizing the impossible.

Moses was slow of speech, but he actualized becoming a great leader for God. Elijah was a rugged mountain man, but he was one of two men who never saw death. Daniel was a slave boy, and he actualized living in the lions' den overnight. Martin Luther was extremely obsessive in some ways, and he actualized the Reformation.

Through Christ we too can actualize the impossible, even if we have experienced failure. Others have done it. After Samson had failed God, he still pulled down a temple and did a great feat for God. David went on to greatness after his fall into sin with Bathsheba.

Actualize the impossible. Emblazon that credo on your brain. Go for the gold just under the grass. Let's do it for Christ.

■ Follow-Up

It is possible to overcome discouragement. You can do it by choosing one of the above twelve tools and applying it daily for one week; then pick another one to practice for one week. Do this for three months, trying a new tool each week. It may be helpful to rate your discouragement on a scale of one (very little discouragement) to ten (extreme discouragement) now and again at the end of three months. You can overcome discouragement. Often gold lies just beneath the grass.

2

Depression

Pursuing Well-Being

The fault, dear Brutus, is not in our stars but in ourselves. Each one of us is free to chart our destiny in the exercise of choice.

William Shakespeare

Depression affects everyone to some degree. Significant, medical-type depression affects more than seventeen million Americans annually. The lifetime prevalence (chance of experiencing the condition during a person's lifetime) approaches a staggering 20 percent. It is more common than coronary heart disease and cancer combined (seventeen million people versus thirteen million people). It can be lethal (leading to suicide). The cost is high in the form of pain, family conflict, and social withdrawal. It also takes an economic toll through work absenteeism, reduced productivity, unemployment, and alcohol and drug abuse.

The cost of treating major depressive disorders is more annually than the cost of treating coronary heart disease, but, still, depression remains undertreated. Less than 25 percent of people afflicted with depression receive adequate antidepressant medication, even though it can often be treated more effectively than can coronary heart disease and cancer. Left untreated, the probability of a more resistant type of depression may increase, with the potential for other lifelong implications.

■ What Is Depression?

Depression is a disturbance of mood. It involves a happy-sad axis. One who is experiencing depression may exhibit a sad affect, have painful thoughts, be melancholy, develop a variety of physical symptoms, and be anxious. Depressed individuals feel blue and often experience anhedonia, a loss of interest in things normally pleasurable. They may experience irritability, a disturbance of sleep or appetite, a loss of energy or fatigue, a decreased ability to make decisions, a diminished self-worth, a tendency to ruminate, recurrent thoughts of not wanting to live, and various medical complaints for which no other medical cause can be found.

In the Middle Ages there was a demonic emphasis in explanations of depression. In the years between 1850 and 1900, there was the idea that depression was due to medical disease. The next fifty years witnessed a shift to an emphasis on psychological factors as the underlying cause of depression. In the 1950s "biological underpinnings" were the focus. In 1984 a new question was considered: Can mental illness be explained on the basis of changes within the brain? Neuroscientists are now at a point in their research at which answers to such questions may soon be possible. During the 1990s, the focus was on the interactions of biological and psychological factors. Thus we are moving closer to the biblical emphasis that we are indeed spirit and soul and body.

■ Types of Depression

Women experience depression at a two to one ratio over men. A major depressive disorder is defined by experiencing five of the following symptoms during a two-week period: increase in unhappy feelings, decrease in interests, change in weight, change in sleep habits, agitation or retardation of speech, decrease in energy, increase in guilt, increase in feelings of worthlessness, decrease in concentration, and increased thoughts of death.

A *manic episode* will have presenting symptoms such as an abnormally elevated, expansive, and irritable mood for more than one week, increase in grandiosity, decrease in sleep, increase in talking and number of thoughts, increase in distractibility, increase in goal-directed activity and in activities with painful consequences (three or more), and marked impairment of occupation, socialization, and relationships.

A *dysthymic disorder* is evidenced by a depressed mood that continues for at least two years.

A *cyclothymic disorder* will continue for a two-year period and is characterized by numerous periods of hypomanic symptoms (mild mania) and alternating periods of depressive symptoms. The depressive symptoms are not as severe as those in major depressive disorder.

A *bipolar II disorder* is major depression with hypomanic episodes. This diagnosis may be indicated when one or more major depressive and hypomanic episodes have occurred that cause significant distress or impairment to one's functioning.

A *mood disorder due to general medical condition* is characterized by one's mood becoming disrupted when there is direct evidence that the underlying cause is a medical disease, such as pancreatic cancer or hypothyroidism.

A *substance-induced mood disorder* may be the diagnosis when there is sufficient physical and historical evidence of a disturbance of mood due to substance use or withdrawal.

An *adjustment disorder with disturbance of mood* may be evidenced when one's emotional or behavioral symptoms increase due to an identifiable stressor(s) during a three-month period.

■ Causes of Depression

Genetic and Chemical Factors

There can be physiological causes for depression. Family studies on major depressive disorders (MDD) indicate that 50 percent of those diagnosed with MDD have a first-degree relative who has also been diagnosed with MDD. Studies also conclude that identical twins demonstrate a common occurrence of 50 percent, while fraternal twins show a common occurrence of 15 percent. In studies of bipolar disorders, the data indicates that 90 percent have a first-degree relative who has been diagnosed with a bipolar disorder. Sixty percent of identical twins have a bipolar disorder common occurrence.

A physiological effect known as kindling in ongoing depression may make the depression more resistant to treatment. Prolonged stress can damage the brain. A PET scan will show the effects of prolonged severe depression on the hippocampus of the brain.

It has been found that abnormalities in chromosome X, 11, or 18 may be present in bipolar disorders.

In depressive disorders, there may be imbalances of neurotransmitters, such as 5HT/NE dopamine, and GABA, along with other biochemical abnormalities, such as high cortisol and low brain-derived neurotrophilic factor (BDNF). Low BDNF may be especially important since it nourishes brain cells. Prolonged, intense stress with resulting high cortisol and low BDNF can reveal brain cell atrophy in the frontal cortex, important in emotions, and in the hippocampus, important in emotional memory that lets us know when a stressor is over.

Psychological Factors

As the brain experiences stress, changes in the neurotransmitters may occur. If a child loses a parent before eleven years of age, for example, he would be predisposed to depression. Although anger has often been proposed, and certainly may be a factor in some cases, as the cause of depression, this has never been proven. In a variety of animal studies, indicators show that learned helplessness may, in turn, lead to depression.

■ Depression in the Bible

There are many instances of depression in the Bible. In some cases the cause is external, such as the behavior of other people, and in others it is internal, such as a feeling of guilt or shame. Some examples are given below.

Threat by man. 1 Kings 19:1–4: And Ahab told Jezebel all that Elijah had done, also how he had executed all the prophets with the sword. Then Jezebel sent a messenger to Elijah, saying, "So let the gods do to me, and more also, if I do not make your life as the life of one of them by tomorrow about this time." And when he saw that, he arose and ran for his life, and went to Beersheba, which belongs to Judah, and left his servant there. But he himself went a day's journey into the wilderness, and came and sat down under a broom tree. And he prayed that he might die, and said, "It is enough! Now, LORD, take my life, for I am no better than my fathers!"

Loss. Job 1:13–19; 3:1–3: Now there was a day when his sons and daughters were eating and drinking wine in their oldest brother's house; and a messenger came to Job and said, "The oxen were plowing and the donkeys feeding beside them, when the Sabeans raided them and took them away—indeed they have killed the servants with the edge of the sword; and I alone have escaped to tell you!" While he was still speaking, another also came and said, "The fire of God fell from heaven and burned up the sheep and the servants, and consumed them; and I alone have escaped to tell you!" While he was still speaking, another also came and said, "The Chaldeans formed three bands, raided the camels and took them away, yes, and killed the servants with the edge of the sword; and I alone have escaped to tell you!" While he was still speaking, another also came and said, "Your sons and daughters were eating and drinking wine in their oldest brother's house, and suddenly a great wind came from across the wilderness and struck the four corners of the house, and it fell on the young men, and they are dead; and I alone have escaped to tell you!" . . .

After this Job opened his mouth and cursed the day of his birth. And Job spoke, and said: "May the day perish on which I was born, and the night in which it was said, 'A male child is conceived.'"

Anger. Jonah 2:10–3:3: So the LORD spoke to the fish, and it vomited Jonah onto dry land. Now the word of the LORD came to Jonah the second time, saying, "Arise, go to Nineveh, that great city, and preach to it the message that I tell you." So Jonah arose and went to Nineveh, according to the word of the LORD. Now Nineveh was an exceedingly great city, a three-day journey in extent.

Genesis 4:6–7: So the LORD said to Cain, "Why are you angry? And why has your countenance fallen? If you do well, will you not be accepted? And if you do not do well, sin lies at the door. And its desire is for you, but you should rule over it."

Wrong perspective. Psalm 73:1–3, 16–17: Truly God is good to Israel, to such as are pure in heart. But as for me, my feet had almost stumbled; my steps had nearly slipped. For I was envious of the boastful, when I saw the prosperity of the wicked. . . . When I thought how to understand this, it was too painful for me—until I went into the sanctuary of God; then I understood their end.

Wrong focus. Psalm 42:5: Why are you cast down, O my soul? And why are you disquieted within me? Hope in God, for I shall yet praise Him for the help of His countenance.

Rejection by man. Jeremiah 15:10: Woe is me, my mother, that you have borne me, a man of strife and a man of contention to the whole earth! I have neither lent for interest, nor have men lent to me for interest. Every one of them curses me.

Sin and guilt. Psalm 32:3–5: When I kept silent, my bones grew old through my groaning all the day long. For day and night Your hand was heavy upon me; my vitality was turned into the drought of summer. I acknowledged my sin to You, and my iniquity I have not hidden. I said, "I will confess my transgressions to the LORD," and You forgave the iniquity of my sin.

■ Biblical Means of Overcoming Depression

The Bible not only illustrates causes for depression but also points to choices that lead to health. Consider how the following men overcame depression.

Refocusing. The sons of Korah found release from depression through refocusing. Psalm 42:11: Why are you cast down, O my soul? And why are you disquieted within me? Hope in God; for I shall yet praise Him, the help of my countenance and my God.

Right perspective. Asaph changed his perspective. Psalm 73:16–17: When I thought how to understand this, it was too painful for me—until I went into the sanctuary of God; then I understood their end.

Refreshment. When Elijah found refreshment, his depression left. 1 Kings 19:5–8: Then as he lay and slept under a broom tree, suddenly an angel touched him, and said to him, "Arise and eat." Then he looked, and there by his head was a cake baked on coals, and a jar of water. So he ate and drank, and lay down again. And the angel of the LORD came back the second time, and touched him, and said, "Arise and eat, because the journey is too great for you." So he arose, and ate and drank; and he went in the strength of that food forty days and forty nights as far as Horeb, the mountain of God.

Repentance. David found relief through repentance. Psalm 32:5: I acknowledged my sin to You, and my iniquity I have not hidden. I said, "I will confess my transgressions to the LORD," and You forgave the iniquity of my sin.

Seeing the big picture. Apparently God wanted Jonah to see the big picture so that he wouldn't be angry. Jonah 4:9–11: Then God said to Jonah, "Is it right for you to be angry about the plant?" And he said, "It is right for me to be angry, even to death!" But the LORD said, "You have had pity on the plant for which you have not labored, nor made it grow, which came up in a night and perished in a night. And should I not pity Nineveh, that great city, in which are more than one hundred and twenty thousand persons who cannot discern between their right hand and their left, and also much livestock?"

Experiencing God. Knowing God better relieved Job's depression. Job 42:5: I have heard of You by the hearing of the ear, but now my eye sees You.

Rejoicing in God's Word. God's Word brings joy to Jeremiah. Jeremiah 15:16: Your words were found, and I ate them, and Your word was to me the joy and rejoicing of my heart.

Responsible behavior. If Cain had confessed his behavior and avoided sin, his sense of well-being would have been restored. Genesis 4:6–7: So the LORD said to Cain, "Why are you angry? And why has your countenance fallen? If you do well, will you not be accepted? And if you do not do well, sin lies at the door. And its desire is for you, but you should rule over it."

The observations we draw from these experiences are not absolute since there are so few cases and each is unique. The causes of their depression were diverse. In all cases, however, the most important insight is that the treatment involved a spiritual change or growth.

Whether the treatment for depression is a spiritual change, counseling, medication, or some combination of all of the above, significant treatment tools are available today. When a person is helped to climb out of depression, the benefits for the individual will be great and the value to the cause of Christ may be immeasurable.

■ Future Treatments of Depression

The future should hold many new and innovative treatments for depression. For example, currently more than twenty new medications are in various stages of testing for depression and/or anxiety. In all probability the new medications will become more and more effective and specific and will have fewer and fewer side effects overall. While the medications will be simpler for the patient, they will become more and more complicated for the physician. As understanding of neurotransmitters increases and medications become more highly specific, the physician must be able to determine what combination of medicines is needed to obtain the desired results.

New methods that we could hardly dream of in the past may move out of the research level to practical application. Transcranial magnetic stimulation (TMS), vagal nerve stimulation, and bright light may be three such methods. For example, with TMS magnetic stimulation to the dorsolateral prefrontal cortex is often not only effective but also efficient, and side effects appear very low in general. TMS may be used increasingly especially in augmenting antidepressive treatments and helping in treatment-resistant depression. It may even become a substitute at times for pharmacotherapy or electroconvulsive therapy (ECT). It could complement cognitive and interpersonal psychotherapy in mild to moderate depressive episodes.

Furthermore, the future is already here in one sense in seeing the brain at work in depressive states through positron emission tomography (PET) scans (see appendix D) and magnetic resonance imaging (MRI). However, at a practical level, the current method of assessing chemical depression based on a specific analysis of different emotions may remain the most useful. This current analysis of emotions may be hard to replace because it is simple, effective, and cost efficient. In fact, in the recent past, various chemical tests (such as DST—dexani-ethasone suppressive test—and thyroid tests) did not prove as reliable as the analysis of emotions that is currently used. Though overall they are excellent now, in time, diagnosis and treatment of depression will surely become more and more specific and reliable.

Counseling will probably continue to move more and more toward a behavioral, short-term approach, such as behavior therapy, cognitive therapy, and interpersonal therapy. The past will be dealt with only as it significantly affects the present.

Finally, spiritual considerations will not change, but new methods of communicating the same biblical truths will be developed.

■ Choices That Could Change Your Life Forever

There are certain choices a person can make that can lift a depressed mood. I've used seven of them through the last twenty-five years in my practice of Christian psychiatry. These seven choices, which you may need to make or help someone else make, could change your life forever, moving you from depression to happiness. Actually, these choices apply not only to those who are depressed but to all who are in pursuit of happiness.

1. Be Kind

One area of my life I enjoy almost as much as any is simply talking with depressed individuals at the hospital every Monday night. Why? Because they are so kind to me. They are polite and complimentary. They go out of their way to be nice to me and it feels good. I have often wondered if they are as kind to themselves as they are to me, a stranger to many of them. I doubt it. Typically depressed people are not kind to themselves and are often unable to forgive themselves even though they forgive others.

I have often asked depressed individuals to imagine that they have been duplicated and that all day long their identical twin talks to them as they talk to themselves. How would they feel about their duplicate at the end of the day? Would they say to their duplicate: "You have criticized me all day even over minor mistakes. You refuse to forgive me. Please let me go. I can't take it anymore." You may laugh, but the way we talk to ourselves affects us just as surely as the way others talk to us. Why not be kind to yourself? Aren't you trying to be a good person (perhaps more than many others)? Doesn't 1 John 1:9 say you can be forgiven? Have you ever known a perfect person? Why not let up on yourself? Why not be kind to yourself as you try to change, as you try to pursue happiness?

2. Focus Initially on Behavior

If you are depressed, then according to Reality Therapy your current daily behavioral plan (plan A) is not working. It is easy for depressed people to get in a rut in their behavior, and that behavior, in turn, reinforces their depression. As I said in the last chapter, feelings follow behavior, so why not change the behavior? We have minimal direct control over how we feel, so why not focus on behavior over which we have maximum control? By changing daily, specific behaviors, many individuals have changed their depressed feelings. Indeed, they have learned to pursue happiness.

By a behavior focus, I am talking not about some abstract concept but rather about simple, specific, daily behaviors—what time you get up, whether you exercise daily, whether you have daily relationship input from meaningful others, whether you go over a daily Bible verse that meets a specific need, whether you stop a specific behavior that obviously is not healthy, and so on.

I remember working with a client twenty-five years ago when I first started using the concept. I was a young psychiatrist in Dallas, Texas. I had been trying to help this lady for a few weeks when one day I said to her, "What are you doing to make yourself depressed? Feelings follow behavior, so how is your behavior making you depressed?"

She replied that she did not know what I was talking about, so I asked, "What time do you get up in the morning?" (Most people who are depressed sleep late because they truly feel so bad.) She said she arose at about 7 A.M. That wasn't what I was looking for, but I wrote it down: Plan A: 1. Get up early—7 A.M.

"What do you do then?" I asked. She replied that she helped her child get ready for school. Again, that was not what I was look-

ing for, but I wrote it down: 2. Be responsible—get child ready for
school.

"What do you do then?" I inquired.

"Well, I hate to admit it," she said, "but then I go back to bed
and I stay in bed all day long."

I said, "So your plan for overcoming your depression is to stay
in bed all day long?"

She laughed and said, "No," and I said, "Yes," and wrote it
down.

I inquired further, "Do you get any exercise?"

She said, "Are you kidding? I don't even take my dog for walks
anymore."

I responded, "So your plan for overcoming your depression is
to plan no exercise?"

She laughed and said, "No," and I said, "Yes."

"Do you have any social contact?" I asked.

"I don't even go to church anymore."

I said, "I understand. Your plan for overcoming your depression
is to have no social contact."

She laughed and said, "No," and I said, "Yes."

"Is there anything else you feel I need to know?" I asked.

"Well, I hate to admit it, but I have been drinking a lot of alcohol," she responded.

I said, "I understand. Your plan for overcoming your depression includes drinking a depressant. Alcohol is a depressant, you
know."

She said, "No," and I said, "Yes."

"Is there anything else I need to know?" I asked.

She continued, "Just before my husband arrives home, I get up,
but I look bad."

"I understand," I replied. "So you plan to look bad to overcome
your depression."

"No," she laughed. I said, "Yes."

"Let's examine your behavioral plan A for daily living," I said.

1. Get up early—7 A.M.
2. Be responsible—get child ready for school.
3. Stay in bed all day.
4. Get no exercise.

5. Have no social contact.
6. Drink a depressant.
7. Plan to look bad.

She looked at the plan in black and white and mused, "That is a terrible plan. No wonder I'm depressed."

I encouraged her, "It's easy to get in a rut when you're depressed. But let's change it. Let's make a new plan—plan B." She did, and in two weeks her mood began to lift.

Behaviors and feelings form a cycle.

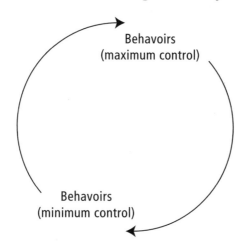

Behavoirs
(maximum control)

Behavoirs
(minimum control)

By going from whatever damaging behavior plan you are in (plan A) to new daily behaviors (plan B), you can go from depression to happiness. You can pursue happiness.

Are you in a rut in your behavior? Is your daily behavior plan not working for you? Why not form a new healthy daily behavioral plan? The new behavioral plan needs to include several things: exercise, relationships, a nutritious diet, spiritual nourishment, stopping or limiting at least one unhealthy behavior, education on overcoming depression, a daily schedule, giving to others, special time with family members, and fun times. What do you have to lose? Commit to a new plan for at least two weeks and see if you feel better.

The success of the new plan will probably depend on whether it includes *small* and *specific* goals and is a plan to which you can give *commitment* with *no excuses*. First, make the goals of the new plan *small*. Do not plan to exercise three hours per day but rather three minutes. Do not commit to memorizing a book of the Bible but rather one verse reviewed and enjoyed daily for two weeks. Do not commit to losing a pound per day but rather to one pound in two weeks. Do not decide to go for one hour of group therapy per day but rather plan a two-minute daily phone call with someone who builds you up. Do not commit to never worrying again but rather to limiting worry time to a problem-solving time of ten minutes per day. Do not plan to read a book per day on problem solving but rather to reading one paragraph per day on problem solving. You can always do more than you've committed to but not less, so start small.

Second, your plan must be *specific*. We do not do what we do not specifically commit to doing. Plans need to be highly specific in regard to what you will do, how long you will do it, and where. Rather than say, "I will start exercising," say, "I will do five push-ups before I leave the house each morning." Rather than say, "I will start memorizing Bible verses," say, "I will review one encouraging verse each night for two weeks just before I go to bed." Rather than say, "I will start doing some fun activities each week," say, "I will have a date with my mate every Friday night." Rather than say, "I will quit worrying," say, "I will do problem solving each evening from 6:00 to 6:10 P.M., and then any time I want to worry, I will remind myself that worry will have to wait until 6:00." If you say, "I may wander over to the hospital for a group therapy session sometime this week," you would probably never go. Say instead, "I will be at the hospital at 8:00 P.M. on Monday night." When plans are specific, we are more apt to do them.

Third, you must commit to your new plan for a period of time. Usually a two- to four-week commitment is necessary before feelings begin to change. Feelings follow behavioral changes, but they often do so slowly. Why not commit to a new seven- to ten-point, daily, specific behavioral plan for a period of at least two weeks? Could a new healthy plan B possibly be worse than your current depressive plan A?

3. Challenge Inaccurate Thinking

We are able to think four hundred to twelve hundred words per minute, and if that thinking is inaccurate and negative, then our mood becomes more and more depressed.

A colleague of mine, Dr. Chris Thurman, along with other cognitive therapists, has described eight depressive thought patterns that need to be challenged as inaccurate and repeatedly replaced with an accurate belief every day.[1] These inaccurate beliefs can be described as magnification, perfectionism, personalization, expectation of happiness when events change, generalization, emotional reasoning, selective attention to the negative, and arbitrary references. If these inaccurate beliefs are not challenged, they will lead the depressed individual further and further into depression. Accurate beliefs will lift a depressed mood. Here are the inaccurate and corresponding accurate beliefs that can help you in your pursuit of happiness.

Magnification. Life is filled with events. Some events are good and some are bad. We tend to think this way:

A produces C.
Events produce responses (emotional, physiological, behavioral).

We tend to think that the event produces the response. Thus we say we had a bad day or a good day, depending on the events of the day. The problem with that thinking is that it leaves out the individual's belief system. In reality, the way we think should look like this:

A, filtered through B, produces C.
Events (good or bad—trials, stressors, losses), filtered through our belief system, produce responses (emotional, physiological, behavioral).

Events can be difficult. Life can be difficult. But depressive individuals, through their inaccurate beliefs, make events worse than they actually are.

Thurman accurately states that our tendency is to take a nickel event and give it a five-thousand-dollar emotional response. Thus the depression intensifies. Rather than give a nickel event a five-thousand-dollar emotional response, why not give a nickel event a nickel emotional response?

Incidentally, the Scriptures can change our belief system dramatically in regard to life events. Consider these verses:

> *Romans 8:28:* And we know that all things work together for good to those who love God, to those who are the called according to His purpose.
>
> *Psalm 103:19:* His sovereignty rules over all (NASB).
>
> *Proverbs 3:5–6:* Trust in the LORD with all your heart, and lean not on your own understanding; in all your ways acknowledge Him, and He shall direct your paths.
>
> *Proverbs 16:9:* A man's heart plans his way, but the LORD directs his steps.
>
> *Jeremiah 29:11:* For I know the thoughts that I think toward you, says the LORD, thoughts of peace and not of evil, to give you a future and a hope.

Perfectionism. Depressed individuals are usually very down on themselves, often to the point of not wanting to live. They believe they are so imperfect that they should not live or at best should live a miserable life. Of course, this belief is not accurate. The accurate belief is that none of us is perfect (Rom. 3:23: "For all have sinned and fall short of the glory of God"). The depressed individual is like a baseball player who expects to hit a home run every time at bat. Every player strikes out at times. We all sin, and there is forgiveness when we do (1 John 1:9: "If we confess our sins, He is faithful and just to forgive us our sins and to cleanse us from all unrighteousness"). We all make mistakes. We all get in trouble. We are all weak at times, and in fact that may be when God can use us the most (2 Cor. 12:9–10: "And He said to me, 'My grace is sufficient for you, for My strength is made perfect in weakness.' Therefore most gladly I will rather boast in my infirmities, that the power of Christ may rest upon me. Therefore I take pleasure in infirmities, in reproaches, in needs, in persecutions, in distresses, for Christ's sake. For when I am weak, then I am strong"). The depressed person must challenge his inaccurate belief that he cannot be forgiven or that only the strong can be effective for Christ.

There is a difference between perfectionism and maturity. None of us will ever be perfect, but we can grow toward maturity in Christ.

Personalization. The depressed person often believes that everything is his fault. He owns emotionally what he did not cause, taking responsibility when it's not his to take. When someone is a jerk to him for no reason, he owns it, he feels bad, he is upset. Why should a person own what he did not cause?

When this happens, challenge yourself with: *Now I am personalizing again. I did not cause this. I am not responsible for another's inappropriate behavior. I refuse to get upset over this individual's being a jerk. I refuse to let it make me feel depressed. I'm going to reject this and shift my mind to something else.*

Expectation of happiness when events change. Often the depressed person has undergone a series of stressors and losses. It becomes easy to develop the belief that happiness will come when events change, when life goes from bad events to good events, when things go your way. The only problem with this thinking is that life will often just be life. Some events you control, but many you do not. Why should you wait on happiness until things go your way? That may never happen. Why not choose happiness in the meantime and then do all you can to change events? The inaccurate belief—*I will be happy when things go my way*—needs to be challenged whenever it occurs and a more accurate belief immediately repeated—*I will be happy in spite of life's events and then do all I can to improve on them.*

Generalization. The depressed person feels that his present state of despair and disappointment will be continued into the future. He feels hopeless. This inaccurate view should be repeatedly challenged with a more accurate belief.

The truth is that in Christ the present state does not have to indicate the future. Christ can change things. Christ is the God of the universe. Your choices through Christ can overcome circumstances. "I can do all things through Christ who strengthens me" (Phil. 4:13). You can overcome your current set of depressing circumstances. This is the accurate belief and should be used to replace the inaccurate belief whenever it occurs.

Emotional reasoning. It is easy to become upset when we do not have all of the facts concerning a problem. Waiting until we have all the information can diminish the problem and reduce the concern. Depressed people worry about what has not occurred. They assume the worst without having the facts. Obtain the facts and then act on them.

Selective attention on the negative. Depressed individuals tend to look at only the negative—where they failed—rather than the many areas where they have succeeded. They focus on the 10 percent they missed on a test rather than the 90 percent they got right; they focus on a specific individual who does not like them rather than the others, including Christ, who love them dearly.

Arbitrary references. Despite the lack of confirmation, depressed individuals tend to think that others don't like them, that others are even talking about them in a derogatory way. It has been said that when a person is twenty years old, he worries about what others think; when he is thirty years old, he does not care what they think; and when he is forty years old, he realizes that they didn't think at all. The depressed individual thinks like the twenty-year-old.

4. Share Feelings

Feelings need to be shared. Depressed individuals need to talk, talk, talk. Talking gets the emotions out. When we don't talk about our feelings, we suppress them, and this usually has a deleterious effect. We may become like a volcano that is ready to explode. It has long been proposed that anger turned inward is the cause of depression. So share your feelings with a friend, a counselor, and especially with God.

5. Gain Insight

We all need love, affection, and attention, but an unhealthy dependency often indicates some form of abuse or abandonment, including the lack of a parent's nurturing; absence of parental warmth;

physical abandonment by a parent; emotional abandonment by a parent because of the parent's own emotional needs; parental neglect caused by the parent's alcoholism, workaholism, perfectionism, or depression; parental abandonment due to divorce; and verbal, physical, or sexual abuse. Because of the pain, relief is sought through some addictive (anesthetic) agent, such as other people, alcohol, drugs, money, work, perfectionism, television, sports, affairs, food, Internet, computers, sex, compulsive behaviors, power, possessions, anger, negative thinking, cleaning, organizing, criticism, physical illness, and many other activities that are carried to extremes. Thus, trying to fill an emptiness on the inside, the individual is driven by an excessive dependency, which results in unhealthy attractions. He is sometimes tormented by experiences with his dysfunctional family of origin.

Insight is the ability to understand the hidden issues that affect us. Gaining insight into the causes for our feelings of emptiness can help move us out of depression.

Five crucial steps often help in the process:

Acceptance. We first must gain insight into what we're trying to numb with our particular form of anesthesia. We will need to look at our family of origin; unhealthy relationships; hurts we've suffered; hidden anger; verbal abuse we've endured; feelings of abandonment; having an emotionally unavailable parent; absence of a nurturing parent; having to assume a parental role as a youth; parental pressure and expectations to fulfill their dreams; distortions of relationships today because of distortions in our family of origin; and hidden dangerous agendas. Acceptance often begins as insight that, even though it shouldn't, a past unresolved issue is truly affecting us today.

Accountability. We may need someone to hold us accountable, such as a counselor, medical doctor, pastor, friend, or spouse—someone we must face on a weekly basis and report success or failure with our temptations to anesthetize our hurt. We need someone we can call if the temptation for an addicting agent is becoming too strong. This must be a person who cares for us and will hold us accountable.

Grief. Grieving our losses, abandonment, or abuse, and grieving what never was—affection, love, time, tenderness, nurturing, bonding, or security—is essential. As Christians we do not grieve as those who have no hope (1 Thess. 4:13), but we do grieve. The Bible has many examples of mourning. "Blessed are those who mourn, for they shall be comforted" (Matt. 5:4).

At first, after a loss, the pain may be almost continual and unrelenting. The first stage of grief is *denial*—"This did not happen." Next comes *anger turned outward,* then *anger turned inward.* Next comes *bargaining.* Finally comes *true grief.* It is all right to cry and grieve. Then resolution can begin. The pain comes sharply at first, but with time it comes at less frequent intervals. The pain may never go away totally, but time is often of great help, so hold on.

A new life. Finally, we begin to realize that a new lifestyle is essential to meet our dependency needs. Dependency needs are facts of life. They are greater in some individuals than others because their needs were never met in youth. However, what is important now is that they be met in a healthy fashion, avoiding extremes. We need healthy relationships that have a healthy emotional aspect, not an unhealthy physical or sexual emphasis.

Sharing is a great help. Sharing the pain with a few good friends helps to rebuild your life and new friendships in a healthy manner. The Bible often talks about the importance of healthy relationships: "Bear one another's burdens, and so fulfill the law of Christ" (Gal. 6:2). "Two are better than one because they have a good return for their labor. For if either of them falls, the one will lift up his companion. But woe to the one who falls when there is not another to lift him up" (Eccles. 4:9–10 NASB).

We may need to say goodbye to the old and say hello to new relationships and activities. Isaiah 43:18–19 is speaking of God and the nation of Israel, but it is a great passage to consider applying today. "Do not remember the former things, nor consider the things of old. Behold, I will do a new thing, now it shall spring forth; shall you not know it? I will even make a road in the wilderness and rivers in the desert."

Spiritual provision. We all have dependency needs, and there is nothing wrong with them. It is how we meet them that produces healthy or unhealthy emotional and spiritual reactions. Christ can and will meet our dependency needs. A person with unmet dependency needs often has an intense spiritual and emotional hunger or vacuum. Only God can satisfy this hunger, not sex, drugs, a person, work, television, the Internet, money, buying, or anything else.

6. Consider Medical Intervention

Should medicine be used in overcoming depression? Consider the following data and you decide (also see the appendixes).

Major depressive disorder (MDD) or serious medical depression has a lifetime prevalence of 5 to 10 percent. Lesser but significant medical depression may approach 50 percent lifetime prevalence. Annually seventeen million Americans have MDD, which is usually recurrent and causes greater functional impairment than do diabetes, arthritis, and hypertension. The cost annually for MDD is $43 billion. Social burdens seen in MDD include dysfunctional families, absenteeism from work, decreased productivity, lost jobs, and failure to advance in career or school. The condition is associated with high morbidity and mortality. Fifteen percent of those with MDD commit suicide. Though it is very treatable medically, few receive adequate treatment.

Today people usually do not have to stay depressed. Modern medicines can change moods, and yet less than 25 percent of the medically depressed population ever receives adequate medical help. I have often said that as good as cardiology and oncology are today, they are not nearly as good as psychiatry. The results from cardiology and oncology vary, but the results of antidepressant medication are usually good and not infrequently excellent. You don't have to feel depressed. Depressed, negative thinking can have a medical dimension, and that medical dimension can usually be corrected today.

The brain is composed of one hundred billion cells, and each cell has about one hundred thousand synapses. Therefore, the total number of synapses in one brain would approach infinity. There are perhaps more synapses in one brain than all the stars in all the galaxies.

Neurotransmitters are chemicals in the synapses between brain cells. They play a major role in emotions. By altering specific neurotransmitters through medication, emotional symptoms can be abated. Through a cascade of chemical reactions initiated by altering

the neurotransmitters, the brain can return to health. The following
medications have various effects.

- The antidepressant Wellbutrin is effective not only in lifting
  a depressed mood but in helping a depressed individual lose
  weight, quit smoking, and decrease his ADHD inattention.
  Wellbutrin is usually free of sexual side effects.
- With antidepressants such as Serzone, Remeron, or Desyrel, not
  only can the depressed mood be lifted, but the depressed individual who can't sleep and is anxious may be helped. Serzone
  and Remeron are usually free of sexual side effects. Remeron
  is also used when a football player wants to gain bulk.
- The antidepressant Effexor can lift a depressed mood and help
  relieve the significant anxiety of a depressed individual.
- Topamax and Zonegran, which are anticonvulsant medications
  that have been used off-label in bipolar depression and mania,
  can lift a depressed mood as well as help in weight loss.
- Lamictal (lamotrigine), another anticonvulsant medication,
  has been used off-label in both depression and mania.
- Not only can a bipolar mood disorder be stabilized in a bipolar individual with a history of drug addictions, but sleep
  also can be improved without fear of addiction with Zyprexa,
  a new neuroleptic approved for use in bipolar disorders.
- Neurontin, an anticonvulsant medication, has been used off-
  label for insomnia and bipolar mood disorders.
- The depressed individual with an anxiety disorder, such as
  obsessive-compulsive disorder, social phobia, panic disorder,
  and posttraumatic stress disorder, may be helped by a selective
  serotonin reuptake inhibitor (SSRI), such as Lexapro, Celexa,
  Luvox, Paxil, Prozac, or Zoloft. In fact, depressed individuals
  with eating disorders may be helped by an SSRI.
- A new antidepressant, Symbalta, should also prove helpful.
- Even for extremely difficult cases, such as those with depression
  and psychosis, it is possible that the new neuroleptics Geodon
  and Abilify will help with both depression and psychosis.

As we can see from the above list, antidepressant medications
are now used for many disorders other than just depression, includ-

ing posttraumatic stress disorder, panic disorder, phobic disorder, chronic pain disorders, fibromyalgia, social phobia, premenstrual dysphoric disorder, generalized anxiety disorder, and obsessive-compulsive disorder.

Medicines are often very effective, selective, and specific in how they work. In short, they are often great. Not only are the new psychiatric medications becoming more specific, but in general they have fewer side effects than the older antidepressants. While almost any medicine can have almost any side effect on almost any organ, the new psychiatric medications often have fewer side effects. Indeed, they are miracle drugs for many people. Please see appendix J for a detailed discussion of the antidepressants.

Occasionally I hear a depressed individual say that he was hurt when a friend said to him, "Christians shouldn't need antidepressant medications." I tell my client that technically that statement may be true. However, it is based on the assumption that a Christian is perfect. Christians, however, are imperfect people for whom a perfect Christ died. If we were perfect, we wouldn't have heart disease. In fact, studies by the thousands document that heart disease is often stress-related in type A personalities. Just as we are not critical of the individual on heart medication, neither should we be of individuals on antidepressants. Stress can damage not only the heart but also the brain, and not treating it would be cruel. God is not against medication or the physician who administers it appropriately. The physician is referred to in both the Old Testament, as in Jeremiah 8:22, and the New Testament, as in Matthew 9:12.

7. Rely on Christ's Intervention

Have you ever had an experience in which it seemed as though God intervened on your behalf—as though he stood in the gap for you? I had such an experience several years ago. It was late fall and the early morning air was crisp. I had arisen early that morning to talk with the Lord about an especially difficult situation: "Lord, you know I love you. You know I need your help. Please intervene on my behalf."

Mary Alice and I, as we often did, went out for coffee and a time of sharing. It was only about 5:00 A.M. As I walked into the restaurant, I met an old acquaintance who, as he greeted me, made a comment. In so doing, he acted as God's instrument to intervene on my behalf in a miraculous way. The odds of my old acquaintance being in that restaurant at 5:00 A.M. were one in a million. The odds of his offhand but invaluable comment were one in a million. I will always believe God intervened on my behalf.

During that time period, there were several such occurrences. They seemed beyond the law of chance. I simply could not explain them. I had not set them up. My memory went back to a sermon I had heard years before by Haddon Robinson from a passage in Isaiah (40:31). God sometimes acts by *interaction*. God works through us as he did when David fought Goliath in 1 Samuel 17:31–54. God sometimes acts by *inner action*. God says no to our request but strengthens us inwardly as he did when he refused Paul's request to have his thorn in the flesh removed in 2 Corinthians 12:8–9. Sometimes God just flat out *intervenes*. God does what we can't do in a miraculous way, such as he did for Moses at the parting of the Red Sea in Exodus 14:21.

Are you depressed? Why not consider asking Christ to intervene for you? He just might do it.

■ Follow-Up

We have seen that there are certain steps you can take to lift a depressed mood. And there are also certain steps that can cause depression. We saw this earlier in the chapter where I encouraged a patient to form a plan B. If you are depressed, ask yourself, *What has been my daily seven-point plan (plan A) for living life this past month?* Remember, feelings follow behavior. You may even laugh at yourself and say, *I can't believe I had that seven-point plan!* We all get in ruts. The important point is to change unhealthy behaviors. Go from plan A to plan B.

Depression has many symptoms. The causes are diverse and comprise medical factors, current stressors, early-life issues, and the choices we make. There is much hope today for treating depression. In fact, it is highly treatable. Why not avail yourself of the medical, psychological, and, most of all, spiritual help you need? Why not do something to get well? Why not take advantage of the best scientific and spiritual tools available today that will allow you to understand the causes of your depression and make the needed changes? You can go from enduring depression to pursuing happiness.

3

Anger

Pursuing Forgiveness

> Be kind and compassionate to one another, forgiving each other, just as in Christ God forgave you.
>
> Ephesians 4:32 NIV

I grew up in a rough, tough community that had a John Wayne mentality. Anger was often handled inappropriately by fighting. I recall that when I was a youth, some men took the pastor out behind the church and gave him a beating for preaching too directly. (If ministers today think they have it rough, it may have been worse then.) It is equally bad to equip people with great psychological tools but fail to emphasize their need for Christ. With these tools, people can become adept at psychologically beating each other up. Let's pray that with a Christ-like sensitivity we can handle anger appropriately. Much may be at stake for the cause of Christ.

Anger often walks with depression. Anger is a subjective emotion when we feel hostility, hurt, and sometimes a desire to get even. Anger, left unchecked, can be a factor in depression, discouragement, anxiety, drug abuse, hurting self, and hurting others. It can also be a factor in psycho-physiological conditions, such as high blood pressure, and is a possible factor, either directly or indirectly, in many deaths.

47

▪ Dealing with Anger

Anger can be turned inward, possibly resulting in depression and bitterness; it can be turned outward as aggression toward others, provoking their anger and hurt; or it can be dealt with in a gently assertive, Christ-like manner. Ephesians 4:15 may be a good verse to apply here: "But, speaking the truth in love, may [we] grow up in all things into Him who is the head—Christ."

The medical importance of handling anger appropriately is immense. Anger is a major health risk in America and probably the leading cause of death. In fact, the single factor most likely to cause a heart attack in the American adult is not high cholesterol, smoking, or a history of heart disease in the family; rather, it is chronic exposure to hostile interactions with other people. Depression (with possible anger) is a better predictor of heart attacks than existing artery damage, high cholesterol, or cigarette smoking. Furthermore, death rates are four to seven times higher in people who are hostile, cynical, and suspicious than in people who are not as angry. Angry, cynical people are five times more likely to die under the age of fifty than people who are calm and trusting. It has been suggested that there is a cancer-prone personality, one that is passive and withdrawn and that suppresses anger. Though never proven, anger has long been postulated as a major factor in many psychological depressions.

Anger with unforgiveness and resulting bitterness not only hurts us spiritually but can also hurt many others. "Looking diligently lest anyone fall short of the grace of God; lest any root of bitterness springing up cause trouble, and by this many become defiled" (Heb. 12:15).

Here are some great choices to help you deal with anger.

1. Gain Insight into Unresolved Anger

It is difficult to deal with a problem if you do not recognize it. Just as insight helps you determine the causes for your depression, it can also help you identify hidden issues that underlie your anger. If you find yourself overreacting to a person today, it may be because of transference from anger in the past. Of course, this is not fair to the current recipient of the anger and will not resolve the damaged emotions of the past. Often an individual is not aware of her hidden anger, but friends and family may see it in facial expressions, passive-aggressive actions, or subtle hostile comments. Insight into the causes for unresolved anger is a great first step in dealing with it.

2. Share the Anger

A burden shared is only half a burden. When you have pinpointed causes for your anger, consider sharing your insights with a wise friend or a counselor. This person may help you gain perspective and see the situation from another vantage point, or it may be comforting just to have a listening ear, even if the person has no advice on what to do. Be sure to tell God about your anger. He will understand and lead you in the way of peace.

3. Sublimate the Anger

Sublimation is a defense mechanism whereby a person can take hostile energy and initially express it in an acceptable manner (through exercise, housework, and so on) just to get the anger under control. For example, a man may be so angry that if he tried to express it, he would be aggressive, so he jogs around the block (sublimation) first. Then he may be able to deal with his anger more appropriately through healthy behavioral choices.

4. Use Helpful Behavioral Techniques

Many techniques can help with anger resolution. For example, write a letter to the offending party and then tear it up, write a letter but frame your comments in a positive way, count to ten before responding, or practice with a friend how to respond verbally in an appropriate way.

5. Use Spiritual Helps

Forgive and turn the issue over to God. From time to time people in our life will make us angry. We may even be angry with God. (Of course, God does nothing wrong, but in our ignorance we may not understand why he has allowed something to happen.) We must learn to trust God and allow him to help us forgive others.

Forgiveness starts with the will, not the emotions. Emotional resolution of feelings takes time, so forgiveness must start with a simple choice of the will. Even without the appropriate feelings, it's interesting that this act of the will releases God to work on our behalf. "Never take your own revenge, beloved, but leave room for the wrath of God, for it is written, 'Vengeance is Mine, I will repay,' says the Lord" (Rom. 12:19 NASB).

Ask God for his help. God does not want us to remain angry and unforgiving. "Bearing with one another, and forgiving one another, if anyone has a complaint against another; even as Christ forgave you, so you also must do" (Col. 3:13). Also, "Let all bitterness, wrath, anger, clamor, and evil speaking be put away from you, with all malice. And be kind to one another, tenderhearted, forgiving one another, just as God in Christ also forgave you" (Eph. 4:31–32).

Our anger may be so difficult to deal with that we need to repeatedly ask God for help as we claim his promises. "No temptation has overtaken you except such as is common to man; but God is faithful, who will not allow you to be tempted beyond what you are able, but with the temptation will also make the way of escape, that you may be able to bear it" (1 Cor. 10:13).

Grow in Christ. When we grow in Christ, we grow in self-control and the other fruit of the Spirit, which preclude our being carried away with anger. "But the fruit of the Spirit is love, joy, peace, longsuffering, kindness, goodness, faithfulness, gentleness, self-control" (Gal. 5:22–23). Much of my anger stems from my being somewhat selfish or suspicious. Whatever the cause, growing in Christ can help.

Make a choice against letting the anger escalate. A few years ago, as I was reading the book of Proverbs, I noticed that there is a choice involved in anger: "He who is slow to wrath has great understanding" (Prov. 14:29). When we choose not to fly off the handle, we can count on God's help in gaining perspective and understanding the situation. This may lessen our anger or do away with it altogether.

6. Consider Medication

In some cases, medication can make a major difference. For example, in depression with anger, the SSRIs, such as Lexapro, Celexa, Prozac, Paxil, and Zoloft, may make a dramatic difference. There has been talk of working toward approval of these drugs for the more severe cases of premenstrual syndrome (PMS) with its associated depression and anger. Also, many other drugs have been suggested as possibly helping in various conditions with anger and aggression:

- beta blockers such as Inderol and Visken
- mood stabilizing medication such as Zonegran, Trileptal, Lithium, Depakote, Tegretol, and Neurontin
- minor tranquilizers such as Ativan and Buspar
- dopamine agents such as Risperdal, Seroquel, Zyprexa, Geodon, and Abilify
- attention-deficit/hyperactivity disorder agents such as Adderall, Strattera, Concerta, Metadate, and Focalin

7. Use a Behavioral and Cognitive Approach on Yourself

Ask yourself if there is an appropriate action that you can take that would help you with your anger. Do you need to challenge your thinking? Are you overly personalizing, magnifying, or generalizing? Are you focusing too much on a few negatives and ignoring many positives? Are you assuming things that may not be true? Are you reasoning more from emotions than actual facts? There are times when we all can answer yes to these questions, and we all need to challenge any thinking that unduly increases anger.

8. Deal with the Anger Quickly

Anger should be dealt with quickly. "'Be angry, and do not sin': do not let the sun go down on your wrath" (Eph. 4:26).

■ Follow-Up

Anger can be handled in appropriate ways. These are eight of the best. Which three do you do best? Which three give you the most trouble? Consider working on one of the above daily for a week and then picking another one. Rate your anger on a scale from one to ten with ten being the highest intensity. Rate yourself now and then again in two and one-half months.

4

Anxiety

Pursuing Peace

Do not be anxious about anything, but in everything, by prayer and petition, with thanksgiving, present your requests to God. And the peace of God, which transcends all understanding, will guard your hearts and your minds in Christ Jesus.

Philippians 4:6–7 NIV

My hands shook in 1967 as I opened the letter from medical school. I felt anxiety. Had I been accepted or rejected? I was accepted, but the subsequent years would be difficult. I had only ninety hours of college, so if for some reason medical school did not work out, I would not have a bachelor's degree. Medical school went fine, but the hours were long with many nights of no sleep. Times were difficult, and anxiety was knocking on the door.

■ What Is Anxiety?

Anxiety is a common emotional state that is characterized by feelings of apprehension, uneasiness, worry, and concern; an unpleasant anticipation of some unknown misfortune, danger, or doom; the feeling that something must be done, but not knowing what;

a basic, underlying factor in most emotional disorders and many physical ones as well; an experience that affects everyone, to some degree, but renders some people nonfunctional.

Years ago I read a book by Gary Collins on anxiety in which he made the following interesting observations.[1] Anxiety can be normal or abnormal. It is normal when a realistic concern exists, as we see in the New Testament: "For I have no one else of kindred spirit who will genuinely be concerned for your welfare" (Phil. 2:20 NASB); "Apart from such external things, there is the daily pressure on me of concern for all the churches" (2 Cor. 11:28 NASB).

Anxiety is abnormal when it implies fretting and worrying. We also find this in the Bible: "Be anxious for nothing, but in everything by prayer and supplication, with thanksgiving, let your requests be made known to God" (Phil. 4:6); "The seed which fell among the thorns, these are the ones who have heard, and as they go on their way they are choked with worries and riches and pleasures of this life, and bring no fruit to maturity" (Luke 8:14 NASB); "Casting all your anxiety on Him, because He cares for you" (1 Peter 5:7 NASB).

When I was growing up, I heard many sermons on Luke 8:14, which speaks about the dangers of worries and riches and the pleasures of this life. All of the sermons, however, were on riches or pleasures, never on worry or anxiety. But in reality worry brings down as many people as riches and pleasure.

If we examine the concept of anxiety psychologically, we find that a little anxiety (a realistic concern) is healthy for better job performance, for example, or as an appropriate response to having surgery. However, when a person goes from a realistic concern to fretting and worry, the job performance goes down and the response is maladaptive.

Anxiety symptoms and disorders are major health problems in America, ranging from a single adjustment disorder to more difficult and debilitating disorders, such as panic disorder and posttraumatic stress disorder. According to the most recent data, the lifetime prevalence for anxiety disorders in general is about 25 percent; social phobia has a lifetime risk of 17 percent, while panic disorder occurs in approximately 1 to 3 percent of the population. Although quite common, anxiety disorders are very treatable with good, persistent medical care.

Below I list thirteen types of anxiety. As you read through the descriptions, you may realize that you are experiencing one of them.

■ Types of Anxiety

Anxiety is a subjective sense of worry, apprehension, fear, and distress. It is normal to have these sensations on occasion, and so it is important to distinguish between normal levels of anxiety and unhealthy or pathological levels. The subjective experience of anxiety typically has two components—physical sensations and the emotions of nervousness and fear. Anxiety, when severe, can affect a person's thinking, decision-making ability, perceptions of the environment, learning, and concentration. It raises blood pressure and heart rate and can cause nausea, vomiting, stomach pain, ulcers, diarrhea, tingling, weakness, and shortness of breath, among other things. Anxiety disorders are the most common psychiatric disorders.

Diagnosis of normal versus abnormal anxiety depends largely on the degree of distress and its effect on functioning. The specific anxiety disorder is diagnosed by the pattern and quality of symptoms as follows:

Generalized anxiety disorder is defined as excessive worry, apprehension, and anxiety occurring most days for a period of six months or more that involve concern over a number of activities or events. The person has difficulty controlling the anxiety, which is associated with restlessness, feeling "keyed up" or on edge, being easily fatigued, difficulty concentrating or having the mind go blank, irritability, muscle tension, difficulty falling asleep or staying asleep, or restless sleep. The anxiety causes significant distress, including problems with functioning.

Panic attacks are sudden, discrete episodes of intense fear and/ or discomfort accompanied by four out of thirteen bodily or cognitive symptoms, often manifesting with an intense desire to escape and a feeling of doom that lasts for twenty to thirty minutes. The thirteen symptoms are heart palpitations or fast heart rate, sweating, trembling or shaking, shortness of breath or smothering, choking sensation, chest discomfort or pain, nausea or abdominal distress, dizziness or lightheadedness or feelings of being faint or unsteady, feelings of unreality or being detached from oneself, fear of losing control or going crazy, fear of dying, numbness or tingling sensations, and chills or hot flashes. Panic attacks are frequently but not always associated with *agoraphobia* (anxiety and avoidance of situations from which escape might be difficult or help might not be available).

Panic disorder consists of recurrent, unexpected panic attacks with interepisode worry about having other attacks. This leads to marked changes in behavior related to the attacks.

Obsessive-compulsive disorder is defined as persistent obsessions (intrusive, unwanted thoughts, images, ideas, or urges) and/or compulsions (intense, uncontrollable, repetitive behaviors or mental acts related to the obsessions) that are unreasonable and excessive. These obsessions and compulsions cause notable distress and impairment and are time-consuming (involving more than one hour a day). The most common obsessions concern dirt and contamination, repeated doubts, the need to have things arranged in a specific way, fearful aggressive or murderous impulses, and disturbing sexual imagery. The most frequent compulsions involve repetitive washing of hands or using a handkerchief or tissue to touch things; checking drawers, locks, windows, and doors; counting rituals; repeating actions; and requesting reassurance.

Posttraumatic stress disorder is when a person experiences, witnesses, or is confronted by an event or events that involve actual or perceived threat of death or serious bodily harm, and the person's response involves intense fear, helplessness, or horror. The traumatic event is continually reexperienced in the following ways: recurrent and intrusive distressing recollection of the event involving images, thoughts, or perceptions; distressing dreams of the event; acting as though or believing that the traumatic event is recurring; intense anxiety and distress in response to situations that resemble the traumatic event; and body reactivity (for example, nausea, vomiting, shortness of breath, heart palpitations, and sweating). The person avoids situations associated with and reminding him of the traumatic event; feelings or conversations associated with the trauma; and activities, places, or people that remind him of the traumatic event. The person with posttraumatic stress disorder may be unable to remember details of the event; have markedly diminished participation and interest in usual activities; feel detached and estranged from others; have a restricted range of emotional expression; sense a foreshortened future or life span; and have persistent signs of physiologic arousal, such as difficulty falling asleep or staying asleep, irritability or angry outbursts, difficulty concentrating, excessive vigilance, and exaggerated startle response. The above symptoms persist for more than one month and cause significant distress and impairment of functioning.

Acute stress disorder occurs when an individual undergoes some traumatic stress issues. This disorder is much like posttraumatic stress disorder, but the symptoms last for a shorter duration.

Social phobia is persistent and significant fear of one or more social situations in which a person is exposed to unfamiliar persons or scrutiny by others and feels he will behave in a way that will be embarrassing or humiliating. Exposure to the feared social situations almost always causes significant anxiety, even a panic attack, despite the fact that the anxiety is seen as excessive and unreasonable. This fear may lead to avoidance of such situations or endurance under extreme distress, leading to marked interference in the person's functioning and routine.

Specific phobia is persistent, significant fear that is recognized as unreasonable and excessive, triggered by the presence or perception of a specific feared situation or object that immediately provokes an anxiety reaction. The distress, avoidance, and anxious anticipation of the feared situation or object significantly interferes with a person's normal functioning or routine. There are various types of phobia: *animal type:* fear of animals or insects; *natural environment type:* fear of storms, heights, water, and the like; *blood-injection type:* fear of getting injections, seeing blood, seeing injuries, or watching or having invasive medical procedures; *situational type:* fear of elevators, flying, driving, bridges, escalators, trains, tunnels, closets, and so on.

Adjustment disorder with anxiety (with or without depressed mood) occurs when emotional and/or behavioral symptoms develop within three months in response to an identifiable stressor. These symptoms and behaviors cause marked distress in excess of that which could be expected and result in significantly changed occupational, social, and/or academic performance. Once the initiating stressor has ceased, the disturbance does not last longer than six months.

Anxiety disorder due to a general medical condition is when the physiologic consequences of a distinct medical condition are judged to be the cause of prominent anxiety symptoms.

Drug-induced anxiety disorder is when the physiologic consequences of the use of a drug or medication are judged to be the cause of prominent anxiety symptoms.

Anxiety disorder not otherwise specified is when the prominent symptoms of anxiety and avoidance exist but do not fully meet any of the above diagnostic criteria.

Subclinical anxiety is not a clinical category; rather, it is the mild anxious feelings that all people experience for brief periods in their lives.

■ Causes of Anxiety

As the preceding list shows, anxiety can result when a combination of increased internal and external stressors overwhelm one's normal coping abilities or when one's normal ability to cope is lessened for some reason. John, fifty-four, came in anxious and depressed. He had recently lost his job and was greatly worried about finances. In addition, his wife had started threatening to separate and even divorce. By attacking John's problem behaviorally, through counseling, by attacking it medically, through appropriate medication, and by attacking it socially, through a support system at his church, John and his wife were able to overcome this challenge.

Several dimensions of anxiety may occur:

Internal. Anxiety occurs when internal competing mental processes, instincts, and impulses conflict, causing distress.

Behavioral. Anxiety is a maladaptive, learned response to specific past experiences and situations that become generalized to future similar situations.

Spiritual. Anxiety occurs when people experience a profound, unquenchable emptiness and nothingness in their lives, often leading to distress concerning their mortality and eventual death. Anxiety can occur when people sin and feel convicted, as King David experienced (see Psalms 32 and 51).

Genetic. Heredity plays a large role in the development of anxiety disorders. For example, studies show that 50 percent of patients with panic disorder have at least one relative affected with an anxiety disorder. Furthermore, there is a higher chance of an anxiety disorder in the parents, children, and siblings of a person with an anxiety disorder than in the relatives of someone without an anxiety disorder. Studies of twins demonstrate varying but important degrees of genetic contribution to the development of anxiety disorders.

Biological. Evidence exists that suggests abnormal function in several regions of the brain of those suffering from anxiety.

Medical. Illnesses such as cardiovascular disease (mitral valve prolapse, arrhythmias), lung disease, certain tumors (pheochromocytoma), endocrine disorders (hyperthyroidism), infections, and neurological diseases can all cause anxiety disorders. Therefore, it is important to see your doctor to exclude medical conditions as potential causes of or contributors to anxiety disorders.

■ Overcoming Anxiety

During my years in medical school, when anxiety threatened, six precious choices encouraged me greatly. They may hold the key to your pursuit of happiness.

1. Read the Bible

I turned as I had as a young child to soothing words from an old black Bible. Let these verses calm your soul as they did mine years ago and still do.

John 14:27: Peace I leave with you, My peace I give to you; not as the world gives do I give to you. Let not your heart be troubled, neither let it be afraid.

Psalm 56:3: Whenever I am afraid, I will trust in You.

Psalm 34:4: I sought the LORD, and He heard me, and delivered me from all my fears.

Isaiah 41:10: Fear not, for I am with you; be not dismayed, for I am your God. I will strengthen you, yes, I will help you, I will uphold you with My righteous right hand.

Psalm 27:1, 14: The LORD is my light and my salvation; whom shall I fear? The LORD is the strength of my life; of whom shall I be afraid? . . . Wait on the LORD; be of good courage, and He shall strengthen your heart; wait, I say, on the LORD!

Matthew 6:25–34: Therefore I say to you, do not worry about your life, what you will eat or what you will drink; nor about your body, what you will put on. Is not life more than food and the body more than clothing? Look at the birds of the air, for they neither sow nor reap nor gather into barns; yet your heavenly Father feeds them. Are you not of more value than they? Which of you by worrying can add one cubit to his stature? So why do you worry about clothing? Consider the lilies of the field, how they grow: they neither toil nor spin; and yet I say to you that even Solomon in all his glory was not arrayed like one of these. Now if God so clothes the grass of the field, which today is, and tomorrow is thrown into the oven, will He not much more clothe you, O you of little faith? Therefore do not worry, saying, "What shall we eat?" or "What shall we drink?" or "What shall we wear?" For after all these things the Gentiles seek. For your heavenly Father knows that you need all these things. But seek first the kingdom of God and His righteousness, and all these things shall be added to you. Therefore do not worry about tomorrow, for tomorrow will worry about its own things. Sufficient for the day is its own trouble.

Philippians 4:6–8 (NASB): Be anxious for nothing, but in everything by prayer and supplication with thanksgiving let your requests be made known to God. And the peace of God, which surpasses all comprehension, will guard your hearts and your minds in

Christ Jesus. Finally, brethren, whatever is true, whatever is honorable, whatever is right, whatever is pure, whatever is lovely, whatever is of good repute, if there is any excellence and if anything worthy of praise, dwell on these things.

I would read or recite the words over and over. I would enjoy them. I would talk with God about them. They calmed my soul. I suggest that you consider memorizing Scripture, then pray the verses back to God each day for a week. Let them calm and encourage your soul. Let the Word of God make you strong: "I have written to you, young men, because you are strong, and the word of God abides in you, and you have overcome the wicked one" (1 John 2:14).

2. Listen to Soothing Music

From the bookshelf I pulled down an old songbook and reviewed precious songs I learned as a youth. The memories were still there, the words were still in my brain, and the warm, calming feelings of years before returned.

I suggest that you listen to music that warms your soul. Your local Christian bookstore will have a large selection of contemporary music and traditional hymns available on tapes and CDs, and most areas have a Christian radio station that plays music that can comfort and inspire. Usually people list music as an important influence in their life. Why not let words and melodies soothe any anxious feelings you may have?

3. Allow for Adequate Sleep

Much anxiety may dissipate with adequate rest. When anxious clients come into the hospital, we usually try to be sure they get a good night's sleep. We know that this alone may help to mitigate much of their extreme anxiety. Anxiety keeps individuals awake, and sleep deprivation creates more anxiety. If insomnia is severe and behavioral tools are not effective, a physician may need to be consulted. My goal is to help individuals go from Job 7:4—"When I lie down I say, 'When shall I arise?' But the night continues, and I am continually tossing until dawn" (NASB)—to Proverbs 3:24—"When you lie down, you will not be afraid; yes, you will lie down and your sleep will be sweet." I first learned in medical school that when I feel anxious I should get a good night's sleep.

4. Allow for Adequate Exercise and Recreation

When I am tempted to be anxious, I swim. Exercise releases chemicals that may help to decrease anxiety. In medical school I learned a valuable lesson about the need for recreation. Since high school, I had studied every night until ten o'clock (even on weekends). Then one day while in medical school, I almost died from an insulin reaction with my diabetes. I decided the intense pressure and lack of relaxation were not worth it. Then my whole life began to improve. Mary Alice and I started going to football games, and I returned to the horseback riding and the wilderness camping of my youth. I even learned to laugh again.

5. Live One Day at a Time

Two thousand years ago, the best advice I know was given for anxiety: "Therefore do not worry about tomorrow, for tomorrow will worry about its own things. Sufficient for the day is its own trouble" (Matt. 6:34). I have often reminded myself to follow this advice and work at living one day at a time, because I don't know the future. No one does. I try to focus on what has to be done today and I try not to think about tomorrow.

6. Consider Medication

As we have seen, anxiety may be caused by a significant alteration in brain chemicals, which can often be corrected. Please see appendix L.

■ Follow-Up

Anxiety is a common subjective emotion characterized predominantly by worry. But it can also have physical manifestations, such as tremors, and emotional manifestations, such as feeling restless or tense. Irritability can be a problem as well. By working with the whole person—spirit, soul, and body—anxiety symptoms can be overcome.

5

Worry

Pursuing Calm

Our tomorrows are determined by the choices we make today.

Walter B. Knight

Keep talking to him. Don't let him go to sleep," the old country doctor told the worried mother as her fifteen-year-old son lay near death with diabetes mellitus. I was that son in the early sixties. I had good reason to have a realistic concern, but, if left unchecked, that concern would have turned to worry that surely would have killed me.

When we worry, we are disturbed or troubled or we experience mental uneasiness. It's a disturbance of our peace of mind. Worry is one component of anxiety, with anxiety being a much broader term.

A young woman came to our clinic, saying she worried incessantly about her children and her husband, even though they were all doing well. She worried when her husband traveled to and from work. She worried when her kids played sports. She even worried when one of them had a test at school. Worry kept her from enjoying her family. She said that many members of her family were worriers. She needed help with strategies to overcome her excessive worrying.

■ Overcoming Worry

Through Christ I learned eleven precious ways to deal with worry.

1. Develop a Driving Desire to Overcome Worry

Worry is not easily abated, but for healthy living, overcoming it is a must. Alexis Carrel said, "Those who do not learn to fight worry die young." Worry is no doubt a factor in many medical conditions, such as heart disease, high blood pressure, some cancers, and even physiological and neurological changes resulting in depression and anxiety. William Lowry said, "The Lord may forgive us our sins, but the nervous system never does."

During World War II, we lost about one-third of a million men, compared to about half a million people per year who currently die of heart disease, much of which is worry related. Plato said, "The greatest mistake physicians make is that they attempt to cure the body without attempting to cure the mind; yet the mind and the body are one and should not be treated separately." The Bible states the concept even better in 1 Thessalonians 5:23.

I recall one of my first psychiatric patients years ago. She told me she was a chronic worrier. She was only thirty-five years old, but she looked forty-five. The years of worry had taken their toll. Her face was lined and the corners of her mouth turned down. She had some premature graying, and she had gained a considerable amount of weight.

Not only does worry age us, it also may be related to infections—worry tends to decrease the lymphocytes, which fight off disease. It has been noted that cancer patients who worry intensely do not seem to do as well as those who don't. Furthermore, worry triggers the autonomic nervous system, which can be a factor in the disease of many organs. In one research study, six of ten heart patients had constricted coronary arteries and decreased blood flow to their heart following emotionally triggered events and worry.

Worry kills in another way. For example, when a close relative dies, there may be extreme stress and worry. If a first-degree relative dies, one's chance of dying at any point in time within the next year is increased sevenfold.

2. See the Big Picture

Many times we worry over issues that, when we consider the big picture, are really quite minor. The big picture is of life and death—a life to live for Christ. When we consider life and death, what really matters? If we had only one week to live, would we spend time worrying about things that matter little?

3. Live One Day at a Time

As I said in the last chapter, I have often reminded myself to work at living one day at a time. *No one knows the future,* I tell myself. *I must enjoy Christ in the present and focus on today.* Worriers tend to live in the future, worrying about a tomorrow that never comes. Obsessive individuals tend to live in the worry of the future, and depressive individuals tend to live in the worry of the past. God holds tomorrow, and he forgives the past. The future is not here, and the past is gone forever. We can live only in the present.

4. Form a Plan of Action

When I want to worry, I sit down and formulate a plan of action to attack the problems that confront me. I write down the problems and many options for solving them. I then pick a few good options and start to implement the plans. Taking action gets my mind off the worries and begins the process that may make a difference. This is a healthy approach to solving problems and overcoming worry.

5. Share with a Friend

Sharing with others is one of the most powerful techniques for dealing with worry that I have ever known. I recommend building a few good friendships and, on a daily basis, sharing with those friends your worries. "A friend loves at all times, and a brother is born for adversity" (Prov. 17:17). Robert Louis Stevenson said, "A friend is a present you give yourself." Of course, the best friend we can ever have is Christ. He loves for us to share our worries with him. "There is a friend who sticks closer than a brother" (18:24). He wants us to become less worry oriented and more heaven oriented, where the days of worries will no longer exist.

6. Realize That God Is Still in Control

Sometimes I laugh at myself. I hear myself say, *Well, there is nothing else I can do; I guess I will just have to pray.* Then I catch myself and think about the person to whom I pray. I pray to the God of the universe, the one who can do anything, who is omniscient, omnipresent, and omnipotent. I pray to someone who can erase a problem in one thousandth of a second. This makes me laugh. Why isn't it my first thought to pray? "Until now you have not asked for anything in my name. Ask and you will receive, and your joy will be complete" (John 16:24 NIV). I remind myself that God has never lost control. He can take care of any of my troubles.

7. Improve on Possibilities

I used to worry about having diabetes; then I decided that diabetes, for me, was a reality and that worrying over having it would not change it. What I could do was take action to prevent possible medical side effects of the disease. I turned from worry to action, and that action worked. I have had diabetes for forty years, and I am still healthy and without side effects. In fact, God used my diabetes to help me develop discipline, which allowed me to have a ministry for Christ.

Often future events are not inevitable but just good possibilities. In these cases it may help not only to prepare to accept what is possible but to try to improve on it. Perhaps good can come from the apparent bad. "And we know that all things work together for good to those who love God, to those who are the called according to His purpose" (Rom. 8:28).

8. Choose Not to Worry

There is a choice involved in worry. Let's choose not to worry, for ourselves and for the cause of Christ, because worry will interfere with our effectiveness as witnesses to Christ's faithfulness. "Therefore we also, since we are surrounded by so great a cloud of witnesses, let us lay aside every weight, and the sin which so easily ensnares us, and let us run with endurance the race that is set before us, looking unto Jesus, the author and finisher of our faith, who for the joy that was set before Him endured the cross, despising the shame, and has sat down at the right hand of the throne of God. For consider Him who endured such hostility from sinners against Himself, lest you become weary and discouraged in your souls" (Heb. 12:1–3).

9. Memorize Scripture Verses

If you want victory over worry, memorize the following verses over the next few weeks, repeating them daily:

Philippians 4:6–7 (NIV): Do not be anxious about anything, but in everything, by prayer and petition, with thanksgiving, present your requests to God. And the peace of God, which transcends all understanding, will guard your hearts and your minds in Christ Jesus.

Matthew 6:34 (NIV): Therefore do not worry about tomorrow, for tomorrow will worry about itself. Each day has enough trouble of its own.

1 Peter 5:7(NIV): Cast all your anxiety on him because he cares for you.

10. Consider Medications

Worry, like anxiety, can be caused by abnormalities in chemicals of the brain. Medication often can help greatly. See appendix L.

11. Consider Counseling

Proverbs teaches us that there is safety in counselors (see 11:14; 15:22; 20:18; 24:6). Counseling can offer encouragement, insight, behavioral tools, education, support, and a chance to share a heavy burden.

■ Follow-Up

There are many ideas in this chapter for dealing with worry, but for any of them to be effective, you will need to apply them. Try taking one of these steps daily for the next three months. Then try a different one, if needed.

Worrying is something we all do, but as we grow in Christ, we worry less, because we learn that we can depend on him to handle all of our cares. Some people worry more than others because of genetic and/or environmental factors. For those with genetic factors, wonderful medications are available. For those with environmental factors, counseling with behavioral and cognitive techniques can be of great benefit. For me, the benefit has come through the memorization of Scripture, which I commend to you highly.

6

Stress

Pursuing Rest

Stress is not stress if one does not perceive it that way.

Frank Minirth

Ice froze on the window of our jet as my daughter and I landed in London, Canada, in February 1988. The stress on our jet was intense. However, the stress on the plane tugged no stronger than the stress that pulled at my heart. About a week earlier at the same airport, another jet had crashed due to ice on the wings. Furthermore, my daughter was ill. I was concerned. We had flown to London to consult with some doctors about her condition. My stress alarm had blown.

■ What Is Stress?

Stress is a close cousin to worry and anxiety. *Worry* and *anxiety* are the terms used to describe the internal fretting, whereas *stress* is the term for the external factors causing the worry or anxiety. In reality, they usually coexist. Stress is a state of physical, mental, or emotional tension caused by external conditions.

A thirty-five-year-old man who came to the clinic is a good example of someone under stress. He said he'd been under tremendous pressure at work and then lost his job. His mortgage and car payments were overdue, and he didn't know how he could pay them.

A stressor (an external event that affects the individual) is the person, thing, or event that causes us to feel stressed. Various evaluations have listed different common stressors. Holmes and Rahe developed "The Stress of Adjusting to Change" evaluation. The accumulation of two hundred or more stress points in a single year correlates with a high probability of developing significant emotional problems. How many stress points have you accumulated over the past year?

The Stress of Adjusting to Change

Event	Scale of Impact
Death of a spouse	100
Divorce	73
Marital separation	65
Jail term	63
Death of close family member	63
Personal injury or illness	53
Marriage	50
Fired at work	47
Marital reconciliation	45
Retirement	45
Change in health of family member	44
Pregnancy	40
Sex difficulties	39
Gain of new family member	39
Business readjustment	39
Change in financial state	38
Death of close friend	37
Change to different line of work	36
Change in number of arguments with spouse	35
Mortgage over $10,000	31
Foreclosure of mortgage or loan	30
Change in responsibilities at work	29
Son or daughter leaving home	29

Trouble with in-laws	29
Outstanding personal achievement	28
Wife begins or stops work	26
Begin or end school	26
Change in living conditions	25
Revision of personal habits	24
Trouble with boss	23
Change in work hours or conditions	20
Change in residence	20
Change in schools	20
Change in recreation	19
Change in church activities	19
Change in social activities	18
Mortgage or loan less than $10,000	17
Change in sleeping habits	16
Change in number of family get-togethers	15
Change in eating habits	15
Vacation	13
Christmas	12
Minor violations of the law	11

©1967 by Pergamon Press, Inc.

Another survey showed the top ten causes of immediate stress.[1]

Situation	Percentage of People Who Worry
1. Being with a group of strangers	78.6
2. Talking with an authority figure	78.6
3. Giving a speech	46.4
4. Meeting a date's parents	39.3
5. Saying something stupid	37.5
6. Asking for a date	33.9
7. Attending a party	32.1
8. Going on a date	26.8
9. Starting a new job	25.0
10. Going on a job interview	23.2

In the Minirth Clinic, the top three stressors we find are:

1. relationship issues

2. financial, job, career issues
3. loss issues

Which of the three stressors above has affected you the most?

■ Our Response to Stress

The way we interpret an event determines how we will respond psychologically, physiologically, behaviorally, and spiritually. What causes stress for one person may not be stressful to another because of the interpretation or cognitive appraisal of the events. For example, if a Christian is assailed by an event involving another individual, his perception can be altered if he remembers God's Word: "The LORD is for me; I will not fear; what can man do to me?" (Ps. 118:6 NASB); "Do not be fainthearted. Do not be afraid, or panic, or tremble before them, for the LORD your God is the one who goes with you, to fight for you against your enemies, to save you" (Deut. 20:3–4 NASB). For the one who is strengthened by verses such as these, stress is diminished.

When events seem out of control, Psalm 91:9–11 (RSV) can have a strong influence on one's perception and resulting response: "Because you have made the LORD your refuge, the Most High your habitation, no evil shall befall you, no scourge come near your tent. For he will give his angels charge of you to guard you in all your ways." Furthermore, Psalm 23:4 fights the most potentially fearful event with a great cognitive appraisal, "Yea, though I walk through the valley of the shadow of death, I will fear no evil; for You are with me; Your rod and Your staff, they comfort me." Clearly, what is stressful to one (such as possible approaching death) may not be as stressful to another. Interpretation makes all the difference in the world.

That snowy February day in 1988, my daughter and I, while on the jet above London, Canada, claimed Genesis 18:14 (NIV): "Is anything too hard for the LORD?" The verse made manageable what otherwise would have been a terrifying event.

Stress can be either good or bad. A little stress sounds an alarm that we need to rise to meet a challenge. In the Scriptures it seems that a little stress or anxiety is good when there is a realistic concern (Phil. 2:20; 2 Cor. 11:28), but it is not good when it goes beyond a signal of danger and causes unproductive worry and fretting (Phil. 4:6; Luke 8:14; 1 Peter 5:7).

With a little stress, work productivity goes up, but too much stress brings it down. Surgical patients with a realistic concern do better than those with intense worry or no concern at all. Indeed, a little stress is helpful, but distress is harmful.

Demands on the body or mind—emotional arousal, humiliation, pain, fatigue, success, failure, fear, effort, loss of blood, bodily injury, or any change in life—can be stressful. The level of stress relates both to the environment and the person's interpretation, evaluation, appraisal of meaning, and appraisal of his coping ability.

Do you read your stressors accurately, or do you tend to misinterpret the event? The following are nine ways people often misread an event and are therefore more stressed by it than they should be. Evaluate how much you allow any of the following to affect your response to an event (1 = a little; 10 = a lot):

- *Magnification*—overstating the danger of the event

  1 2 3 4 5 6 7 8 9 10

- *Generalization*—reading more than is warranted into the implications for the future

  1 2 3 4 5 6 7 8 9 10

- *Personalization*—overpersonalizing events that have more to do with the misbehavior of others

  1 2 3 4 5 6 7 8 9 10

- *Perfection*—demanding perfection from yourself or not forgiving your personal faults

  1 2 3 4 5 6 7 8 9 10

- *Selective attention to the negative*—focusing too much on the negative and missing many positives

  1 2 3 4 5 6 7 8 9 10

- *Arbitrary reference*—assuming a negative personal reference to oneself when it does not exist in reality

  1 2 3 4 5 6 7 8 9 10

- *Polarization*—seeing events as black or white and not seeing possible advantages as well as dangers of an event

  1 2 3 4 5 6 7 8 9 10

- *I can't live without her (or him)*—overly dependent on one person and missing the importance of the entire body of Christ

  1 2 3 4 5 6 7 8 9 10

- *I can't be forgiven*—missing the concept of forgiveness (see 1 John 1:9) and grace (see Eph. 2:8–9)

  1 2 3 4 5 6 7 8 9 10

Which one of the above nine do you do the most? _____

Stress is multifaceted and is affected by our drives, our conflicts, and our worldview. Which of the following apply to you? Grade yourself on a scale of one to ten.

- *Drives*—Drives exist internally in the Christian and may produce stress, as we read, for example, in Galatians 5:17: "For the flesh lusts against the Spirit, and the Spirit against the flesh; and these are contrary to one another."

  1 2 3 4 5 6 7 8 9 10

- *Conflicts*—Three types of conflicts can produce stress:
  Approach-Approach. The choice between two good alternatives (for example, the choice between attending one of two equally prestigious universities)

  1 2 3 4 5 6 7 8 9 10

  Approach-Avoidance. The existence of a single choice that has both positive and negative results (for example, an individual can choose marriage but loses some freedom)

  1 2 3 4 5 6 7 8 9 10

  Avoidance-Avoidance. Two choices, each having undesirable results (for example, a student can study for a test in a course he hates, or he can flunk the test)

  1 2 3 4 5 6 7 8 9 10

- *Worldview*

  Are there incompatibilities between what you feel should be true in Christianity and what you have seen in reality in Christianity?

  1 2 3 4 5 6 7 8 9 10

  Are there incompatibilities between what you want your character to be and what it is?

  1 2 3 4 5 6 7 8 9 10

  Are there incompatibilities between what your goals are and what you have obtained?

  1 2 3 4 5 6 7 8 9 10

  Are there incompatibilities between what you know Scripture says about trials and your perception in reality? "Wherein ye greatly rejoice, though now for a season, if need be, ye are in heaviness through manifold temptations" (1 Peter 1:6 KJV). Individuals under trial are "distressed."

  1 2 3 4 5 6 7 8 9 10

Any system, person, or machine under stress can wear out; eventually exhaustion and even death can ensue. Our reserve of energy for adaptation can be compared to a bank account. Withdrawals from the account can be made only so long without making deposits. Are you making deposits, or is your account near depletion? The type A personality may be in more danger than other people of a depletion that results in heart disease. The following characteristics identify a type A personality. Check the ones that sound like you.

_____ Often feels angry and hostile. (This may be the most dangerous component in regard to the development of atherosclerosis—a hardening of the arterial vessels.)

_____ Overly time-oriented.

_____ Eats, walks, or speaks fast.

_____ Tense demeanor.

_____ Highly competitive.

_____   Does two things at once.

_____   Interrupts others.

_____   Schedules too many events to do in too little time.

_____   Feels guilty with leisure time.

_____   Aggravated while waiting in lines or driving.

■ Effects of Stress

Stress can have an emotional, physical, or spiritual effect.

Physical Effects

Stress can affect almost any organ of the body and is a factor in numerous diseases.

Stress certainly can alter the neurotransmitters of the brain with profound influence on the emotions and body. With stress, the body is poised for either "fight or flight." This reaction causes chemical changes that may have far-reaching implications. When we encounter stress, corresponding behavioral changes may take place, such as making angry verbal responses, being ready to run, exercising, drinking, smoking, binge eating, and so on. The autonomic nervous system balance is altered and the blood pressure increases (which, in some individuals, may trigger a heart attack), along with many other physiological reactions.

After a stressful occurrence, the blood pressure may not go back down totally and may result in hypertension and acceleration of atherosclerosis. Also with stress the hypothalamus is affected, which in turn affects the pituitary gland, which in turn affects the adrenal medulla (with the resulting release of adrenaline). The adrenal cortex releases cortisol, which eventually can result in accelerated aging, decreased bone mineral density, alterations in immune system response, and possible permanent alterations in the functioning of the brain through their effects on the hippocampus, the amino acids of the brain, and the neurotransmitters themselves. Because stress may alter the hippocampus (which controls memory), continued stress may result in an inability to access the information needed to decide that a situation is no longer a threat. Thus stress begets stress. In fact, according to an article in the *New England Journal of Medicine:* "Magnetic resonance imaging has shown that stress-related disorders such as recurrent depressive illness, posttraumatic stress disorder, and Cushing's disease are associated with atrophy of the hippocampus. Whether this atrophy is reversible or permanent is not clear."[2] Furthermore, ongoing stress may result in a dysregulation of the hypothalamus-pituitary-adrenal axis, resulting in cognitive impairment. Finally, stress alters the neurotransmitters of the brain that control mood, logic, disposition, sleep, attention, weight, and pain perception.

As a result of the physical implications of stress, there are other, secondary, conditions that people under stress may experience:

depression	sweating
anxiety symptoms	trembling
mood swings	shortness of breath
outbursts of anger	anxious appearance
intense worry	angina attacks
confusion	irritable bowel syndrome
eating issues	impotence
panic episodes	menstrual disorders
obsessive worry	nervous tics
phobias	asthma attacks
health worries	frequent urination
sexual issues	outbreaks of skin problems
hair pulling	hair loss
sleep problems	appearing older than age
decreased concentration	increased infections
chest discomfort	high blood pressure
nightmares	coronary heart disease
increased crying	hypervigilance
rapid heartbeat	

The effects of stress vary, depending on the stage of the stress: alarm reaction, adaptation, or exhaustion. If you have any of the above symptoms, they may be stress related.

Emotional Effects

To deal with stress mentally, many individuals develop defense mechanisms. Defense mechanisms can be either good or bad, just as the physical effects of stress can be good or bad.

Following is a list of defense mechanisms that may be unhealthy. You may want to put a check by the ones that you use most often.

Denial is when you refuse to believe that the stressors you are undergoing are affecting you, even though to others you are obviously depressed, anxious, worried, or having other mental or physical signs of stress.

Rationalization, like denial, is a largely unconscious mechanism whereby you deal with stress by developing reasonable explanations for unreasonable behavior, such as having an affair, becoming intoxicated, being rude. In short, the behavior is unhealthy but rationalized.

Displacement is a largely unconscious defense mechanism whereby you cope with stress by displacing it to another individual or even an animal that is undeserving of the displacement. For example, if a person is under stress at work, he may go home and kick the dog or spouse.

Somatization is an unconscious defense mechanism whereby you deal with stress by overly focusing on possible health issues. Thus a person may become convinced he has hypoglycemia, heart disease, or a variety of other possible medical problems that may in fact not exist.

Introjection is a largely unconscious defense mechanism whereby you deal with stress by accepting responsibility beyond what is realistic. The individual thus assumes blame he doesn't deserve or feels guilt beyond what he should feel.

Projection is somewhat the opposite of introjection. In projection, you deal with stress by projecting emotions onto others. Thus a person may assume that others are angry, demanding, untrustworthy, guilty, and so on, when they are not, or at least not to the degree the individual feels they are.

Passive-aggressive. In the passive-aggressive defense mechanism, you respond to stress in a passive way. Thus, for example, you fail to complete jobs or arrive late for appointments or through various other behaviors act passively rather than straightforwardly and assertively.

Acting-out behavior. With this defense you deal with stress by acting out in various ways—sexually, financially, vocally, physically, and so on. Rather than face the stress directly, you act sinfully or inappropriately. Of course, this being a defense mechanism does not excuse the behavior.

Intellectualization is a defense whereby you deal with stress by becoming more and more intellectual. You do not face your feelings of stress but instead become focused on the intellectual. For example, an individual under stress may spend hours in some theological pursuit, such as in determining how many angels can stand on the head of a pin.

Controlling. Individuals under stress may deal with it and the insecurity it fosters by becoming overly controlling of others around them. The others may have very little or nothing to do with the immediate stress.

Dissociation is rare but is certainly very interesting and worthy of mention. In this case, stress is dealt with by dissociating into another personality or by having amnesia for a period of time during which inappropriate and unacceptable behavior may occur.

Idealization is overly admiring other individuals. Only Christ should be idealized. Everyone else is only human. It is easy to deal with stress by idealizing others only to be disappointed when one realizes that they too are human with human limitations. The reality is that people are on a spectrum from immature to mature. It is when we get to the far end of the spectrum, thinking that someone is totally perfect, that we have moved into idealization.

Defense mechanisms can also be healthy.

Anticipation, looking forward to future, happy events, is a simple, healthy defense in times of stress. For years I have enjoyed the defense of anticipating my vacations with Mary Alice and the girls. I dream about these and enjoy the anticipation almost as much as the vacation itself. The Christian looks forward to heaven. He anticipates wonderful times with the Lord. Of course, this defense needs to be kept in proper balance.

Daydreaming is a wonderful defense. There is nothing wrong, for example, with daydreaming about times of laughter and joy with Christian friends. And there is certainly nothing wrong with daydreaming about Christ and the wonderful promises God gives us in his Word. We must be careful, however, not to daydream our life away.

It is interesting to look at what people daydream about. According to one poll, 49 percent dream of being rich, 44 percent of global travel, 32 percent of the future, 32 percent of being smarter, 29 percent of a better job, 24 percent of the past, 11 percent having power and influence, 10 percent of being a great athlete, 9 percent of being involved in the media, 8 percent of getting revenge, and 4 percent of being elected to political office.[3] Perhaps you have had similar daydreams.

Laughter is a wonderful defense because it releases as much tension as crying and is a lot more fun. When women are asked what they enjoy most about a man, humor is usually very high on the list. Humor releases endorphins and enkephalins, which are our natural antidepressants.

Forgiveness. Bitterness can defile many, according to Hebrews 12:15: "Looking diligently lest anyone fall short of the grace of God; lest any root of bitterness springing up cause trouble, and by this many become defiled." Through forgiveness we can relieve a tremendous stress. Apparently we can control whether or not we let go of anger and forgive. Ephesians 4:31–32 says, "Let all bitterness, wrath, anger, clamor, and evil speaking be put away from you, with all malice. And be kind to one another, tenderhearted, forgiving one another, just as God in Christ also forgave you." Since the number one stress factor we see at this clinic is anger at other individuals, forgiveness may be one of the greatest defenses against stress.

Faith, of course, is more than a defense, but it probably relieves stress better than anything else. Faith in Christ, faith in what he can do, faith in the veracity of the Scriptures, faith in God's promises, faith for a wonderful future—faith offers help that is almost beyond description. Faith is what brought us to Christ and faith is what allows us to live the Christian life, even if it is filled with stressors.

Love. The giving and accepting of genuine Christian love is a wonderful defense against feelings of inferiority and loneliness that cause stress. Love is a choice. Love is a behavior. Love is a defense that we can choose. Since calm feelings tend to follow loving behavior, this defense should be primary.

Confession. Guilt causes unbelievable stress. First John 1:9—"If we confess our sins, He is faithful and just to forgive us our sins and to cleanse us from all unrighteousness"—offers relief from any guilt that the Christian may be facing. Christians are also encouraged to confess their sins to each other; this will promote healing. James 5:16 says: "Confess your trespasses to one another, and pray one for another so that you may be healed. The effective, fervent prayer of a righteous man avails much."

Redirection. In redirection an individual may become aware of some unwanted psychological or spiritual issues or inappropriate behavior and choose a different course of action. The different course of action reduces the stress.

Restitution is correcting a wrong. If individuals have been hurt, then restitution may be appropriate. If you have truly wronged someone, the mental stress you feel could be relieved by an apology.

Conscious control means dealing with stress with appropriate behavior, choosing against hostile retaliation or inappropriate acting-out behavior. Christ can give you the ability to deal with stress in a healthy manner by conscious control.

You may want to put a check by the healthy defense mechanism you use the most and a star by the one you would like to use more.

Spiritual Effects

Stress can affect our spiritual life. It may cause us to lose a sense of the Lord's presence and caring. For example, Elijah was an extremely godly man, but under stress he lost perspective and wanted to die. He thought he was the only one left who loved the Lord.

■ Overcoming Stress

1. Change Your Perception through the Scriptures

Perception is everything when it comes to stress. The Scriptures were written to alter our perception. It is possible to be under stress and yet not distressed. "We are troubled on every side, yet not distressed; we are perplexed, but not in despair; persecuted, but not forsaken; cast down, but not destroyed" (2 Cor. 4:8–9 KJV).

In the table below, consider common perceptions versus the reality of the Scriptures.

Common Perception	Reality Perception from the Scriptures
This situation is hopeless.	Behold, I am the LORD, the God of all flesh. Is there anything too hard for Me? (Jer. 32:27). The LORD has established His throne in the heavens, and His sovereignty rules over all (Ps. 103:19 NASB).
There is no one to help me in this stress.	And when the servant of the man of God arose early and went out, there was an army, surrounding the city with horses and chariots. And his servant said to him, "Alas, my master! What shall we do?" So he answered, "Do not fear, for those who are with us are more than those who are with them." And Elisha prayed, and said, "LORD, I pray, open his eyes that he may see." Then the LORD opened the eyes of the young man, and he saw. And behold, the mountain was full of horses and chariots of fire all around Elisha (2 Kings 6:15–17). If you make the Most High your dwelling— even the LORD, who is my refuge—then no harm will befall you, no disaster will come near your tent. For he will command his angels concerning you to guard you in all your ways (Ps. 91:9–11 NIV).

My stress is an individual who is being just plain mean to me. I am afraid.	The LORD is for me; I will not fear; what can man do to me? (Ps. 118:6 NASB).
I am alone facing this stress. Doesn't God know or care?	I will never desert you, nor will I ever forsake you (Heb. 13:5 NASB).
I love Christ, but if you only knew the many people who are against me . . .	Do not be fainthearted. Do not be afraid, or panic, or tremble before them, for the LORD your God is the one who goes with you, to fight for you against your enemies, to save you (Deut. 20:3–4 NASB).
These stressors will never end.	Be merciful to me, O God, be merciful to me! For my soul trusts in You; and in the shadow of Your wings I will make my refuge, until these calamities have passed by (Ps. 57:1).

Now, go back and put a check by problem perceptions that you need to alter with the reality of the Scriptures. Christ is ever so gentle and will help you work on your faulty perceptions. You may want to commit one of the above Scriptures to memory so it will be there when a problem area causes distress.

2. Develop a Fighting Spirit

Seventy women with breast cancer and subsequent mastectomies were divided into four groups—those who felt hopeless, those who were indifferent, those who were in denial, and those who had a fighting spirit or the attitude of "I will beat this thing." Ten-year survival rates were evaluated. Only 20 percent of the hopeless group (they felt there was nothing they could do) survived. Only 25 percent of the indifferent group (they showed no signs of distress) survived. Fifty percent of those in the denial group (they felt the mastectomy was just preventive) survived. However, 70 percent of those with a fighting spirit survived the physical and emotional stress.[4]

An aging sage said to me years ago, "Pray to God but row to shore." In other words, God will help, but we must do our part and fight. Nehemiah 4:9, 14 says, "But we prayed to our God and posted a guard day and night to meet this threat. . . . After I looked things over, I stood up and said to the nobles, the officials and the rest of the people, 'Don't be afraid of them. Remember the Lord, who is great and awesome, and fight for your brothers, your sons and your daughters, your wives and your homes'" (NIV). Indeed, we must fight back. God wants us to have a fighting spirit to combat the effect of the stressors in our life. How much fighting spirit can you muster with God's help?

3. Alter Your Lifestyle

Do you live a high-stress lifestyle? Perhaps altering your lifestyle would help alleviate some of your stress. You may need to slow down, get a different job, go on a vacation, move to the country, lay aside some of your burdens, avoid certain individuals, or bring to an end some other ongoing stressor. It's worth making changes in your lifestyle if they mean you will be less stressed.

■ Follow-Up

Our world is filled with many stressful people and events that can make you feel overwhelmed. Stress does not have to defeat you, however. You can gain insight into why you are prone to stress, memorize the precious Scriptures, develop a fighting spirit, and alter your lifestyle. Trust Christ to help you calm a stressful life.

7

Loss and Grief

Pursuing Comfort

Holy influences from this right choice flowed down through the
generations to come, and resulted in untold good.

Dr. and Mrs. Howard Taylor

I have never felt such a pain as I felt on May 8, 1989, when I
heard that my mother had died. My life had always been tough
because I had grown up having diabetes mellitus, which meant
daily injections, special diets, and being sickly in general. However,
I had always had one unbelievable ally—my mother. She had led
me to Christ; she had always been there to encourage me; she had
always believed that God had a special purpose for me and that he
had gifted me for that purpose.

Now, suddenly, she had died of a heart attack. My heart ached
with a burden I cannot explain. For one of the few times in my life,
I had been knocked to my knees.

What losses have you suffered in the past two years? Have you
lost a relationship through death, conflict, or a move? Have you
experienced a financial loss? Have you lost health or self-esteem?
Are you suffering from lost youth? Have you lost a job or your
career through missing a promotion?

With loss, it is easy to become discouraged. We often view a loss
as catastrophic, impossible, hopeless, negative, personal, or altering
our life forever. Do Christians tend to view loss from the wrong

perspective? What if that perspective were altered? I have found that it is possible to gain from our losses. Here are six choices that may help you do that.

■ Gaining from Loss

1. Allow for Time

Often time helps with the pain of loss. As a psychiatrist, I am especially concerned if someone's grief is intense past a few months. Usually with most major losses, the emotions are continually intense at first. Then the emotional pain seems to come in periodic waves. Eventually it abates.

2. Share

Sharing really does help. When my mother died, I spent many nights talking with my wife, Mary Alice, and my sister, Georgia, who is a lot like my mother. And sharing my grief with a few dear friends was comforting.

Sharing lifts a burden. There is no need to carry your loss alone. Galatians 6:2 states, "Carry each other's burdens" (NIV). Then verse 5 says, "For each one should carry his own load." Do these verses seem contradictory? The Greek word for *burden* in verse 2 is different from the word for *load* in verse 5. The word for *burden* in verse 2 actually means excessive burden. We need to share excessive burdens with someone who cares—our mate, a close friend, a counselor, our pastor, or another Christian with a spirit of encouragement. With whom do you share your burdens of loss?

3. Change Your Behavior

Are you in a grieving rut? It may be time to move beyond the loss. Isaiah 43:18 states, "Forget the former things; do not dwell on the past" (NIV). The emphasis seems to be on the word *dwell*. Are you preoccupied with a loss? Have you thought about it too much and for too long? Are you dwelling on it? Grieving is necessary, but you may need to change your day-to-day behavior. Because you are so focused on your loss, you may be missing current blessings. The Isaiah passage goes on to say, "See, I am doing a new thing!

Now it springs up; do you not perceive it? I am making a way in the desert and streams in the wasteland" (v. 19 NIV). As I've said before, feeling follows behavior. If you believe your grieving is more extended than it should be, try returning to some of the healthy activities you did before your loss. You may find that your feelings of grief and loss will lighten.

4. Gain Insight

You may be stuck in one of the stages of grief (denial, anger turned inward, anger turned outward, bargaining). Perhaps you can't let go because you need insight into an unhealthy, unfinished agenda before you can move forward. If you had an unhealthy dependency on the person you have lost, you may need someone to help you gain insight into this and how you can meet your needs in a healthier way, such as by developing relationships with several members of the body of Christ. A wise counselor can often help an individual gain insight. Proverbs 20:5 states, "Counsel in the heart of man is like deep water, but a man of understanding will draw it out."

5. Consider Medication

If the grief is prolonged and unrelenting, it may be that the brain chemistry has changed from the stress of loss. With the alteration of brain chemicals, thinking becomes perpetually negative and focused on the past. Seemingly the brain loses the ability to realize that the loss has been sufficiently grieved. Even when God wants to do a new thing and send new blessings, a state of grief and high alert persists. When this is the case, it may mean that you are medically depressed. In that case, antidepressant medication should be considered and can make a world of difference. You may need only a short-acting sleeping pill, such as Ambien, or a mild tranquilizer, such as Xanax, which is effective especially for a short period of time.

6. Have a New Perspective

In circumstances of loss there may exist both a human and divine element. They do not negate each other in any way. For example, from a human perspective the individual may feel that he should have done more to prevent the loss, but we understand from a divine perspective that a Christian's length of life ultimately depends on God (see Ps. 31:15). Sometimes, for our mental health, it is good for a while to focus on the divine element. I often share the following verses with my Christian friends who are lost in the human element.

Issue	Seven False Beliefs of Christians	Biblical Truth
Life Length of life and death	If only I had done more, she would have lived.	All the days ordained for me were written in your book before one of them came to be (Ps. 139:16 NIV). My times are in Your hand (Ps. 31:15).
Promotion Success or failure	If only I had tried harder, I would have succeeded in this endeavor.	For exaltation comes neither from the east nor from the west nor from the south. But God is the Judge: He puts down one, and exalts another (Ps. 75:6).
Loss Tragedy and calamity	This event will destroy me. My life is ruined. Nothing good can ever come out of this.	And we know that all things work together for good to those who love God, to those who are called according to His purpose (Rom. 8:28).
Jerks People who are mean to you	These people have set out to destroy me, and they will succeed.	As for you, you meant evil against me; but God meant it for good, in order to bring it about as it is this day, to save many people alive (Gen. 50:20). Who shall separate us from the love of Christ? Shall tribulation, or distress, or persecution, or famine, or nakedness, or peril, or sword? . . . Yet in all these things we are more than conquerors through Him who loved us (Rom. 8:35, 37).

World events out of control The six o'clock bad news	The world is in horrible shape—economic crises around the globe, wars, and terrorism. There are so many dangers, I feel very nervous. My world will surely fall apart also. I think God has finally lost control.	All the inhabitants of the earth are reputed as nothing; He does according to His will in the army of heaven and among the inhabitants of the earth. No one can restrain His hand or say to Him, "What have You done?" (Dan. 4:35).
Why do things always go wrong?	I might as well give up. Look at all that has happened to me.	Then the LORD said to Job, "Will the faultfinder contend with the Almighty? Let him who reproves God answer it." . . . Then the LORD answered Job out of the storm and said, "Now gird up your loins like a man; I will ask you, and you instruct Me. Will you really annul My judgment? Will you condemn Me that you may be justified? Or do you have an arm like God, and can you thunder with a voice like His?" (Job 40:1–2, 6–9 NASB).
Happiness is gone forever	Life can never be any better. It can never turn around after this loss.	I will restore to you the years that the swarming locust has eaten (Joel 2:25).

■ Six Lessons on Grief

God used my mother's death to teach me six lessons on grief that I hope will be of help to you. As you know, we can grieve any kind of loss (a person through death, divorce, separation; an object; health; prestige; self-esteem; finances; and so on). Here are the lessons I learned. They pertain more to the grief of death, but with a little adaptation they can apply to any type of grief.

1. It Is Okay to Grieve

As Christians, we do not grieve as those who have no hope (1 Thess. 4:13), but we do grieve. Even Christ cried at Lazarus's death. The Bible is filled with examples of mourning. "Blessed are those who mourn, for they shall be comforted" (Matt. 5:4 NASB).

2. God Is Still with You

God uses people to love and care for us, but ultimately he is the one who is loving us through them. It can help immensely to realize that, just as he used one individual who is now gone, he can use another. He alone will always be with you: "When you pass through the waters, I will be with you; and through the rivers, they shall not overflow you. When you walk through the fire, you shall not be burned, nor shall the flame scorch you" (Isa. 43:2).

3. God Is Able to Help

I believe God loves to hear from us. Tell him your sorrow and your grief. Ask him to please help. He is omnipotent, omnipresent, and omniscient. He *can* help! "Casting all your anxiety on Him, because He cares for you" (1 Peter 5:7 NASB).

4. Scripture Comforts

Scripture has always soothed my soul during times of trouble. Being able to recall a verse I've memorized at just the right moment has been precious to me. If you memorize some of the following verses, they will comfort you in your times of mourning and loss.

> *Psalm 23:4 (NASB):* Even though I walk through the valley of the shadow of death, I fear no evil, for You are with me; Your rod and Your staff, they comfort me.
>
> *Hebrews 4:15–16 (NASB):* For we do not have a high priest who cannot sympathize with our weaknesses, but One who has been tempted in all things as we are, yet without sin. Therefore let us draw near with confidence to the throne of grace, so that we may receive mercy and find grace to help in time of need.
>
> *Isaiah 41:10 (NASB):* Do not fear, for I am with you; do not anxiously look about you, for I am your God. I will strengthen you, surely I will help you, surely I will uphold you with My righteous right hand.

2 Corinthians 1:3–4 (NASB): Blessed be the God and Father of our Lord Jesus Christ, the Father of mercies and God of all comfort, who comforts us in all our affliction so that we will be able to comfort those who are in any affliction with the comfort with which we ourselves are comforted by God.

Psalm 119:50 (NASB): This is my comfort in my affliction, that Your word has revived me.

1 Peter 5:7 (NASB): Casting all your anxiety on Him, because He cares for you.

Psalm 139:16 (NIV): All the days ordained for me were written in your book before one of them came to be.

5. We Have Our Hope of Heaven

We can be comforted when we realize that, if a deceased person knows Christ, he or she is far better off in heaven with Christ than here on earth. Our loved one is doing well, but we grieve because we miss him or her.

6. God Is Still in Control

No matter what has happened, it was not beyond God's control. Ultimately he permitted it, he can control it, and he can still bless you if you let him. "He does according to His will in the army of heaven and among the inhabitants of the earth. No one can restrain His hand or say to Him, 'What have You done?'" (Dan. 4:35).

◼ Follow-Up

My friend, Christ loves you. He knows you are hurting. My prayers are with you. As for me, I know my precious mother is in heaven, and I came to realize that I must go on for Christ, and, my dear friend, so must you.

8

Trials

Pursuing Victory

Choosing Christ makes us heirs to all the wealth and glory of the Father's kingdom.

Walter B. Knight

A number of years ago a man who ran a country store went broke and spent ten years working out of the bankruptcy. Later he ran for the Senate two times and lost, and ran for the House two times and lost, but finally he was elected to office. He lived for years in an unhappy marriage. At times in his life he was moody. Yet this man's life and a speech he gave shook the halls of history. He was a man who learned to beat the odds. He was a man who simply signed his name Abe Lincoln.

As I thought about the difficulties Abe Lincoln had to overcome, my mind was drawn to Gideon in the Old Testament. We saw in chapter 1 that he was the least member of his family and his family was the least in the tribe, yet God chose Gideon with an army of three hundred men to beat an enemy with an army in the thousands of thousands. God chose the least of the least and led him to victory. The odds were perhaps four hundred to one against him; and yet I sense that those are just the kind of odds God likes.

I was pondering the story of Gideon the night of March 24, 1985, as I was driving home late from medical rounds. My mind then went to a dear mentor of mine in Christianity and psychiatry who lost out to the odds and committed suicide. Although he was an extremely gifted man, the difficulties of life had beaten him. *Why do some beat the odds and others do not?* I asked myself as I thought about my mentor, Lincoln, and Gideon.

When I arrived home, Mary Alice greeted me and said that a very interesting manuscript had come in the mail and perhaps I should read it. The hour was late and I was tempted to toss it aside, but, fortunately, I read the first page and could not put it down.

The storyteller told a heart-tugging and romantic narrative. Like the story of Esther in the Bible, God was ever present behind the scenes. It was a story from bygone years when time was not so rushed, when one could relax in front of a crackling fire as the family gathered around. Those were gentler days when old-fashioned values and a God who was there in trials were accepted parts of life. The storyteller wove a beautiful picture of beating the odds. Here are the words I read that night that changed my life forever.

> When I got married and acquired me a wife, I also gained the possession of a dog. Having found just the "right" girl, I was doubtful I had found just the "right" dog! However, he was my wife's dog and, having been given to us with the blessings of my mother-in-law, how could I refuse?
>
> They called him Boy Dog. He was a mongrel of sorts and his most distinguishing feature was a dark red, shaggy coat. A dog of great size, he weighed sixty to seventy pounds, and resembled an Irish Setter more than any other blood line. However, his head was much broader. His mighty chest, strong shoulders, and sturdy legs showed he must have had some German Shepherd ancestors. . . . One day I needed to make a trip into town, and I knew that Boy Dog would enjoy the ride, because he was always eager to keep me company. I whistled for him, and he came running from around front of the house. He liked to sleep on an old meat block there that Mr. Taylor had given me when his grocery store had gone out of business.
>
> "You keep an eye out for him, and don't let him get into any fights, you hear!" my wife warned.
>
> "Don't you worry now. I'll watch out for him," I said (recalling very well that I'd been told once before that Boy Dog could take care of himself in a scrap).

When I stopped at the International Harvester place at the edge of town to purchase some new plow points, I commanded Boy Dog to "stay." When a huge, white bulldog appeared and walked over to the strip-down, sniffing the tires and growling, with his teeth bared and his fur bristling, little did I know how great a temptation this would be for Boy Dog. It was plain to see that the bulldog was inviting a fight, and it didn't take long for Boy Dog to accept the invitation.

Boy Dog took a single leap from the front seat, meeting his aggressor head-on. A continuous roar arose as the two angry dogs tumbled back and forth with a gnashing and snarling of teeth, each dog waiting for the right moment to grasp a deadly hold.

As I ran from the building to get a better look, the thought raced through my mind of how many times in such fights a bulldog is known to go for the throat, holding on without letting go until its victim lies motionless and dead. I reached down and picked up a nearby stick, ready to step in if need be; for this dog was heavier in weight than my dog, and I had heard of his reputation. . . . Never having seen Boy Dog fight before, I didn't know that he had a few tricks of his own. As the tremendous form lunged for his throat, Boy Dog seemed to duck. With his mighty jaws he took a good, firm bite into the bulldog's tender, left foot. There he held on with a grip as tight as a mighty steel trap. The bulldog let out a distressful, lingering yelp and fell limp, unable to move. He lay there helpless in the dusty gravel. Seeing as how the bulldog was unable to do any more harm and evidently was in much pain, I hurried over to Boy Dog, reached down, took hold of his collar, and issued a command.

"That's enough, Boy. Let him go now."

The big bulldog got up and took off like a scared rabbit. I seriously doubt he ever picked a fight with Boy Dog again.

"You old rascal," I said to him. "That's a pretty good trick. Where in the world did you learn to fight like that? We won't say anything to Dollie about this, except I imagine she'll know what's gone on by the looks of you." In every fight that I observed him in after that, he always used the same method of biting squarely into a tender paw, thus paralyzing his victim. . . . It wasn't unusual for us to learn things from the animals on the farm; but Boy Dog was something else. He didn't know that the odds seemed to be against him, so they didn't bother him. He just expected and looked for a way to win! Little did I know then how much I would need to remember Boy Dog's example in the years to come. . . . Six years passed. Things couldn't have been better. The farm was beginning to pay for itself, and we had hopes of replacing our three-room bungalow with a new-style farmhouse. Boy Dog proved to be a constant, loving companion. The year was 1941 and with it came rumors of war and then the bombing of Pearl Harbor.

I was thirty years old at the time, with no dependents except for my wife, Dollie, and, of course, Boy Dog (whom the Army didn't count as one). Although thirty was considered old for an enlisted man, single boys and men without children were issued their notices first. This made me a number-one draft choice and shortly word came that my departure date would be on October 17, 1942.

Dollie, Papa, and Boy Dog took me to the train station at Blytheville. From there I would travel to Little Rock, the state capital, and then be assigned to an army base. I thought of how Mama would have been there to see me off, too; but she'd passed on from us years before.

I stepped onto the train. Boy Dog ran alongside trying to get a footing on the first step. I reached down and patted his head.

"So long, Boy. You stay and look after Dollie while I'm gone, you hear?" With those words I gave him a gentle push backwards.

Waving goodbye, I fought hard to hold back the tears. Boy Dog didn't understand why he couldn't make this trip with me, nor did I understand at the time the dangers that lay ahead for me and the loneliness that lay ahead for my wife and him as they remained behind. . . . At Camp Beal we drew our overseas equipment. Rumors were circulating that our division would be heading out for the Philippine Islands, but nothing was yet official. On July 26, 1944, once again I kissed my wife goodbye and left out of San Francisco Bay—destination unknown!

After forty-two days on board ship we found ourselves unloading on the shores of the Hawaiian Islands. However, this was no vacation trip. Here we took our jungle training and more amphibious training, and I continued my training as first scout.

By this time I had received my first letter from Dollie, and with it came exciting news.

Dearest Husband,

I have thrilling, wonderful news. I am expecting a baby and come late March you'll be a papa. I saw Dr. Fox this week and he said that was what those sick spells I'd been having were all about. I can't tell you how happy I am and how much I wish you to be here with me.

I fear for you greatly, and Boy Dog must, too, for the other night after I had gone to bed he raised up the most lonesome howl I've ever before heard. I've never known him to howl and the sound was awesome, sending chills up and down my spine. He was wet from the rain, but I let him come into the house and from that night on he has slept on the floor by my bed. When I cook for myself I also cook enough for Boy Dog. He is so much company to me with you being so far away.

I had to sell Gin and Doll and the cattle, as they were getting too much for me to take care of with the winter coming on. Gin didn't seem to mind, but Doll really threw a fit, and I had to leave the window as the men loaded her.

Mama stays here with me part of the time. Don't worry about me; just take care of yourself and be thinking of a name for the baby. May God be with you.

Love,
Your wife,
Dollie

Just think—me a papa, finally! I read the letter over and over. I told everyone whom I met about my good news and I prayed that God would let me live to see this child.

Our first step into combat was on the island of Leyte, in the Philippines. From there we traveled to Guam and Mindoro and Mindanao, each time sustaining heavy losses. The days were filled with violent attacks and fright, and the nights with sleeplessness because of the crashing sounds of artillery.

It was here that I came to know the Lord in a truly personal way and only He sustained me. The words of Psalm 56:3, "What time I am afraid, I will trust in thee," were always with me.

Once I was sitting next to a tree for protection. The position seemed to be a good one, but I felt I should move, so I did. A moment later the tree was blown up. I will always feel the Lord took care of me then.

Our biggest push was on the island of Okinawa, where we lost practically our whole division. We went in with one hundred and twenty-five men and only twenty-five of us, twenty percent of our division, walked out alive. . . .

So far, for what reasons I didn't know, God was still protecting me, and I was still beating the odds. However, I was escaping all that danger only to ship out for mainland Japan.

We left Okinawa on an L.T.C. cargo ship headed for Japan proper. Not long after we boarded the ship, we ran into a terrible storm at sea. The storm grew so violent that the captain ordered all of us below. We were below the main deck, where the trucks, jeeps, and tanks were stored. With every crash of the waves, the ship would make a loud cracking sound. With the storm raging so, I said, "Boys, the next one's going to get us!"

We had weathered the storm for one day and one night. It was nearing dusk when the storm began to pass over us. We were back port-side when the captain's voice blew out through the loudspeaker. "Now hear this, now hear this: It is a fact that the emperor of Japan has unconditionally surrendered to the United States of America."

Stunned, no one said a word. We all just looked at each other.

Once again the captain's voice rang out. "Now hear this, now hear this: It is a fact that the emperor of Japan has unconditionally surrendered to the United States of America." It was the fourteenth day of August, 1945. . . .

As we stepped from the gang plank to American soil, the first thing we did was to kneel and kiss the ground, and I said "Thank You" to God in my heart! There were people lined up on each side waiting to shake hands with the men who'd helped win the war and had returned home.

The army had efficiently gathered information and had arranged for each soldier a five-minute telephone conversation with a member of his family. Since we had no telephone, I had sent word for Dollie to be at the central telephone office in our hometown of Leachville on the afternoon of December 21. We were taken to a large depot in San Francisco and ushered into a long hallway where telephone booths stood on each side for a distance of two hundred yards or more. As each soldier's call was placed, his name was spoken over an intercom. You could have heard a pin drop as everyone sat quietly awaiting his turn.

As my name was called and I walked to the booth, I kept going over all the important things I wanted to say. My hand trembled as I picked up the telephone. I managed to utter a single, "Hello," before my voice failed me. Dollie picked up the conversation on the other end, and I listened intently as she tried to hurriedly cover all the topics she knew I'd want to hear about. I heard my daughter jabber and I knew that she was saying "I love you, Daddy." It was nearing Christmas Day, but I knew that I'd never make it home by then.

In the meantime, the Army was going all-out to treat us. After each soldier had a chance to talk, we were taken to a large cafeteria in the same building and allowed to order anything. Being, oh, so hungry for some southern cooking, I ordered steak with white soup, beans, and cornbread.

After three days in San Francisco, I found myself on a southern-bound train headed for Arkansas. I arrived in Little Rock and continued my journey on to Blytheville with a buddy of mine. As I stepped off the train, I thought of how this was the very spot where I'd said my farewells an eternity ago, it seemed to me.

I made my way to the outskirts of town. With my army pack on my back, I was going to try my luck at hitchhiking the remaining twenty miles.

As I stood there beside the edge of the highway, a car began slowing down to stop. The man inside rolled down the window and said, "Get in soldier!" Then he looked over at me again. "Well, well, Ike, is that you?"

It was Mr. Kennett, a man I knew from Leachville. We shook hands and he tried to catch me up on all the news from home.

"You know, Ike," he said, "that big, red dog of yours has been seen all over this country! He's been seen in town and at practically all the neighbors' houses, especially when you and your wife were both gone. Looking for you all, I suppose. Everybody just seemed to watch out for him. I suppose the folks here at home thought they might be helping you out in the war, in some small way, by looking out for him. He'd stay somewhere a day or so and then move on. He's quite a dog."

"Yes, that he most certainly is," I replied. "Thanks for looking out for him and thanks for the ride," I said as we approached the road that led from the highway to my house.

"Don't you want me to run you on down to your house?" he asked.

"If you don't mind, Mr. Kennett, I'd rather just walk from here. Thanks again for the ride. Goodbye."

It was the twenty-eighth day of December 1945, and there was a chill in the morning air as I stepped out of his car and onto the dirt road—the dirt road that led home.

As I stood there buttoning up my overcoat, I looked toward my house and then over toward Papa's house. I wondered how he was feeling today. Dollie had said that he hadn't been feeling well lately. I looked at the stalks left standing there in Mr. Moore's cotton field and I wondered if he'd had a good crop this year.

I felt the anticipation growing inside as I picked up my bag and started walking, knowing that shortly I'd be seeing my daughter and my wife. This was the day I'd dreamed of, night after night, as I'd laid in the foxholes. I almost had to pinch myself to realize that I was no longer dreaming.

A little over halfway, where the tall cottonwood stood, I could see the house in full view. I stopped and whistled, wondering if Boy Dog would hear. I watched as he raised his head in a curious manner from where he lay resting on the old meat block. At first he didn't move, but his ears were standing upright and he was watching me. I whistled again. This time he bounded off the front porch onto the frozen earth and here he came! He had remembered the whistle! He knew who I was!

I dropped my bag and knelt down on one knee as he came closer. "Here, Boy," I said, observing his actions closely. No human face could have shown more emotion than did Boy Dog's. As I put my arms around his mighty neck, I felt his old heart pounding heavily and I noticed the streaks of gray that were mingled in among the red. Boy Dog had become an old dog. The years had taken their toll and he had aged greatly in the four years that I'd been away.

"I'm home, fellow," I said. "You don't have to go out looking any more. I'm home to stay." He barked as if to say he understood what I was saying.

"Now, Boy Dog, let's you and me get on toward the house. I've been looking forward to this day for a long time and, by the way, fellow, I think that you've got somebody to introduce me to, haven't you?"

The story above shows how, time after time, God did protect me and how, with Him, I did beat the odds. He was there. He did care.

A couple of years after I returned home, Boy Dog died; but by then I was blessed with a son. I wish I could have spared him some of the trials he would have to face, but then that wasn't God's way. I guess I should have known that God would have to lead my son through trials, too. It was all in His perfect plan.[1]

The above story was told by my dad and recorded by my sister. In it valuable lessons are hidden on how to avoid drowning emotionally. He has long since passed on, but his lessons live on today. Dad was a first scout and a machine gunner during World War II. Of his original company of around six hundred, he was one of only a handful who survived. He beat the odds!

■ Overcoming Trials

Have you ever felt as though you were drowning emotionally—having gone down once, twice, and about to go down the third and final time? Have you ever felt like you were being beaten down by the odds of life? I want to share seven choices with you that may very well mean the difference for you in beating the odds and overcoming trials. Some I have learned from my years in medicine, psychiatry, and theology; but perhaps the best lessons are from my dad.

1. Partner with God

The first lesson I learned is the most powerful and comes from the Bible. The story of David and Goliath is in 1 Samuel 17. Goliath was a giant in the land, and David ran to meet the giant, although in his human strength the odds were against him. In 1 Samuel 17:45 are recorded these words that send chills up my spine: "David said to the Philistine, 'You come to me with a sword, a spear, and a javelin, but I come to you in the name of the LORD of hosts"(NASB). We know the story goes on to tell how David killed the giant with only a slingshot. Surely God was with him.

Even when I read David's amazing words, my mind wants to re-tort, but does God really care about me? Does he really hear? I am reminded of an incident in Numbers 12:1–2, 9: "Then Miriam and Aaron spoke against Moses. . . . And the LORD heard it. . . . So the anger of the LORD was aroused against them." Many of the dear people who have called in on my radio show over the years remind me of Moses. They are godly and humble. Often others have hurt them for no reason. Does God care? Does God hear the schemes and odds against them? The passage says, "Miriam and Aaron spoke against Moses. . . . And the LORD heard it." He knows what we're going through and he cares. He will give us the help we need.

2. Develop a Mission for Christ

Close to 50 percent of individuals who retire die within a year or two. Could it be that they lose out to the "odds," because part of their mission in life—their job—is missing? A mission is what keeps us going against seemingly insurmountable odds. Have you kept going because of your children or your spouse or some other purpose? The best mission is one that can never be taken from us—a mission for Jesus Christ. Why not make your mission that of The Navigators: "To know him and make him known."

As a child, you may have sung a song in Sunday school about a man who beat ominous odds in the lions' den because he had a mission:

> Dare to be a Daniel,
> Dare to stand alone!
> Dare to have a purpose firm!
> Dare to make it known![2]

3. Never Give Up!

The best commencement address ever given at Harvard consisted of three words repeated seven times. The orator was Winston Churchill, and he said: "Never give up. Never give up. Never give up. Never give up. Never give up. Never give up. Never give up." Then he sat down. Those words are still the best advice on how to beat the odds of life.

Persistence gives you an unbelievable advantage in fighting the odds of life. Even Christ advised it when he told about the desperate widow who persisted with the judge until he gave her what she wanted in Luke 18:1–5.

While I am perhaps best known for encouraging others to take care of themselves physically and psychologically, there are times when, for the cause of Christ, one must persist against all odds. Hopefully these times will be brief and infrequent. There are times when the theme of an old quote should be applied: "The heights of great men were not achieved by sudden flight, but while their companions slept, they were toiling through the night." Perhaps for many it's a matter not of toiling through the night but rather of being persistent and resilient and never giving up. When you are going through a trial, you may want to picture in your mind's eye that you are in a race. Christ is just on the other side of the finish line. He is urging you on. You must finish the race for him.

4. Don't Fight the Battle Alone

When I was in college, a friend of mine, States, often talked about a brunette journalism major who sat just behind him in class. One day at the Baptist Student Union, there she sat. States had not introduced me. In fact, no one had told me Snow White's (that's how she appeared to me) name. I just knew that this must be the girl he had been talking about. *Would she go out with me? Might she even consider it? I probably don't have a chance,* I thought. Well, I couldn't help it—I had always been attracted to brunettes.

The B.S.U. was having a Christmas carol sing, and a group of my friends went. Snow White happened to go too. My heart thumped each time I glanced at her dark eyes. However, I was with my current girlfriend.

I didn't have any psychological training then, but I knew what guilt felt like. What was I doing? I was with one girl but thinking about another. My best friend had told me about the other girl, so he must be interested in her too. I, however (ashamed as I ought to be to say so), fought off such rational thinking. The thought that threw off all others was, *Would she go out with me?*

A few days later I picked up the phone to call her. My hands trembled as I dialed. The phone rang. "Hello," she said. My heart jumped. I valiantly fought the quiver in my voice as I tried to tell her who I was and ask her for a date. Just as I expected, she said no. I knew it; I knew she wouldn't go! Well, while I had her on the phone, I thought I might as well ask her if she would go out with me the next week. "Yes." Did she say yes? I almost fainted but maintained my composure as I coolly told her that I would see her then.

The date worked out fine. I was struck with the fact that she loved Christ. She had a quiet and gentle spirit and was very different from any girl I had met. Believe it or not, she seemed to like me! At last I could identify with the last verse of an old song I used to sing, which after we had dated awhile I would often sing to her:

> God gave to the wise men their wisdom,
> To the poets He gave them their dreams,
> To father and mother, their love for each other,
> But He left me out, though, it seemed.
> I went around broken-hearted
> Thinking life was an empty affair.
> But when God gave me you,
> It was then that I knew
> He had given me more than my share.

After she heard my singing, I was surprised that Mary Alice ever consented to marry me; but she did! With Mary Alice, I found the best human element to beating the odds—always there, always on my team, always at my side fighting along with me.

God sent Mary Alice to me. He knew together we could beat the odds. However, the important lesson is this: No man is an island. No man or woman can win alone. Throughout the New Testament the theme of "one another" appears over and over. We need each other in the body of Christ to be victorious in trials. I quoted this verse earlier and it applies here as well: "Two are better than one, because they have a good reward for their labor. For if they fall, one will lift up his companion. But woe to him who is alone when he falls, for he has no one to help him up" (Eccles. 4:9–10).

5. Find Help in a Mysterious Triangle of Strength

There exists a mysterious triangle of strength that allows you to beat the odds through dimensions that cannot be seen or heard. The first leg of that triangle is *God's Word* (see Deut. 32:46–47; Pss. 1:2; 119:162; Matt. 7:24–25; 24:35; Luke 24:32; John 6:63; 1 Thess. 2:13; Heb. 4:12; 11:3; and 1 John 2:14). Some of the comments in the above verses about God's Word are beyond interesting. For example: "It is your life." "I rejoice at Your word as one who finds great treasure." "Therefore whoever hears these sayings of Mine, and does them, I will liken him to a wise man who built his house on the rock: and the rain descended, the floods came, and the winds blew and beat on that house; and it did not fall." "And they said to one another, 'Did not our heart burn within us while He talked with us on the road, and while He opened the Scriptures to us?'" "The words that I speak to you are spirit, and they are life." "For the word of God is living and powerful." "The worlds were framed by the word of God." "I have written to you, young men, because you are strong, and the word of God abides in you." There is no doubt that God's Word empowered by the Holy Spirit offers supernatural help in beating the odds.

The second leg of the triangle of strength is *prayer* (see 1 Kings 3:12; 1 Chron. 4:10; Dan. 10:12; and James 5:17). Interesting words, are they not? "God granted him what he requested." "Your words were heard; and I have come because of your words." "Elijah was a man with a nature like ours, and he prayed earnestly that it would not rain; and it did not rain."

The third leg of the triangle is the *body of Christ* (see Acts 2:42 and Heb. 10:25). Support and encouragement can be found in our close relationship with other Christians.

This triangle of strength has allowed men and women through the ages to beat the odds. The mysterious power of God's Word, prayer, and the fellowship of believers has not diminished.

6. Help for Our Trichotomous Being!

In our trichotomous being (spirit, soul, and body), the spiritual is of tremendous importance. We wrestle with an unbelievably powerful spiritual enemy who wants to beat us. "For we do not wrestle against flesh and blood, but against principalities, against powers, against the rulers of the darkness of this age, against spiritual hosts of wickedness in the heavenly places" (Eph. 6:12). Therefore, we need to walk closely with Christ.

Many of you may remember the old movie *The Invasion of the Body Snatchers*. The movie was about individuals who fell asleep and then their bodies were invaded by an outside force from space. All of a sudden they would no longer be the people they once were. In one of the final scenes were a couple of individuals who had still beaten the odds; they had not been invaded by the body snatchers. They were hiding in a cave when the lead character said to his girlfriend that he needed to step out of the cave for a moment and look for any intruding body snatchers. He did so and then in just a moment returned and kissed his girlfriend. In so doing, the horrible realization came over him that she was no longer the person she once was.

There is a tremendous analogy in that old movie for us today. Have you ever known a friend who walked with Christ and then fell into sin? I was recently talking by phone with just such an old friend. He had once loved Christ and walked with Christ daily, but on the phone he told me he no longer loved his wife and had fallen in love with another woman. As I listened, I had the eerie feeling that he was no longer the person I had once known. In a sense, Satan had snatched him.

We face a powerful enemy in Satan. Only through a daily walk with Christ can we beat the odds of falling into sin.

Concerning the physical, it is very hard to fight the odds when you are sick physically. You can increase your chances of beating the odds by such simple techniques as a healthy diet, increased exercise, and the appropriate use of medicines.

Concerning the psychological, consider just one recent research study of the effects of stress on the body. Positive emission tomography (PET) scan studies were done on individuals with ongoing stress (major depression, Cushing's disease, and posttraumatic stress disorder). A very important part of the brain (the hippocampus) showed atrophy. This is extremely important since the hippocampus controls emotional memory. Thus with continued stress, the brain could lose the ability to recognize when the stress is gone. Then the brain would stay in a constant hyperalert and vigilant state.

What a shame this is when many times a few simple principles may help in beating the odds of psychological disease:

- Share your *feelings* with someone every day.
- Strive for godly, appropriate, *healthy behavior,* regardless of how you feel. Feelings tend to follow behavior.
- Challenge *false thinking* on a minute-to-minute basis. Challenge *magnification* ("This is the end of the world"), *personalization* ("Their action was just because of me"), *perfectionism* ("I can never make a mistake"), and *selective attention on the negative* (a focus on your mistakes and not your successes).
- Gain, with the help of a godly Christian counselor, insight into *personality weaknesses* and unresolved past issues that still haunt you today.

The well-worn adage "We have met the enemy, and the enemy is us" is far too true when it comes to overcoming trials—the biggest fight may be within.

7. Remember Eternity

It is difficult to grasp the concept of eternity. Picture a bird walking around a steel ball the size of the earth until he wears it down so that it breaks in two. The time it takes for the bird to do that could represent just the first moment of the first day of eternity. However, the analogy is a poor one because there is no time in eternity. It is forever.

My dad beat the odds. He survived World War II. More important, however, he knew Christ. He is now with Christ for eternity. What about you? There is more to life than the trials of the moment. We must choose Christ today so that our eternal destiny is with him.

■ Follow-Up

As I pondered my dad's story on the night of March 24, 1985, my mind went back to a time when I was six years old. I was swimming near what we called Buffalo Bridge, and I almost drowned. I went down once; I went down twice; and then my dad grabbed me and lifted me out of the water, saving my physical body. His story taught me lessons on surviving spiritual and psychological trials.

Life is difficult. The odds are strongly stacked against you. For the cause of Christ, fight back. With his help you can be victorious over every trial.

9

Loneliness

Pursuing Relationships

Mary has chosen what is better, and it will not be taken away from her.

Jesus

The noted Swiss psychiatrist Paul Tournier tells the story of a lady who would turn on her radio in the evening just to hear the announcer say in a friendly voice, "We bid you a very pleasant good night!" She was so lonely that even an impersonal but friendly voice comforted her. I shared this story in one of my group therapy sessions, and at the end of the story I commented, "Of course, none of us is that lonely."

An elderly lady interrupted me and said, "Why, I am."

I should not have been surprised. Every week people come to see me who, in their own way, say, "I am so lonely; no one really cares for me. All I want is just one person to care for me."

There are many symptoms of loneliness. Some are obvious, and some are more disguised. In general, loneliness can be described as a state of not feeling accepted or of not belonging. Loneliness may involve intense emotional pain, an empty feeling, a yearning to be with someone, or a restlessness.

The following inventory may be useful in determining if you have some symptoms of loneliness. Complete it as quickly as you can. Your first response is often your most honest answer.

	True	False
I frequently do not feel accepted in a group.		
At times I feel as though I do not belong to the group I am with.		
I have a feeling of inner emotional pain and loneliness.		
I often have an empty feeling on the inside.		
I find myself yearning to be with someone.		
My friends often think that I have no problems and that I am always happy, even though on the inside I feel lonely.		
Although I can be adept at entertaining others, I feel lonely on the inside.		
I have felt rejected by friends.		
I like to talk about theories and carry on intellectual conversations but rarely feel really close to people.		
I find myself wishing that I could be more open about my hurts and pains.		
I desire acceptance by others but fear rejection.		
I have fewer than a half dozen friends with whom I am very close.		

How would you describe your symptoms of loneliness?

Loneliness is a common experience for millions of Americans. It is the reason for singles bars, encounter groups, drug experiences, free sex, and Eastern religions that are so popular today and to which so many have turned to overcome loneliness.

One survey revealed that 26 percent of those surveyed had felt very lonely at some point during the preceding few weeks. Psychiatric research shows that a majority of those seeking help feel very lonely. Loneliness is a problem especially for the elderly, who often escape through suicide. However, loneliness strikes all ages and all classes. People can feel lonely even when they are with many people. The top five stress factors on the Holmes and Rahe stress test have to do with loneliness (see chapter 6). Changes involving loneliness are the most stressful of all.

David, the great king and leader of God's people, felt lonely. He wrote: "Turn to me and be gracious to me, for I am lonely and afflicted. The troubles of my heart are enlarged; bring me out of my distresses. Look upon my affliction and my trouble, and forgive all my sins" (Ps. 25:16–18 NASB).

The first step in overcoming loneliness is to admit that it is a real problem for you. The second step is to make choices that can enable you to truly overcome it.

■ Overcoming Loneliness

1. Determine the Reasons for Your Loneliness

There are many causes of lonely feelings, and experiences that make one person lonely may not affect another in the same way. Here are some common reasons for loneliness:

Being rejected by others. You may be lonely because you have been rejected by others—a spouse, friend, business associate, or others. Often the rejection is totally unfair. It hurts and leaves a feeling of loneliness.

Lack of affection in youth. In our culture, people divorce; fathers are busy; children are left lonely. Children have tremendous dependency needs. If these needs are not met in their youth, an emotional vacuum is created that may be very difficult to fill. I spent time some years ago with an adolescent who had tried to kill himself. As I talked with him, he seemed so happy to have my attention, even for a brief period of time. He had been very lonely because his father was seldom at home.

Our changing society. We live in a society that tends to promote loneliness. Our society is fast, mobile, and changing.

Every two years, 40 percent of families move. Walking on a street in Manhattan, one can come in contact with 220,000 people within a ten-minute period. We meet many people, but, because our society is so mobile, there is not enough time to build relationships. So people are lonely. Also, because of television, people spend much less time talking, so even what little time people have for each other in our mobile society is often spent in loneliness in front of a TV set. Psychiatric research shows that television watching causes individuals to trust others less and thus promotes even more loneliness. Our changing society has also produced changing values, such as individualism and independence, that encourage loneliness.

Rejecting others. In my psychiatric practice, I have observed that sometimes people are lonely because they have rejected others. Fear of rejection, an inferiority complex, shyness, and many other reasons can cause a person to reject others and remain lonely rather than risk reaching out to develop friendships. An individual may decide to reject others before others have the chance to reject her.

Isolation from God. There is a God vacuum in each of us. We may deny it, we may fight it, but we cannot fill the lonely void that only Jesus Christ can fill. Of course, Christians can also experience to some degree this isolation from God as a result of breaking fellowship with him through sin. Adam and Eve experienced that loneliness. So did David. I talk with Christians weekly who are experiencing that loneliness as a result of a break in their fellowship with God.

Other causes. There are many other causes of loneliness. I may not have touched on your particular circumstances here, but the information in this chapter should help you deal with your loneliness, whatever the cause.

2. Be Active

Becoming physically, mentally, and spiritually active may help you overcome loneliness. Since loneliness at times has to do with internal issues, this principle may seem superficial, but it is certainly a good starting point because initiating specific behaviors may help to begin altering lonely feelings. Since feelings (over which we have little immediate control) may follow specific behavior (over which we have maximum control), why not start with a focus on new behavior? What will you do today to feel less lonely? Why not repeat a specific new behavior every day for two weeks and see if some of the loneliness lifts? This suggestion is inadequate by itself but is a beginning for finding your way out of loneliness.

3. Try to Be Involved with Other People

We have so many places to turn today for support. Below are resources that are commonly used. I am not necessarily recommending these, since I do not know many of them personally or agree with all of their principles. However, the list may be generally helpful.

Your local church and its support groups

Community support groups (many of these will be listed in your local phone directory)

    Overeaters Anonymous

    Victims of Violent Crimes

    National Organization of Victims 202-232-6682

    National Victim Center

    Schizophrenics Anonymous

    Alcoholics Anonymous

    Al-Anon (for families of alcoholics)

    Narcotics Anonymous

    Alateen (for teenage alcoholics)

    Anxiety/Agoraphobia/Panic Attacks Support Group

    Families Anonymous

    Grief Resource Foundation

Conferences

    Zig Ziglar (Christian motivational seminars) 972-233-9191

    Promise Keepers for Men 800-456-7594

Singles groups (check activities at local churches)

Residential care facilities for seniors and retirement villages

Psychiatric hospitalization in a Christian environment
888-646-4784

Discipleship ministries

Compassionate Heart Ministries 972-231-4960

Young Life 214-265-1505

Campus Crusade for Christ 800-989-7130

Fellowship of Christian Athletes 800-289-0909

K-Life Ministries 501-327-4357

The Navigators 719-598-1212

Conflict Resolution

PeaceMakers 406-256-1583

4. Focus on Three Spiritual Principles

There are three spiritual principles that are keys to a meaningful and complete life:

1. A close walk with God gives life meaning.
2. A life that produces the fruit of the Spirit is attractive.
3. As God's children, we can be secure in our relationship with him.

A close walk with God gives life meaning. This is an important key to the answer to loneliness.

First Samuel 30 tells the story of David returning home from battle to find that the women and children of his village had been taken captive by the enemy. Soon David found himself in a lonely position because all of his soldiers, whose families had been taken, turned against him. Note the solution David found: "Then David was greatly distressed, for the people spoke of stoning him, because the soul of all the people was grieved, every man for his sons and his daughters. But David strengthened himself in the LORD his God" (v. 6). John 16:32 tells us that Christ found comfort in his Father's presence: "Indeed the hour is coming, yes, has now come, that you will be scattered, each to his own, and will leave Me alone. And yet I am not alone, because the Father is with Me."

I recall a lonely lady whose mother had committed suicide and who had not known her dad. She found comfort in the following verse, which illustrates this point well: "For my father and my mother have forsaken me, but the LORD will take me up" (Ps. 27:10 NASB). Truly the most basic step in overcoming loneliness is a close walk with God through daily time spent with Christ. God loves us and longs to walk with us during lonely times.

> One night I dreamed I was walking along the beach with the Lord. Many scenes from my life flashed before me. In each one I noticed footprints in the sand. Sometimes there were two sets, but at other times there was only one. This bothered me because I noted that during periods of depression, when I was suffering from anguish, sorrow, or severe testing, I could see only a single set. So I prayed in my distress, "You promised, Lord, that if I followed you, you'd walk with me always; but I've noticed that during the most trying periods of my life, there has been just one set of prints in the sand. Why, when I needed you most, haven't you been with me?" To which the Lord replied, "The times when only one set of footprints were made, my child, were the times when I *carried* you!"
>
> Author unknown

A life that produces the fruit of the Spirit is attractive. "The fruit of the Spirit is love, joy, peace, patience, kindness, goodness, faithfulness, gentleness, self-control; against such things there is no law" (Gal. 5:22–23 NASB). These and similar attitudes cause others to want to be with us. When people have a critical, unkind, unhappy spirit, others tend to avoid them. A judgmental attitude drives others away. Being grounded in love is probably the best cure for any emotional problem, including loneliness. In Ephesians 3:17–19, the apostle Paul prayed, "That Christ may dwell in your hearts through faith; that you, being rooted and grounded in love, may be able to comprehend with all the saints what is the width and length and depth and height—to know the love of Christ which passes knowledge; that you may be filled with all the fullness of God." I believe that receiving the love that God imparts is an outstanding cure for loneliness, but giving love can also be a cure for loneliness. Solomon recorded, "He who waters will himself be watered" (Prov. 11:25 NASB). Having the fruit of the Spirit in your life not only produces a positive attitude in you and the ability to love others, but it also produces peace. You know that a feeling of loneliness is not exactly a feeling of peace.

When Christ lives in us, we also have the ability to forgive. It may be that you are lonely because you hold grudges against others. If you forgive others, you will open the way for relationships to continue and deepen.

As God's children, we can be secure in our relationship with him. For a baby to grow up without inner loneliness and with mental health, research has shown that she must feel that her parents will never forsake her and that she will always belong to them. Likewise, we as God's children need to continually remind ourselves of the security of belonging to him. Christ stated:

> Let not your heart be troubled; you believe in God, believe also in Me. In My Father's house are many mansions; if it were not so, I would have told you. I go to prepare a place for you. And if I go and prepare a place for you, I will come again and receive you to Myself; that where I am, there you may be also.
>
> John 14:1–3

Surely we will belong to God for an eternity—never to be lonely again.

5. Resolve Conflicts if Possible

Conflicts often lead to loneliness, so, if possible, resolve conflicts as quickly as possible. In this regard, an interesting verse is found in Romans 12:18: "If it is possible, as much as depends on you, live peaceably with all men." In resolving conflicts, you may wish to go to the other party by yourself to seek resolution. At other times it may be advisable to take a Christian friend along for support. In serious conflicts, rather than go to litigation or arbitration, many individuals are turning to Christian mediation, using such groups as PeaceMakers (406-256-1583).

6. Study Biblical Characters

Perhaps one of the best ways to understand how to overcome loneliness is to study people of the Bible who fought loneliness and won. Certainly high on the list of common factors that tie the following men together is that they faced loneliness. In fact, almost inherent in walking with God is a certain degree of loneliness. Walking with God requires that we dare to be different, which means that at times we dare to walk alone. Individuals such as Elijah (1 Kings 19), David (1 Samuel 30), Abraham (Genesis 12), Job (Job 1), the apostle Paul (2 Timothy 4), and Christ himself (John 16:32) experienced loneliness when they dared to be different, when they dared to stand alone. Their relationship with the Father, however, helped deter their human loneliness. We can learn from men and women of conviction how to be alone and yet not be or remain lonely.

7. Seek Counseling

Every major personality type can have symptoms of loneliness, and a counselor may be able to help you pursue techniques to combat the particular causes of loneliness in your personality type.

Individuals with obsessive-compulsive personality traits are characterized by being perfectionistic, having a decreased expression of warmth, being workaholics, being stubborn, and having underlying insecurities. They are neat, clean, orderly, and dutiful. They are conscientious and meticulous. They often work so hard that they may have a difficult time relaxing. They are concerned about everything and have an overly strict conscience. To deal with this, they use intellectualization to avoid emotions. Individuals with obsessive-compulsive personality traits tend to be overly demanding. They may need to lighten up. They may need to open up more to others, to let others get close so as not to be lonely.

Individuals with hysterical personality traits, such as being overly emotional, may seem very open. Sometimes physical relationships come easily, but the emotional closeness they so desire may elude them. They may benefit by working on healthy emotional closeness while setting boundaries in the sexual realm.

Individuals with paranoid personality traits, such as being overly suspicious, may benefit by working on showing trust, mercy, forgiveness, and the love of God as they attempt to become close to others. Individuals with borderline personality traits, such as instability in regard to mood, relationships, and self-image, may want to work on extreme type thinking, on black-and-white thinking. Perhaps they can work on realizing that others are not totally saint or totally sinner but somewhere in between. Having a balanced view may help in becoming closer to others.

Some personalities (narcissistic and sociopathic) are self-centered and not others-centered. They would benefit from trying to focus on others. Some individuals who are passive-aggressive may benefit by working on any self-defeating behavior that sets them up for loneliness.

Insights into your personality, which can come through counseling, may help in overcoming longstanding maladaptive behavior patterns that contribute to loneliness. A wise counselor may be of great help.

8. Consider Medication

Some people feel lonely because they are distressed with chemical depression, anxiety, or even thought aberrations. In these cases, part of the lonely feeling is caused by a chemical imbalance, and it may well be that appropriate medication would make a world of difference. Medications are also available for other conditions that can produce loneliness, such as obsessive worries, panic, attention deficit disorders, schizophrenia, paranoia, bipolar disorder, and anger. Consult your physician.

9. Be Hopeful

God can help you do anything. He can bring people into your life. Ask for his personal touch in this matter.

■ Follow-Up

Loneliness can be overcome. Tools such as the ones in this chapter are among the best techniques to combat loneliness. Try the ones that seem to fit your situation. Consider consulting a counselor or physician. Loneliness may be tough at times, but it can be defeated.

10

Drug Abuse

Pursuing Freedom

Choose for yourselves this day whom you will serve.

Joshua

A twenty-five-year-old male came into our clinic. He said that during college he would occasionally become intoxicated. About three months ago he had come under tremendous stress and increased workload at his job and had begun to binge drink on weekends. Recently he had begun to drink daily, not just on weekends, and was having trouble going to work. His story is more and more common today.

Do you or does someone you know have a drug problem? Here is a quick check called the TWEAK test:

T: increasing *tolerance* of the effect of drugs

W: *worry* of friends

E: *eye opener* needed to get going

A: *amnesia* experienced

K: has tried to *cut down*

Drugs and alcohol play significant roles in destroying the mental and physical health of twenty-first-century Americans. Today drug abuse is a major mental health problem. The number one cause of death in our country relates to smoking and the abuse of nicotine. The number one cause of highway accidents is related to alcohol, which is also a significant factor in family violence. And alcohol is involved in 50 percent of homicides.

In the late 1970s there was a decrease in the use of hallucinogens, PCP, and marijuana, and barbiturate abuse was not increasing. Cocaine use increased in the 1980s, then leveled off, but recently has begun to increase again. Heroin use is on the increase in middle-class families.

Illicit drugs have a stranglehold on America. More than 50 percent of young adults have experimented with marijuana. Heroin and cocaine abuse has moved from the back streets into the upper middle class of corporate America. Inhalants are beginning to rob us of our preteens. Some athletes use anabolic steroids, in some cases resulting in aggression, depression, and even death. Probably one hundred thousand deaths per year are due to drug abuse.

Drug and alcohol abuse costs $85 billion per year. Most often, abuse in the workplace involves alcohol, marijuana, and cocaine. Intoxication and drug abuse increase accidents, decrease performance, increase broken equipment, and create defective goods. Chronic use causes increased absenteeism, increased job termination, a demoralized workforce, and theft.

Ironically, although they are alluring and seem to offer relief from the pressures of this life, drugs of abuse will never bring their users the joy and peace for which they yearn. The only true answer for our deep dependency needs rests in a personal relationship with Christ, who offers an abundant life.

■ Definitions

Substance abuse occurs when one experiences a maladaptive pattern of use of an addictive substance, developing significant impairment or distress as exhibited in recurrent interpersonal, social, occupational, psychological, or physical problems within a twelve-month period. In addiction, individuals may continue to abuse substances repeatedly, even when they know it is physically hazardous.

Substance dependence may create intolerance and withdrawal problems. Chemical substance–dependent people may use increasingly larger amounts of chemicals or use them for longer periods than intended. They may have a desire to stop and may have made unsuccessful attempts to stop. Because much time is spent obtaining and using the substances, those who are substance dependent may give up social, occupational, and recreational activities. Substance use continues despite the user's knowledge of the problems it engenders.

The following are the most common drugs of abuse today:

Caffeine may cause anxiety, irritability, decreased sleep, and headaches.

Nicotine. On the average, one of every three people smokes. Fifteen percent of deaths in our country are the result of smoking, due to organ damage, lung cancer, and heart attacks—five hundred thousand per year.

Alcohol. Seventy percent of the population drinks alcohol, including two out of three Protestants. There are fifteen million alcoholics today (compared to three million in 1950). Alcohol problems are more common in men than in women and more common in young people than in other ages. Today alcohol problems in young women are showing a sharp increase. Women are more likely to drink in secret. Cirrhosis of the liver from alcoholism is the number three cause of death.

Marijuana breaks down into a chemical called THC (tetrahydrocannadinol). THC becomes part of the fatty tissues of the brain and may be a cause of amotivational syndrome, the inability of those who have smoked too much marijuana to be motivated to do anything.

Amphetamines may cause cardiovascular problems and central nervous system problems, such as psychosis and depression.

Cocaine, which can result in sudden death, is the fastest growing drug of abuse.

Barbiturates, other sedatives, and benzodiazepines create problems with tolerance, withdrawal, and seizures.

Sleeping pills, prescription and over-the-counter, may be abused.

Opium, including heroin. Only one in three opium users lives past his thirties. HIV issues are also a problem since opium users may inject the drug with infected needles.

Hallucinogens (LSD, STP, DMT, MDMA [or Ecstasy], PCP, mescaline, and morning glory seeds) create problems with judgment and may cause psychosis and death.

Inhalants. One-third of inhalant users are below the age of seventeen. Inhalant users' organs (liver, kidney, and heart) are affected, leading to possible psychosis and death.

Anabolic steroids may cause aggression and a sense of being invulnerable. Discontinuation of the use of steroids can result in severe depression.

■ Causes of Drug Abuse

Curiosity, peer pressure, desire to reduce dysphoric (sad) feelings, and a wish to enhance functioning may entice someone to drug abuse. Family instability, parental rejection, and divorce may be factors in drug abuse. Psychological factors as well as behaviors learned through conditioning may be involved.

There may also be a physiological factor in drug abuse. For example, the nucleus accumbens of the limbic brain, which is one of the reward centers of the brain, is affected by drugs of abuse through the neurotransmitter dopamine. By enhancing dopamine transmission, the addictive drugs disturb the natural feedback and control in the system causing a disturbance in functioning that can be temporary but may be permanent in some cases. As the brain adapts to excess dopamine from the drugs of abuse, natural production decreases and dopamine receptors become less numerous and less sensitive. Tolerance to the drug increases and pleasure is decreased until more of the drug of abuse is used, leading to a never-ending cycle of increasing drug use.

Factors affecting drug abuse may include personal choice issues; early environmental factors, such as codependency issues; precipitating stress issues; and genetics, such as an acetaldehyde metabolism issue in which a son is three to four times more susceptible. If his twin is a drug abuser, an identical twin is twice as likely to abuse drugs as is a nonidentical twin.

■ Overcoming Drug Abuse

1. Get Medical Help

ReVia and Zofran are two medications that may decrease the craving for alcohol. Antabuse makes the intake of alcohol impossible. Antidepressants that are not addicting can help some alcohol abusers stop their use. Zyban decreases the cravings for cigarettes. New antiseizure medications may stabilize not only seizures but mood instability and insomnia in drug addictions.

2. Deal with Dependency Needs in a Healthy Way

There is nothing wrong with having dependency needs, but trying to meet them in the wrong way through drugs will never work. It is healthy to accept the help of individuals in the church in finding ways to meet your needs.

3. Develop an Accountability Friend

Find a friend to whom you report on a routine basis your progress in refraining from drug abuse. This should be a friend who has your welfare at heart and will hold you accountable for not using alcohol or drugs. Ideally it will be someone in your church who understands chemical dependency addictions and who is bold enough to suggest hospitalization if relapse should occur.

4. Don't Play Games

Be determined to be more direct and stop playing games, such as "See how hard I've tried"; "Poor me!"; "It's all your fault"; "Yes . . . but . . ."

5. Consider Counseling

Are there issues you need to deal with involving dependency, anger, self-image, family of origin, sex, guilt, grief, or aggression? A good counselor could help.

6. Consider a Change in Lifestyle

Many times, a person's plan for living life is just a poor one. Do your day-to-day activities encourage substance abuse? You may need to make some changes in places you go, your friends, or even your place of employment because it may encourage drug abuse. Feelings often follow behavior. Do the specifics of your daily behaviors need to change so that drug abuse is not encouraged?

7. Watch Your Thinking

Despite your addiction, it is not the end of the world. Life does not have to be horrible forever; whatever you do, don't quit trying to stop abusing drugs. If you have begun the process of getting off drugs, don't be discouraged. Keep working at it and believing that you can do it. Here is a great poem by an unknown author called "Don't Quit."

> When things go wrong, as they sometimes will,
> When the road you're trudging seems all uphill,
> When the funds are low and the debts are high,
> And you want to smile, but you have a sigh,
> When care is pressing you down a bit,
> Rest if you must, but don't you quit.
>
> Life is difficult with its twists and turns,
> As every one of us sometimes learns,
> And many a failure turns about
> When he might have won had he stuck it out;
> Don't give up, though the pace seems slow—
> You might succeed with another blow.
>
> Often the goal is nearer than
> It seems to a faint and faltering man,
> Often the struggler has given up
> When he might have captured the victor's cup,
> And he learned too late, when the night slipped down,
> How close he was to the golden crown.
>
> Success is failure turned inside out—
> The silver tint of the clouds of doubt—
> And you never tell how close you are,
> It may be near when it seems afar;
> So stick to the fight when you're hardest hit—
> It's when things seem worst that you must not quit.

■ Follow-Up

Drugs of abuse are a major problem in America today. Never before in history have we had the medical tools available to counter the drug abuse problem, but individuals must now be willing to work with their doctor to take advantage of them. In addition, Christ is available and he is stronger than even drug abuse.

If one of your family members or a friend is a substance abuser, you need to make every effort to lead him or her to Christ. Without Christ, people, especially children, are no match for the pull of addicting drugs. Give them a goal to reach. If they know Christ as their Savior, help them find a mission for Christ they can pursue. In a child's early years, it is of utmost importance that parents give children time and affirmation. And share with them your heart for Christ.

11

Marriage

Pursuing Unity

A happy marriage is a choice.

Frank Minirth

I f being married thirty-five years and having five daughters over three decades qualify a couple to offer marriage suggestions, then Mary Alice and I qualify. It has been a wonderful trip.

Through a happy marriage individuals can avoid many heartaches for themselves, their mate, and their children in years to come. Marriage is one of the two institutions ordained by God and deserves our highest attention. The majority of the individuals I see in the clinic are having symptoms partially because of problems in their marriage. What if these problems could be prevented, anticipated, and overcome? Indeed, they can.

■ Making Your Marriage a Happy One

Here are eight choices that are keys to a happy marriage.

1. Be Romantic

I have always been deeply in love with Mary Alice. However, there probably are certain behaviors we both do that help keep our love

123

alive, such as walking and talking together; holding hands; short, romantic vacations for just the two of us; a wink of the eye; early morning coffee; snuggling and cuddling; sleeping close together; a single red rose; and eye-to-eye contact with focused attention when we're talking.

Remember that God is not against sex and romance. In fact, he thought it up.

> "May your fountain be blessed, and may you rejoice in the wife of your youth" (Prov. 5:18 NIV).
>
> "Let him kiss me with the kisses of his mouth—for your love is more delightful than wine" (Song of Songs 1:2 NIV).
>
> "How handsome you are, my lover! Oh, how charming! And our bed is verdant" (v. 16 NIV).

One has only to be exposed to any of the media today to realize the power of sexual emotions. Why not deal with those emotions in marriage? God understands sexual feelings and has given us marriage so that we can deal with them in a healthy way. The Bible says of a married couple, after they have abstained from sex to spend time in prayer, "Then come together again so that Satan will not tempt you because of your lack of self-control" (1 Cor. 7:5 NIV).

2. Go Ahead and Be "Codependent"

Before you think I have recanted every ounce of psychiatry I was taught, please let me explain what I mean when I say, "Go ahead and be codependent." In our culture we may carry the term *codependent* too far at times. It is true we should not be addicted to anything or any relationship in an unhealthy sense. We need to be careful about extremes and maintaining a healthy balance in meeting our natural dependency needs; but it is also probably true that the definition of codependency has been twisted at times to mean more than it should.

Unfortunately, I have heard sad stories of how a person took courses on assertiveness ("Let me tell you . . ."); boundaries ("I can be self-centered"); and codependency ("Get rid of him or her"); and how he or she then left the marriage after finding a new partner with whom he or she could be assertive, draw boundaries, and not be codependent.

In a healthy marriage there is a dependency; there is an extreme closeness. One cannot get much closer than Genesis 2:24 (NIV): "For this reason a man will leave his father and mother and be united to his wife, and they will become one flesh."

Go ahead and, in a healthy sense, depend on each other for the encouragement to fight the fight of life together for Jesus Christ. Go ahead and be on the same team.

3. Treasure What You Have

In our early years of marriage, I often enjoyed reading the following verses: "He who finds a wife finds what is good and receives favor from the LORD" (Prov. 18:22 NIV); and "A prudent wife is from the LORD" (19:14 NIV). These verses reminded me to treasure my wife.

Two Greek words have helped me in treasuring Mary Alice and attempting to act accordingly. The first one is the word *blessing,* which in the New Testament is *eulogia.* It is based on two words: *eu,* which means "well," and *logos,* which means "words." Thus, in treasuring Mary Alice, I must bless her with words or speak well of her. The second word is *edify.* In the New Testament the Greek word for *edify* is *oikodomeo,* which means "to build up." It is actually a derivative of two Greek words: *oikos,* which means "home or family," and *demo,* which means "to build." Thus, to edify my wife, I must do all I can to build a home.

4. Be Kind

Recently at the checkout counter of a bookstore I saw an interesting sign that stated why customers stop patronizing places of business: 1 percent of the customers die, 3 percent move, and so on, but 67 percent stop because of rudeness on the part of employees, or in other words, because of a lack of kindness. If kindness is valuable in business, then how much more so in a marriage?

As a psychiatrist, I have been deeply steeped in the importance of gaining insight; but in all honesty, I must say that I believe simple, kind behavior is by far more important than the deepest insight. I have often reflected on such Bible verses as "If I speak in the tongues of men and of angels, but have not love, I am only a resounding gong or a clanging cymbal" (1 Cor. 13:1 NIV) and "What a man desires is unfailing love" (Prov. 19:22 NIV). When marriage partners show love and kindness to each other, their relationship will deepen.

Some of the latest research on healthy, happy marriages is of extreme interest. It seems that secular research has shown that all the communication techniques do not necessarily produce the best marriages. Could it be that the techniques are too technical or rehearsed or abstract to be effective? I do not believe there is anything wrong with communication techniques, but they pale in significance when compared to being Christ-like in attitude and general behavior. From secular research, it seems that the best marriages are those in which the husband does not argue a lot.

5. Understand the Passages of Marriage

A marriage goes through certain stages of development, just as a child does. Each stage has its challenges.

In *young love,* the first two years, challenges will center around power, intimacy, and in-laws. Who will be in charge? How emotionally close will you be? How will you deal with in-laws?

In *realistic love,* years three through ten, challenges may center around working through hidden and dangerous agendas, such as "I must complete the life tasks that my parents never accomplished"; "Men are only interested in sex and I will prove it and fight it"; "All women are bad tempered, so don't get too close"; "Sex is the only weapon I have"; "If I can't get sex at home, then I am justified in taking an outside lover"; "Maybe I can feel closeness if I enter into another intimate relationship"; "I will be nonsexual in the marriage to pay penance for what I have done wrong"; "I will release the anger I have at other people on my spouse"; "My spouse is the extreme opposite of a parent who hurt me, so now I no longer have to suffer"; "I need to be punished in my marriage because of shame I carry from my past."

Comfortable love, years eleven through twenty-five, is similar to the latency years of childhood—those less troublesome years before adolescence. The marriage identity has been established, and even though there are still issues to confront, they are often not as intense in some respects as they were earlier in the marriage.

In *renewing love,* years twenty-six through thirty-five, there are inevitable losses of youth and dreams. These losses must be dealt with and grieved together.

During the remaining years of *transcendent love,* the next generation must be further nurtured so they will be ready when it is time to pass on the mantle of sharing the gospel for Christ. In this passage, if the proper foundation has been laid in the preceding passages, the couple becomes even more deeply committed and deeply in love.

6. Don't Forget the Medical

Sometimes being aware of the medical dimensions can really help in marital issues. For example, for depression alone, antidepressants are available today that tend to increase sex drive; others increase motivation and energy; some tend to decrease weight; some help insomnia; others help focus; and some tend to decrease anger. Some medications help impotence; others help in premature ejaculation. The psychiatric medications today tend to be highly specific, and the results are usually very encouraging. Even more important than the curative aspects of medicine are the preventive measures that can be taken for good health, such as exercise and a healthy diet. Physical and mental well-being have a lot to do with marital happiness.

7. Enjoy Laughter

Mary Alice and I laugh and kid a lot. Whenever possible, we try to look on the lighter side, and it really seems to help. Laughter relieves as much tension as crying and is a lot more fun. It is probable that laughter releases endorphins and enkephalins, which are among the neurotransmitters in the brain that control the perception of pain and pleasure. I have often pondered the truth of an interesting comment in Proverbs: "A cheerful heart is good medicine" (17:22 NIV).

8. Together Commit to a Purpose

In the fall of 1973, *Reality Therapy* by Dr. William Glasser was sweeping the Christian world. Dr. Glasser was not a Christian as far as I know, but in many respects he was like a breath of fresh air to counseling. In the preface of his book, Dr. Glasser even quoted an old hymn. Conservative biblical counselors such as Jay Adams studied reality therapy, as did I that fall. Dr. Glasser said that people are drawn together for one of three reasons—*speed* (romance with the speed of its attraction), *quality* (the perceptions of the other person being a quality person either socially or occupationally), or *depth* (common life goals). This last one is an especially good point. Why not base one's married life on a common life goal?

Soon after that Mary Alice and I discovered Habakkuk 1:5: "Look among the nations and watch—be utterly astounded! For I will work a work in your days which you would not believe, though it were told you." "Oh, Lord," we cried out, "we would love to take that verse as our life goal. Please do a work in our days for you." Since then we have based our lives on that verse, and it has always guided us. Our faces are fixed on it through any trial. It has kept us on track. It burns in our hearts and dreams. Countless issues between us have fallen in the light of that one-heartbeat goal.

The brain has upward of one hundred billion cells, and each cell has upward of one hundred thousand synapses. Its power is awesome. It holds life and death. And all of the brain's power can be marshaled in one direction to fulfill a single overriding goal. What power there is when we join our spouse in pursuit of a goal! And that goal can have eternal meaning when it is a goal for Christ.

■ Follow-Up

I believe that most couples do want to stay married. I also believe it is possible to be not only married but happily married. If you're a couple reading this book, consider applying at least one of the principles in this chapter per week for the next several weeks.

12

Teens

Pursuing Basic Needs

I have set before you life and death, blessings and curses. Now choose life, so that you and your children may live.

Moses

I have raised five daughters. Rachel, our oldest, is a social worker and has the composure and gentleness of her mother. Renee, our second daughter, is in pre-med, is intellectual, and may be prone to working too hard. Carrie is creative and interested in music. Alicia is a pre-teen and is just beginning what in psychiatry we call separation/individuation as she becomes more of her own person. Mary Elizabeth, our youngest, is still in her happy latency—pre-adolescent—years. One lesson I have learned is that each daughter is unique, particularly during her teen years.

■ The Needs of Teens

Indeed, teens are in a unique world, an in-between world. Because teens are in that in-between stage, their needs are very different in some respects but like everyone else's in others. If you are a teen, you might consider asking others to help you with knowing how to meet your basic needs. If you are in a position to help a teen, you might assist the teen in discovering how to meet these basic needs.

1. Belonging

Research reveals that healthy young people are those who feel their parents love them and that they will always belong to their family. Anytime one of my daughters asks me how I am doing, I always respond, "Better now that you're here." If you are a parent, be sure your teens know they belong in your family and in the family of God. If you are a friend, be sure they know you care about them.

Incidentally, if the teens in your life are not sure if they know Christ, you may want to encourage them to pray this simple prayer: "Christ, I realize I am a sinner (Rom. 3:23); I know you died on a cross in payment for my sins (6:23); I am accepting you as my Savior right now (John 1:12)."

2. Boundaries

Because teens are growing up, stepping out on their own, and separating from their parents, at times they will go too far, and a boundary needs to be drawn for them.

One of the best ways I have found is what I call contracting. I ask my daughters to draw up contracts. They are given increased privileges for responsible behavior, and they list privileges to be withdrawn if they fail. I look over the contract and add my modifications. I try to be fair and not harsh and stay in the present or near future when considering discipline. Thus I would not usually ground them for a long time.

Research has shown the relationship between love and effective discipline: The most effective method of helping young people is to give them a lot of love with appropriate discipline. The least effective method is little love with harsh discipline.

3. Individuation (Graduated Freedoms)

One of the biggest struggles teens and parents will go through is called individuation. The teen must be allowed to grow up, to separate from parents. Just knowing this may help a parent back

High Degree of Love (Sense of Belonging)		
Little Discipline (Boundaries)	**2** second most effective	**1** most effective	High Degree Discipline (Boundaries)
	3 third most effective	**4** least effective	
Little Love (Sense of Belonging)		

off at times in certain situations that are not critical. I recall how my heart ached when I left my two oldest daughters at college. They were separating and becoming their own individuals, and though I wanted this for them, I knew it meant a change in our relationship.

4. Modeling

Young people desperately need models of good behavior. They often tend to be a reflection, in some form, of their parents. I recall a story that a pastor told me several years ago. He was visiting in a home of a parent. On seeing a bar for alcoholic beverages (and also knowing a youth in the home had been in legal trouble for drinking), the pastor asked the parent, "Do you think the open bar for alcohol could be part of the problem?" The parent responded, "Yes, I should have locked it up."

We need to understand that teens tend to do what we do more than just what we say.

5. Peers

Next to parents, peers are the most important influence in a young person's life. Therefore, it is important for parents to monitor their child's peers. We become like those with whom we associate. Proverbs 27:17 states, "As iron sharpens iron, so a man sharpens the countenance of his friend." Godly peers can make a difference.

6. A Challenge

In early adolescence, the ability of teens to think abstractly increases, and with this ability comes a tendency to become more argumentative. (Early teens rebel against things, mid-teens rebel against people, and late teens rebel against philosophies.) With their new skill of abstract thinking, they may become more skeptical, challenging, and idealistic. Why not give them a true challenge—a life lived for Christ?

I recall many years ago hearing a Christian leader (LeRoy Eims of The Navigators) say that he once asked a young person what he was going to do with his life now that he had graduated. The young man thought and thought, but no words came forth. The Christian leader was wondering what grand plan the young man was trying to voice—perhaps he would invade China with the gospel. Finally, the young man said, "I think I'll buy a Buick." The vast majority of teens need more of a challenge than that, but they may need help in identifying it. Help the teens in your life decide how Christ is calling them.

7. The Sensation of Being Somebody

As I mentioned in chapter 1, I have often sung an old song by Bill Gaither to my daughters: "You are something special. You're the only one of your kind." I want them to know that they are unique and special, the best in the world at the ministry Christ has for them.

Every teen has the need to feel unique and special. We must help them identify and develop their unique gifts.

■ Special Issues

Teens deal with many issues that may be causing them distress and having an impact on their ability to function well in school and with family and friends. If a teen becomes withdrawn, angry, or defiant, or if the teen's grades are falling, the adult can use the following questions to help the teen sort through special concerns.

A confession need. Are you experiencing guilt over something you've done involving drugs, sex, lying, or stealing? Do you need to confess or share?

A *discouragement/depression issue.* Are you so depressed you hardly want to live? Sometimes medication can really help in severe depression. Do you need to talk with a doctor?

A *school issue.* Are you having trouble in school? Are you having trouble paying attention? Sometimes individuals have a biochemical problem called attention deficit disorder, and medication can make a world of difference.

A *shame issue.* Sometimes teens will experience shame because of something done to them. Do you need to ask for help? Is there something you need to share?

■ Follow-Up

Identify the three greatest needs of your teen (or your three greatest needs, if you are a teen). Consider sharing these with your spouse or your teen (or with your parents, if you are a teen) and then implementing a plan this week to begin meeting the areas of need that are most critical.

For you created my inmost being; you knit me together in my mother's womb. I praise you because I am fearfully and wonderfully made; your works are wonderful, I know that full well. My frame was not hidden from you when I was made in the secret place. When I was woven together in the depths of the earth, your eyes saw my unformed body. All the days ordained for me were written in your book before one of them came to be.

How precious to me are your thoughts, O God! How vast is the sum of them!

Psalm 139:13–17 NIV

13

Troubled Teens

Pursuing Help

We must think anew—and act anew.

Abraham Lincoln

Our precious teens hold the future for America, our families, and our legacy for Christ. Our hearts ache when they are in trouble.

Stan was seventeen when his mother brought him to our clinic. He said that although his parents divorced a year ago, he was fine; he'd been doing well. However, over the past several months he had started periodic binge drinking and staying out with friends. This was very atypical behavior for him since he attended church on a regular basis. Stan was headed down the road to trouble, and his mother knew it. She was wise to bring him in for help.

Here are some of the signs of trouble in teens.

- chronic truancy
- extreme change in appearance
- interest in the occult
- mood swings
- withdrawal or isolation
- low self-esteem

- inability to cope with routine matters or relationships
- unexplained accidents
- a drop in grades at school
- defiance of rules and regulations
- withdrawal from family functions
- not informing family of school activities
- taking money or alcohol
- weight losses or gains
- legal problems
- having drug paraphernalia
- calls from school regarding behavior or grades
- verbal or physical displays of anger or hostility
- drug or alcohol abuse
- blatant sexual behavior
- general apathy
- sleeplessness or fatigue
- excessive sadness or frequent crying
- suicidal thoughts
- poor impulse control
- switching friends
- becoming more secretive
- changes in physical hygiene
- many excuses for staying out late
- selling possessions
- being short-tempered
- defensiveness
- abusive behavior
- coming home high or drunk

■ Causes of Trouble in Teens

The causes of trouble in teens may fall into at least four categories:

Peer oriented: There are many teens who are basically healthy but who may, with the increased peer pressure of the teen years, temporarily act out for a season.

Depression oriented: Teens tend to act out their depression through irresponsible behavior. Teens may become depressed for many reasons—loss of family through divorce or death, loss of a significant relationship, loss of self-esteem, guilt, shame, family issues, and peer issues, among others.

Character oriented: With character or personality problems, long-standing maladaptive behavior patterns are seen. The behavior may become irresponsible on a consistent basis over time. The conscience may be lacking in some areas.

Medically oriented: Major depression disorder, ADHD, bipolar disorder, obsessive-compulsive disorder, other anxiety disorders, autism, and schizophrenia can have a significant medical dimension. These disorders can have a genetic factor and can actually be seen on PET scans of the brain.

■ Types of Trouble in Teens

There are several types of specific disorders with specific symptoms:

Adjustment disorder with disturbance of behavior. Many teens will have temporary irresponsible behavior when they are going through a difficult situation or adjustment in their life.

Major depression. The classic symptoms of a major depression may include depressed mood, diminished interest in daily activities, weight changes, sleep changes, fatigue, agitation, feelings of worthlessness, decreased concentration, and recurrent thoughts of death. In teens, acting-out behavior or irresponsible behavior often accompanies major depression. Depression may result from losses, guilt, shame, and many other issues.

Bipolar disorder is characterized by mood swings from high positive or angry to low. During the high times the person may have rapid thinking, rapid speech, grandiosity, agitation, distractibility, and poor judgment that results in much trouble.

Attention-deficit/hyperactivity disorder (ADHD) is characterized by inattention with forgetfulness and distractibility. This means that the person does not follow instructions, which often causes feelings of inadequacy. In some individuals it is also characterized by hyperactivity and impulsivity, which cause trouble. This disorder can have a genetic cause and can be seen on a PET scan.

Obsessive-compulsive disorder (OCD) causes excessive worry and only indirectly causes trouble in the sense that persons become so discouraged. This too runs in families and can be seen on a PET scan.

Asperger's disorder is characterized by a high IQ but an inability to relate socially. Isolation often results. There is often a fine line between genius and trouble. Thomas Edison and Albert Einstein had terrible inattention; Winston Churchill and Ernest Hemingway had bipolar disorder; Martin Luther and John Bunyan had OCD; Beethoven and Abraham Lincoln had depression; and Asperger's disorder is almost synonymous with genius.

Posttraumatic stress disorder (PTSD) is a disorder precipitated by a life-threatening situation, such as child abuse. In this disorder PET scans document that the hippocampus of the brain that controls emotional memory has atrophied, and this may explain why the nightmares and fear will not abate and why these individuals are in trouble and always on high alert.

Personality disorders tend to be characterized by many years of maladaptive behavior. There may be problems with perception and interpretation of self, others, and events. There may be instability in emotions and the expression of them. There may be problems with impulsiveness and relations with others. Personality disorders that are often accompanied by irresponsible behavior include antisocial, borderline, histrionic, and narcissistic disorders.

One may have only traits and not the complete disorder. In *antisocial disorder,* there may be a failure to conform to social norms, resulting in deceitfulness, impulsivity, aggressiveness, irritability, disregard for others, consistent irresponsibility, and lack of remorse. In *borderline disorder,* there may be abandonment issues, unstable interpersonal relationships, identity disturbance issues, impulsivity, suicidal behavior, emotional instability, chronic feelings of emptiness, and intense anger. In *histrionic disorder,* there may be patterns of being emotional, egocentric, expressive, seductive, rapidly shifting expression of emotions, dramatic, suggestible, and considering relationships to be more intimate than they actually are. In *narcissistic disorder,* there may be a grandiose sense of self-importance; preoccupation with success, power, beauty, brilliance, or ideal love; a requirement of excessive admiration; a sense of entitlement; a pattern of being interpersonally exploitative; a lack of empathy for others; arrogant behaviors; and envy of others.

Eating disorders are characterized by a disturbance in one's perception of body weight and shape. Many teens, especially young women, have an intense fear of becoming fat. Eating disorders include anorexia nervosa and bulimia. In anorexia nervosa, there is a refusal to maintain normal body weight so that the body weight is less than 85 percent of what it should be. Amenorrhea often accompanies anorexia nervosa. In 5 to 10 percent of the cases, anorexia nervosa ends in death. In bulimia there are recurrent episodes of binge eating with recurrent inappropriate compensatory behavior to prevent weight gain, such as vomiting, laxative abuse, fasting, and excessive exercise.

Regardless of the causes of inappropriate behavior, we are always responsible for our choices. In reality, this is what offers hope. We may make some bad choices, but we can always decide to make better choices in the future.

Disorders Usually First Diagnosed in Infancy, Childhood, or Adolescence

Certain disorders often involve behavioral problems and are usually first diagnosed in youth.

Attention-deficit/hyperactivity disorder (ADHD): There may be inattention, hyperactivity, and impulsivity, all three of which can cause behavioral problems and be misunderstood as being primarily psychological when they may be more physiological.

Oppositional defiant disorder (OPDD): There may be negativism and defiant or hostile behavior. Those with OPDD are known for losing their temper; arguing; refusing to comply; blaming others; being easily annoyed, angry, and vindictive; and attempting to deliberately annoy people.

Conduct disorder: There may be aggressive acts toward people and animals (bullying, threatening, intimidating, fighting, being cruel, or stealing), destruction of property, deceitfulness, or serious violations of rules.

Substance Abuse

A major mental health problem in America is drug abuse, which is also a leading cause of death. Irresponsible and dangerous behaviors are often associated with the abuse of drugs. These drugs include nicotine, alcohol, marijuana, amphetamines, cocaine, barbiturates, opium, hallucinogens, and inhalants (see chapter 10).

■ Helping Troubled Teens

When there is a troubled teen in our lives, we must do all we can to help her face her problems and find solutions to them. The following are just the basics of what we as adults can do.

1. Inquire

If you note signs of trouble in your teen, do not be afraid to ask her about it. Be gentle but specific in your inquiry: "Has something happened that you need to share?" "Are you suicidal?" "Are you using drugs?" If the teen is unwilling to talk, let her know you're always available to listen when she needs to talk.

2. Reassure

Teens desperately need to know that you will always love them and that they will always belong to your family, regardless of what they do, and that you are always on their team. Because you are on their team, however, limits must be set. It works best if the teen helps determine the limits. Let her write a contract with you so that she will agree with the contract's provisions.

3. Help in Their Own Language

Teens tend to have their own language, and it may be a language that only their peers speak. This is one reason Christian peers can be invaluable. They may be able to talk with your troubled teen, and you should not hesitate to enlist their help.

And don't underestimate the value of Christian music. Music is often a part of the teen's world to which she can easily relate. Christian music may provide comfort, encouragement, and emotional release.

4. Encourage a Life Mission

It may be that your teen needs to make a decision to follow Christ or to renew her commitment. Look for an opportunity to talk to her about God, and then encourage her to think about the life mission that Jesus Christ is calling her to. Encourage teens to verbalize their mission or write it out for their review in years to come. Teens need a major life mission—something to live for—why not Jesus Christ?

5. Intervene

As much as we may hate to do so, sometimes parents must intervene. We may have to intervene medically, socially, or spiritually. We may need to enlist medical help. At times we will have to impose social limitations. And we must be sensitive to our teen's need for spiritual encouragement. When I have to intervene, I remind myself, "Be as gentle as possible, but do what you must for her welfare." In one of John Wayne's best-known movies *(True Grit)*, one of the characters makes this comment: "Enough that you know I will do what I have to do." In like manner, may we as parents, with a Christ-like sensitivity and tone, say to our teen when necessary, "Because I love you and because I love Christ, 'enough that you know that I will do what I have to do' to help you, even if that means an intervention."

6. Get Medical Help

Great choices exist today for treating such disorders as ADHD, bipolar disorder, depressive disorder, OCD, Asperger's disorder, and schizophrenia. If you can help your teen who has one of these disorders to get the appropriate medical help, it may dramatically decrease the trouble (see appendix M).

■ Words of Encouragement for Discouraged Parents

If you're a discouraged parent, I have words of encouragement for you. You may feel like you have tried but failed. First, you may be looking too much at your faults. Adolescents make choices. Even the godly Samuel had children who chose sin. Second, the fight is not over yet. Adolescents may have maturity issues that last until age thirty. Many come around in time. Third, there may be medical dimensions, as discussed above, and treatment of these can make a major difference.

■ Follow-Up

Our precious teens hold our legacy for Christ. May God grant us the grace to spot any signs of trouble and respond accordingly.

14

The Mature Years

Pursuing Fulfillment

He who does not make a choice makes a choice.

Michael Reagan

Every night as I would make my rounds at the hospital, an aged gentleman would tell me good-bye for the last time. He had lost his purpose for living. One morning at four o'clock the dreaded call from the nurse came. The aged gentleman had passed on. I have thought much about him. The following are some choices I wish he could have understood.

■ Making the Mature Years Happy

1. Correct Erroneous Beliefs Concerning Age

I can no longer be productive. Old age is a state of mind. Individuals can be elderly at age fifty, or they can be young at age ninety. Many individuals excel in their more mature years. For example, at age ninety-one, Eamon de Valera served as president of Ireland; at age eighty-nine, Arturo Rubinstein gave one of his greatest recitals; Albert Schweitzer at age eighty-nine headed a hospital in Africa. When he was eighty-eight years old, Michelangelo designed the Church of Santa Maria degli Angeli; at age eighty-two, Winston Churchill wrote his four-volume work *A History of the English-Speaking Peoples;* and Benjamin Franklin at age eighty-one effected the compromise that led to the adoption of the United States Constitution. Finally, the following is recorded of Moses in Deuteronomy 34:7 (NASB): "Although Moses was one hundred and twenty years old when he died, his eye was not dim, nor his vigor abated." Truly, one can be very productive in his or her more mature years.

Traditionally, age sixty-five and above has been defined as elderly. If one holds to this definition, there are currently over twenty-six million people in America who are elderly. This figure is compared to only three million in the year 1900. Nearly 20 percent of the population is now in this age range.

In early biblical times, people lived to be much older than they do today. For example, Adam, the father of the human race, lived to be 930 years old; Noah lived 950 years; and Methuselah lived to be 969 years old. As time continued (probably more so after the flood), life spans shortened. For many years, people who lived to be in their thirties or forties were doing very well.

Today people live to be about three score and ten years (seventy years of age), just as they did in the days of King David (Ps. 90:10). The average life expectancy of males at birth is seventy years and females about seventy-eight years; but as people survive to age sixty-five, the figure significantly increases, and the individual can look forward to another fourteen to twenty years of life. Medical research is greatly increasing longevity. There is no reason we could not soon live to be 110 to 120 years old. These years can be the most productive of all because of the wisdom and wealth of experience gained through the years.

All my friends are dead and gone. It is only in relatively recent years that many people live to age sixty-five. Of all the people who have ever lived to age sixty-five, more than half are currently alive. More than twenty-six million in the United States are above age sixty-five. If you are included in this number, there are many people out there who are in your age bracket. Take steps to make new friends—at church, at senior and retirement centers, or on a bus tour for seniors. Even if many of your friends have died, your best friend, Jesus Christ, is not dead and gone.

Since I am over sixty-five, I will probably die soon. As I have already noted, although the average life expectancy of a male at birth is around seventy years, if a person survives to sixty-five, the figure significantly increases, probably another fifteen to twenty years on average. Don't sit around waiting to die. Make the years you have left productive and rewarding by developing good relationships with younger family members, pursuing a hobby, doing volunteer work, taking a course, traveling, and doing many other activities you will enjoy. Remember the man in the story at the beginning of this chapter. Our attitude has something to do with how long we live.

America is a youth-oriented culture; there is no place for me. A few years ago, this seemed to be true, but it is no longer the case. Though much of our culture is still geared to young people, individuals sixty-five and above have become a major economic and political force, simply because of their number. Advertisers are appealing more and more to this age group, and many businesses are catering to the older market. Politicians are extremely eager to be sensitive to senior citizens. Many individuals in this age range are vigorous, healthy, and very productive. More and more of them are well-off financially. Seven out of ten own their own homes. More and more of this population segment are continuing in the active work force and choosing not to retire.

Some people think almost all elderly people live in retirement or nursing homes. However, approximately 63 percent live in families, 31 percent live alone, and only 6 percent are in institutions. Among older men, one out of five is still in the labor force. The proportion for women is one of twelve.

I am sick just because I am old. This is not true. A quote from gerontologist Neil Resnick is interesting. He said, "Old people are sick because they are sick, not because they are old. It is never too late to be the person you might have been." Normal aging can be attenuated by lowering one's blood pressure, not smoking, increasing exercise, avoiding a sedentary lifestyle, and having a goal—a reason to live.

No one needs me anymore. The highest incidence of suicide in the United States is among white men over age seventy-five. What a shame! These people are needed by society, their families, and God. Each person has a mission to fulfill and must go on for the cause of Christ (see below on depression).

There is no hope. Spiritually there is always hope. Christ died for you. If you are depressed, antidepressants accompanied by counseling can help. Medicines are becoming more and more effective with fewer side effects. I challenge you to try to live your life to the fullest for the cause of Christ. Is there no hope? Remember, 8 percent of those above the age of eighty function well and are independent. Even for those who are less healthy, if they have Christ as their Savior, they can find joy within the body of Christ and peace in their hope of heaven.

I cannot go on without my mate, my friends, and my job. Life may be difficult, but remember Philippians 4:13: "I can do all things through Christ." Christ is loving you through this. He knows life is difficult, and he wants to help you. Rely on him and expect him to show you how to live a life that is fulfilling and useful.

2. Be Proactive

Be on the watch for depression. Approximately 25 percent of all suicides occur among the elderly. Depression is the single most common psychological disorder in senior citizens, and it may be precipitated by losses—physical, family, financial, and friends. It may be disguised and manifested in worries over health, sleep disturbances, appetite loss, decreased concentration, decreased energy, and concerns over body functions.

The following may indicate depression: a sense of failure, loss of interest in usual activities, feeling as though you are finished, a pronounced dissatisfaction, increased guilt, feelings of worthlessness, difficulty making decisions, increased crying, a sad mood, and suicidal ideations or increased thoughts of death. Sometimes senility or dementia can look like depression, and it's important to know the difference, since depression can often be treated effectively with medication, counseling, and a good support system.

In Major Depression . . .	In Dementia . . .
there are depressive symptoms/anxiety.	there is euthymia (a normal mood).
the person experiences subacute onset of dementia associated with mood changes.	the person experiences insidious onset.
there is a history of depression.	a history of depression is less common.

In Major Depression . . .	In Dementia . . .
aphasia (difficulty with words) and apraxia (difficulty performing physical tasks) are absent.	aphasia and apraxia are present.
orientation is generally intact.	orientation is impaired.
concentration is impaired.	recent memory is impaired.
the person emphasizes memory complaints.	the person minimizes memory complaints.
the person tends to give up on cognitive testing.	the person makes an effort in cognitive testing but does poorly.

Be on the watch for senility or dementia. Dementia is often a worry as we grow older, but now with all the recent medical discoveries, elderly people have every reason to be hopeful that dementia will have little effect on them. New and better medications keep appearing. And nothing is more encouraging than the Word of God. The Bible gives this gloom-dispelling and challenging word to God's aged children: "The righteous shall flourish like a palm tree, he shall grow like a cedar in Lebanon. . . . They shall still bear fruit in old age; they shall be . . . flourishing" (Ps. 92:12, 14). Long ago David said, "My times are in Your hand" (Ps. 31:15). We can trust God to be with us, no matter what the future holds.

The vast majority of people over sixty-five years of age do not develop senility or dementia, so you could be worrying prematurely. Often depression is mistaken for dementia. If you are concerned, review the above chart and contact your doctor.

Dementia is a term that refers to a group of multifaceted, different disorders, all of which are characterized by a decline in memory functions, as well as apraxia—difficulty in performing physical tasks, such as using hand tools, buttoning a shirt, and brushing teeth, that one previously was capable of performing. They also may have agnosia—the inability to recognize familiar objects, sounds, textures, tastes, and people—and aphasia—difficulty in comprehension, expression, naming, reading, writing, and repeating words. Other mental tasks (called executive functions) that become impaired include planning, judgment, impulse control, forethought, troubleshooting, attention, self-awareness, abstract thinking, and sequencing. The loss in memory and function may either be a slow, subtle process or occur fairly quickly, either in a continuous progression or in a more limited fashion.

In dementia of the Alzheimer's type (DAT), the etiology is unknown. On autopsy, characteristic neuritic plaques and neurofibrillary tangles are found. These are believed to be involved somehow in the neurotoxic process that leads to nerve cell death and subsequent dementia. Abnormalities in several brain neurotransmitters—acetylcholine (ACh), norepinephrine (NE), and serotonin (5HT)—are commonly found.

About 85 percent of all dementias are accounted for by DAT. The remaining 15 percent of dementias are made up of many different disorders, the most common of which is called vascular dementia or multi-infarct dementia. Atherosclerosis typically leads to multiple strokes, causing multiple circumscribed areas where brain tissue and function are lost. It can also be seen with multiple emboli (clots) that lodge in the small arteries of the brain and cause islands of brain loss.

Alcohol abuse can also induce dementia. Alcohol itself is directly neurotoxic. In addition, in the metabolism of alcohol, certain vitamins essential for nerve growth and function are depleted, especially thiamine (vitamin B_6).

With dementia there may be delusions and hallucinations. *Delusions* may include fears of theft of belongings, abandonment by family, spousal infidelity, and bodily harm. *Misinterpretation delusions* may include fears that others are living in the house, one's house is not one's home, dead individuals are still alive, one's caregiver has been replaced by an impostor, and characters on television are real. *Hallucinations* may involve people or animals that do not exist.

Often other conditions accompany dementia: 60 percent have agitation; 70 percent become psychotic; 50 percent have behavioral problems at any given time; 70 percent have apathy; 50 percent have anxiety, and 40 percent have depression.

Many well-known people have suffered from some form of dementia, including former President Ronald Reagan (DAT). Although the majority of dementias are irreversible, approximately 10 to 15 percent of dementias can be corrected, or at least not permitted to worsen, with proper medical treatment. For this reason, it is important to consult with a physician if dementia is suspected. New medicines are already on the scene and more will be coming (see appendix N). There is certainly reason for hope.

Watch for pathologic processes. Sometimes with age individuals become more paranoid. There may be an accentuation of basic personality traits, or the person may become rigid and cautious. There is a decrease in performance and speed, and there may be a relaxing of defense mechanisms, so a person may take actions he would not ordinarily take. Sometimes medications can help.

Be on the watch for drug dependency. Alcohol consumption often increases after retirement. The use of sleeping pills could become a problem also, as could the use of minor tranquilizers. However, minor tranquilizers and sleeping medications are sometimes needed, so consult your personal physician concerning their use.

Be alert to anxiety disorders. Anxiety symptoms, such as fearfulness, insomnia, agitation, irritability, gastrointestinal problems, chest pains, feeling on edge or keyed up, worry, trouble concentrating, fatigue, and muscle tension, may develop in the elderly. Antianxiety medications may help along with increased emotional support and a chance to share one's feelings and fears.

Be alert to changing sleep patterns. With increased age, sleep may be more restless. Avoid daytime naps. Consult the doctor regarding medical problems (for example, restless leg syndrome or sleep apnea) that may be part of the problem.

Be aware of drug reactions. As individuals age, they may need smaller doses of medication. Also, it is easy to take too many medications with the risk that they will interact with each other and cause problems. Seventy-five percent of the elderly take over-the-counter medications, so be careful. Be sure your physician and/or pharmacist is aware of all the medications you take.

Be aware of a feeling of social isolation. Evaluate your current living condition. Is it best for you? For some individuals a retirement home is best because of the medical and social help available. If you are living alone, be sure to encourage regular visits and calls by family and friends. Take advantage of other resources, such as senior citizen clubs, home health care, day health care, Meals-on-Wheels, home health aids, transportation services for the disabled, visiting nurses, social security benefits, old age assistance, and Medicare.

Be careful with retirement. Perhaps 50 percent of retirees die within one year. So don't retire (stop all productive work), but redirect your energies to service projects, hobbies, or an avocation. Stay active for Christ.

Be careful with some common physical problems. Orthostatic hypotension, when untreated, may result in falls, which may result in breaking a hip.

Incontinence may be a problem. Fifty percent of females over eighty have this problem as do 25 percent of males over eighty. Many are too embarrassed to mention it to their doctor, but many cases are treatable. The causes vary and include delirium, infection, atrophic vaginitis, drugs, psychological depression, diuresis, excessive intake of liquids, malnutrition, cirrhosis, stool impaction, and prostate enlargement.

Take practical steps to treat immobility. The most common cause of stiffness is osteoarthritis. To remain mobile with this condition, you may want to install handrails, lower the bed, use chairs with arms, use rubber shin guards, and consider a cane or walker.

Take preventive measures. Much can be done to prevent the onset of disease. For example, discontinue using tobacco and alcohol; take a daily multiple vitamin; treat high blood pressure; talk with your doctor about a pap smear; consider immunizations for influenza, pneumococcal pneumonia, and tetanus; consider a periodic mammogram; exercise daily (it may help blood pressure, glucose, bone density, insomnia, and constipation); consider the refresher driving courses AARP offers; and, finally, use a hearing aid if you have diminished hearing.

Let the church help. Every member of the body of Christ is important, according to 2 Corinthians 12. Let the deacons of the church know what your needs are. Be willing to accept help from other church members. By so doing, you are allowing them to exercise their gifts.

Be aware of helpful phone numbers. Take advantage of the many organizations that offer helpful services:

Alzheimer's Association 800-272-3900
American Association of Retired Persons 800-523-5800
American Diabetes Association 800-252-8233
Arthritis Foundation 800-283-7800

Eldercare Locators   800-677-1116
National Adult Services Association 202-479-6682
National Aging Information Center 202-619-7501
National Counsel on the Aging 202-479-1200
National Victim Center   800-394-2255
Veterans Administration   800-827-1000

3. Consider Medications

Medications today offer great hope for seniors. Be sure to check with your physician if you have a physical or emotional problem. He or she will probably be able to prescribe a medication that will help. It is encouraging to see the advances being made in the treatment of disease. This should give seniors hope for the years ahead (see appendixes N and O).

4. Enjoy Scripture

From a biblical perspective, there is great value in the maturity that comes with age. Over half of the exploits of faith that are recounted in God's "Spiritual Hall of Fame" in Hebrews 11 were done by individuals who were past age sixty-five.

When Enoch was sixty-five years old, he became the father of Methuselah. At this point in his life, Enoch "walked with God" (Gen. 5:24). After walking with God for three hundred years, God found Enoch so pleasing that he took him home to himself without his experiencing death (Heb. 11:5).

In the violent world before the great flood, Noah found grace in the eyes of God. Being warned of the coming destruction, Noah built the ark. He was six hundred years old when the flood came (Gen. 7:6; Heb. 11:7).

Abraham, Isaac, and Jacob lived in tents in the land of promise. All three knew the meaning of patient waiting for the promises of God to be fulfilled in the maturity of their latter years (Heb. 11:8–10). By faith Sarah received the ability to conceive Isaac when she was almost one hundred years old and past any possibility of childbearing (Gen. 21:2; Heb. 11:11–12). Abraham was one hundred years old when his son Isaac was born (Gen. 21:5). By faith Abraham was willing to offer up his dearly loved son, Isaac, knowing that God could raise Isaac from the dead if he so desired (Heb. 11:17–19).

On their death beds, Isaac, Jacob, and Joseph made great prophetic statements of faith (vv. 20–22). Joseph, whose life was marked by great exploits, performed his most remarkable act of faith when he was one hundred and ten years old (Gen. 50:22–25; Heb. 11:22). He commanded that his bones be carried out of Egypt and buried in the Promised Land when the children of Israel went to their homeland.

Moses chose to identify himself with God's people at age forty. At age eighty, he accepted the challenge of leading the people of Israel out of Egypt (Heb. 11:24–29).

In both the Old and New Testaments, God gave great emphasis to the importance of maturity when he chose the term *elder* for the spiritual leaders of Israel and of his church (Exod. 12:21; 17:5; Num. 11:16; 1 Kings 8:1; Acts 4:8; 16:4; 1 Tim. 5:17; Titus 1:5).

Are you troubled at the thought of growing old? Following are some great verses that may help:

Isaiah 43:1–2: But now, thus says the LORD, who created you, O Jacob, and He who formed you, O Israel: "Fear not, for I have redeemed you; I have called you by your name; you are Mine. When you pass through the waters, I will be with you; and through the rivers, they shall not overflow you. When you walk through the fire, you shall not be burned, nor shall the flame scorch you."

Hebrews 12:1–3: Therefore we also, since we are surrounded by so great a cloud of witnesses, let us lay aside every weight, and the sin which so easily ensnares us, and let us run with endurance the race that is set before us, looking unto Jesus, the author and finisher of our faith, who for the joy that was set before Him endured the cross, despising the shame, and has sat down at the right hand of the throne of God. For consider Him who endured such hostility from sinners against Himself, lest you become weary and discouraged in your souls.

John 14:27: Peace I leave with you, My peace I give to you; not as the world gives do I give to you. Let not your heart be troubled, neither let it be afraid.

Psalm 27:13–14: I would have lost heart, unless I had believed that I would see the goodness of the LORD in the land of the living. Wait on the LORD; be of good courage, and He shall strengthen your heart; wait, I say, on the LORD!

John 3:16: For God so loved the world that He gave His only begotten Son, that whoever believes in Him should not perish but have everlasting life.

Every member of the body of Christ is very important (1 Corinthians 12), and each has a part to contribute. We must bear one another's burdens: "Bear one another's burdens, and so fulfill the law of Christ" (Gal. 6:2).

■ Follow-Up

The aged gentleman in the introduction to this chapter had no purpose in life. I trust that with the above choices you, the senior citizen, can find purpose in your life. We need you. Christ needs you to live for him.

If you are a friend or relative of an elderly person, there are two things you can do for him or her. Watch for financial concerns. Sometimes the concern is realistic; sometimes it isn't. In either case, family members and friends can offer reassurance. If there is a reason for concern, talk to the elderly person about options that may help.

Finally, tell the elderly person in your life how much you love and need him or her. Say it often.

15

Reviving Hope

Once a decision is carefully reached, act! Get busy carrying out your decisions—and dismiss all anxiety about the outcome.

Dale Carnegie

I hear you all talk about hope, but I just don't think there is any!" my young client said in anguish.

"Well, please don't give up yet," I said. "We all encounter tough times in life, but you can choose to include your name among those who faced adversity and countered it with hope. Make hope a habit. In doing so, you will find challenges, disappointments, trouble, and burdens much easier to take. Even though you may think nothing good can happen in your life whatsoever, still there is hope. Please consider the following points."

■ Always Hope in Something Better

We are inundated each day with stress and worry. We worry about our kids, family, finances, work, friends, and health. With each new worry, with every pressure we endure, hope begins to get squeezed out of the picture. Rather than enjoy life, we fight each day just to survive life and maintain a balance.

Prior hurts and disappointments also work to destroy hope. A painful past can sometimes leave no apparent opening for a happier

153

future. Many choose to remain within negative circumstances and endure hardships rather than boldly reach for something better. This type of "learned helplessness" traps the unsuspecting and fools them into believing that "this is the best for which I can hope."

Near the end of the movie *Old Yeller,* Fess Parker makes a sage comment when he states that sometimes, for no reason at all, life will just knock a person to his knees. But we have to be honest and admit it's not always like that. Often better times are just ahead. We can hope in that.

Despite all of the obstacles and barriers in our way, we have discovered something unique about hope. Even in the depths of pain, discouragement, depression, and adversity, hope can survive; it is always there.

Sometimes when individuals are losing hope, it is because they have a physical problem. There are powerful chemicals in the brain that may be abnormal for one of several reasons (physiological, stress, hormonal, disease factors, and so on). With the depletion of these neurochemicals, there can be negative thinking, low energy levels, sleep abnormalities, impaired concentration, and feelings of hopelessness.

Many times, appropriate medical treatment can restore the ability to see the hope that is always available through Christ.

■ God's Word Gives Hope

The following are verses of comfort:

Jeremiah 29:11 (NIV): "For I know the plans I have for you," declares the LORD, "plans to prosper you and not to harm you, plans to give you hope and a future."

Psalm 42:5 (NIV): Why are you downcast, O my soul? Why so disturbed within me? Put your hope in God, for I will yet praise him, my Savior and my God.

Psalm 130:7 (NIV): Put your hope in the LORD, for with the LORD is unfailing love and with him is full redemption.

Jeremiah 17:7: Blessed is the man who trusts in the LORD, and whose hope is the LORD.

Psalm 62:5–8 (NIV): Find rest, O my soul, in God alone; my hope comes from him. He alone is my rock and my salvation; he is my fortress, I will not be shaken. My salvation and my honor depend on God; he is my mighty rock, my refuge. Trust in him at all times, O people; pour out your hearts to him, for God is our refuge.

■ Find Hope in Prayer

Jeremiah 33:3 is a powerful verse: "Call to Me, and I will answer you, and show you great and mighty things." When life seems futile, when circumstances are tough, when you feel lonely, you can renew your heart through prayer. God promises that if you call on him in times of trouble, he will deliver you (Ps. 50:15).

■ Hope in Christ

John 3:16 gives us ultimate hope through the message of Christ. As followers of Christ, we are promised life everlasting—a hope that is real.

■ Follow-Up

My friend, there is always hope in Christ. Do not be deceived by the simplicity of these suggestions. The Bible and prayer are powerful resources for giving and renewing. The latest research with PET scans reveals that brain chemistry can be altered for the better with simple behavioral techniques. My prayer for you is that in Christ and his Word, you will find hope!

Woodrow Kroll's poem is most fitting for any problem, any choice you may need to make for health and starting over. Regardless of the choices you may have made in the past, happiness can be yours today for the choosing, but you may need to start over in some area of your life.

Start Over

When you've trusted Jesus and walked His way,
When you've felt His hand lead you day by day,
But your steps now take you another way . . . Start over.

When you've made your plans and they've gone awry,
When you've tried your best till there is no more try,
When you've failed yourself and you don't know why . . . Start
    over.

When you've told your friends what you plan to do,
When you've trusted them, but they didn't come through,
Now you are all alone and it's up to you . . . Start over.

When you failed your kids, and they're grown and gone,
When you've done your best but it turned out wrong,
And now your grandchildren have come along . . . Start over.

When you've prayed to God so you'll know His will,
When you've prayed and prayed but you don't know still,
When you want to stop 'cause you've had your fill . . . Start over.

When you think you're finished and want to quit,
When you've bottomed out in life's deepest pit,
When you've tried and tried to get out of it . . . Start over.

When the year's been long and successes few,
When December comes and you're feeling blue,
God gives a January just so you . . . Start over.

Starting over means victories won.
Starting over means a race well run.
Starting over means the Lord's . . . "Well done!"

Woodrow Kroll
President, Back to the Bible

So don't just sit there! Have hope and start over!

16

Changing Your Life Forever

History does not teach fatalism. These are moments when the will of a handful of free men breaks through determinism and opens up new roads.

Charles de Gaulle

Choices are the hinges of destiny! But what are the most important choices in life? Four stand out:

■ Be in Control of Your Feelings

We have many choices. Some events are unfortunate, tragic, and wrong. They may produce strong feelings with a desire for revenge. We can choose either to let the unfortunate circumstances control us or to control them with Christ-like alternatives for our behavior. Controlling our feelings begins with controlling our behavioral choices. Below are six important issues involving choices and feelings.

Forgive yourself if you have let feelings overly control your choices in the past. Perhaps you chased the illusive butterfly of love into an affair and now feel extreme *guilt*. Perhaps you chose

157

to let your anger get away from you and were abusive and now feel *shame*. Perhaps you made choices that let the circumstances of life escalate, and now you are incapacitated by *anxiety*. Perhaps you chose an *addicting agent* in response to life's stressors. Turn to Christ and forgive yourself.

Succumbing to guilt and shame is a bad choice; choose instead to pursue health in Christ. In 1 John 1:9 God promises forgiveness when we confess our sins. This promise is still operative. Psalm 103:13–14 still applies: "Just as a father has compassion on his children, so the LORD has compassion on those who fear Him. For He Himself knows our frame; He is mindful that we are but dust" (NASB).

God can deal with the bad choices of your past. Allow him to redirect you away from guilt and shame. "I will restore to you the years that the swarming locust has eaten" (Joel 2:25). Though there have been bad times, God can and will restore.

Never underestimate the power of feelings. I have often seen feelings drive very logical and intelligent individuals to behaviors that are incongruent with who they are. Feelings may be positive, but they can also be sinister. They may be straightforward, but they can also be treacherous. They may be overt, but they can also be covert. They may be strong for Christ, but they can also be strong for Satan.

To understand the power of feelings, just read the newspaper. You'll read about a pastor with a thriving ministry and a beautiful wife who is found to be involved in an affair; a church leader who is held in respect but charged with voyeurism; a missionary who has served God for years in a foreign country charged with incest; a church deacon who is guilty of spouse abuse; a medical doctor with a good practice found to be addicted to drugs; or a beautiful teenager from a professional family who has starved herself and now weighs only fifty pounds. Indeed, feelings are stronger than logic. When we are led by the power of our feelings, we'll wind up in immoral, abusive, and self-destructive behaviors.

Share difficult feelings. The only way to deal with troubling feelings is to talk about them. Don't stuff them; don't hide them. Talk about them, grieve, and cry. First, we must admit our feelings to ourselves.

I recall talking to a fourteen-year-old whose parents had divorced. I asked, "Doesn't that hurt?"

He responded, "Yes, I guess so." He was hurting immensely but had never shared his feelings, had never even really admitted them to himself.

You can, if you choose, override your past programming by choice. We have seen countless individuals just like you overcome what seemed to be insurmountable odds because they chose to do so. We need to gain insight into how feelings are disguised in ourselves and how they may have had powerful influences on our choices. Feelings are often disguised by defense mechanisms, games, and transference issues. A therapist can help you deal with underlying negative feelings.

Defense mechanisms are conscious or subconscious mechanisms that may strongly affect our choices and cause us to deceive ourselves. They include *denial,* by which we deny feelings that may be obvious to others and should be obvious to us; *projection,* by which we project our faults onto others and resent those faults in others; *rationalization,* by which we excuse sinful behavior; *reaction formation,* by which we go to an opposite extreme in dealing with an unacceptable feeling; *pharisaism,* by which we become overly critical of others; *passive-aggressive behavior,* by which we deal with aggressive feelings through passive behavior; *displacement,* by which we unfairly displace feelings from one person or object to another; and *somatization,* by which we deal with feelings through an overconcern with possible physical illnesses.

Games we play to disguise our feelings include taking the position of victim, persecutor, and/or rescuer. In the process of disguising our feelings through games, we may hurt ourselves or others. We may play the "Poor me" game; "Yes . . . but . . ." game; "It's all your fault" game; "Now I've got you" game; "I'm defective" game; and "Let me do that for you" game.

Finally, *transference issues* involve unfairly transferring our feelings from someone in our past to someone else today.

Seek to understand the power of unresolved feelings in yourself and others. These feelings affect your choices.

When experiencing the power of others' feelings, try not to personalize their issues. Bad choices in others may revolve around past issues of abandonment, abuse, or feeling unskilled or inferior. Don't take personally what you had nothing to do with in any way.

Don't let feelings control your choices. As we have seen, if you allow your feelings to be your master, you will find them leading you into bad choices. They may seem to promise satisfaction of your basic needs but in the long run often lead to sexual or anger issues. On the other hand, *don't ignore all gut feelings in decision making*. The brain has an amazing ability to sift through various pieces of information and quickly produce ideas, so some hunches may be good, and it makes sense to consider them. Many CEOs are good at recognizing a good hunch. If we ignored all feelings, we would become like Mr. Spock. We need the right brain, which in most people controls our emotional and creative side.

■ Be in Control of Your Behavior

The Bible repeatedly emphasizes the need to consider our behavior, because our behavior determines our destiny. What we do today has a powerful impact on our life tomorrow. Satan's trap is to encourage us to swap moments of pleasure for weeks of pain. But before being ensnared, consider the high cost of behavior that focuses on momentary pleasure or is motivated by a vengeful spirit.

If you realize that some changes in your behavior are needed, start making those changes now. Learn to smile, use a kind tone of voice, share sincere appreciation, listen carefully to others, and avoid useless arguments. These behaviors can make a big difference in your life and the lives of others. An old Chinese proverb says, "A bit of fragrance always clings to the hand that gives the rose."

Life is too short to waste it in poor behavior. You can begin now to make changes and turn things around. Think of the benefit for the future. What momentum this could create for you! Think of what you could accomplish! You will experience great pleasure in knowing that you have walked with Christ and pleased him. How wonderful to hear our Lord say, "Well done, good and faithful servant" (Matt. 25:23)!

In any area of your life where you are not satisfied with your behavior, ask yourself four questions:

1. What is the problem?
2. What are my options?
3. Which ones will I choose?
4. When will I start?

Thomas Carlyle said that our main business is not to see what lies dimly at a distance but to do what lies clearly at hand. Insanity has been said to be "doing the same thing over and over again and expecting a different result." We must face our old unhealthy behaviors, search for alternatives, and replace the unhealthy behaviors with new healthy ones. For example, if you easily lose your temper, learn how to avoid situations that cause your anger; if you have a problem with drinking too much, stay away from places where you would be tempted to drink; if you are a workaholic, discuss time management with your superior or take a course on the subject; if you often overeat, plan activities that will keep you busy during times when you are tempted to eat too much. Use the principle of positive reinforcement on new healthy behavior. Reinforce any behavior you want to repeat with a positive reward—treat yourself to something special when you have behaved as you desire.

Study the Bible to discover the behaviors that God rewards. Look at the behaviors of the heroes of the Bible. What helped them succeed in their mission? Try adopting their behaviors. Then think through your life's mission. What has God called you to do? Determine behaviors that will reinforce and help you achieve your mission. For example, if you feel called to teach the Bible, set aside time for daily Bible study, sit under good teachers and observe their methods, and be willing to learn from others. But don't fall into the trap of being driven to achieve a certain goal. We need God's daily guidance to have the right balance.

By recognizing behaviors that need to change and taking steps to replace them with healthy behaviors, you can change your daily life, and by so doing you can change your destiny. Remember, choices are the hinges of destiny.

■ Be in Control of Your Thinking

The Bible says that your thinking is important. "As he thinks in his heart, so is he" (Prov. 23:7). "And do not be conformed to this world, but be transformed by the renewing of your mind, that you may prove what is that good and acceptable and perfect will of God" (Rom. 12:2). "Finally, brethren, whatever things are true, whatever things are noble, whatever things are just, whatever things are pure, whatever things are lovely, whatever things are of good report; if there is any virtue and if there is anything praiseworthy—meditate on these things" (Phil. 4:8).

Our brains are able to think four hundred to twelve hundred words per minute, and thoughts can have great impact, holding the power of life and death. Everything ever done began with a thought. Every great discovery began with a thought. We may even prolong our own life by wanting to live and hasten our demise when we give up. Thinking really does hold the key.

According to Dr. Chris Thurman, we need to be careful that we do not take a nickel event and assign a five-thousand-dollar reaction to it or that we do not take a five-thousand-dollar event and assign a nickel reaction to it. In his book *The Lies We Believe*, Dr. Thurman details several lies we need to challenge, often on a moment-by-moment basis:

Self Lies
I must have everyone's love and approval.
It is easier to avoid problems than to face them.
I can't be happy unless things go my way.

Marital Lies
It's all your fault.
If it takes hard work, we must not be right for each other.
You can and should meet all my needs.
You owe me.
I shouldn't have to change.
You should like me.

Distortion Lies
This is the end of the world.
It's all my fault.
Things can never change.
I will only look at the negative.

Worldly Lies
You can have it all.
You are only as good as what you do.
Life should be easy.
Life should be fair.

Don't wait.

People are basically good.

Religious Lies

God's love must be earned.

God hates the sin and the sinner.

Because I'm a Christian, God will protect me from suffering
and pain.

It is my Christian duty to meet all the needs of others.

All my problems are caused by my sins.

God can't use me unless I'm spiritually strong.

Recognizing that lies like these have entered our thinking is the first step in controlling our thoughts. We may have to remind ourselves often of the truth.

Be careful with negative input—television, books, magazines, and movies. These and other sources can put negative thoughts into your brain, actually changing the brain chemistry. The neurotransmitters change with input, and it is the neurotransmitters that control who we are from a physiological and pathological standpoint, so be careful of what goes into your brain. It is also important to refuse to dwell on negative thinking, because it can cause and increase depression. Instead, try to stimulate good thoughts by choosing uplifting books and television programs, Christian radio, and Christian music. Einstein said, "The problems we face cannot be solved at the same level of thinking we were at when we created them." New input can change our thinking, and new thought patterns will change our behavior.

Let the Scriptures transform your thinking. This is what God intended. "So shall My word be that goes forth from My mouth; it shall not return to Me void, but it shall accomplish what I please, and it shall prosper in the thing for which I sent it" (Isa. 55:11). The more of God's Word that gets into our minds, the more it will change us. It is especially effective in refuting the lies listed above.

■ Change Your Attitude

Attitude is a way of living that reflects both one's feelings and thinking. It is one's disposition, and it can be changed. Attitude is mental. Attitude is a choice.

During World War II, Viktor Frankl was imprisoned by the Nazis. He lost everything and saw many family members put to death. Finally, he decided the only thing that could not be taken from him was his attitude. He developed a wonderful attitude. Soon even the guards were coming to him for help. Later he wrote about living with hope through great tragedy in his book *Man's Search for Meaning:*

> We who lived in the concentration camps remember the men who walked through the huts comforting others, giving away their last piece of bread. They may have been few in number, but they offer sufficient proof that everything can be taken away from a man but one thing: to choose one's attitude in any given set of circumstances, to choose one's own way.

The importance of attitude is summarized well by Charles Swindoll:

> The longer I live, the more I realize the impact of attitude on life. Attitude, to me, is more important than facts. It is more important than the past, than education, than money, than circumstances, than failures, than successes, than what people say or think or do. It is more important than appearance, giftedness or skill. It will make or break a company, a church, a home. The remarkable thing is we have a choice every day regarding the attitude we will embrace for the day. We cannot change our past. . . . We cannot change the fact that people will act in a certain way. We cannot change the inevitable. The only thing we can do is play on the one string we have, and that is our attitude. I am convinced that life is 10 percent what happens to me and 90 percent how I react to it. And so it is with you. We are in charge of our attitudes.

It is up to you to choose what your attitude will be. Will you let the difficulties of life make you bitter and discouraged, or will you decide to trust God for his help to get you through trials and disappointments? When we are trusting and hopeful in spite of circumstances, we have an attitude that is pleasing to God.

■ Follow-Up

This book is centered around choices that offer hope and allow you to start over no matter what the stressors are in your life. Regardless of the choices you may have made in the past, happiness can be yours today if you pursue it.

We make daily choices in regard to feelings, behavior, and thinking. Through these choices we have the ability through Christ to change our lives. Some choices carry eternal weight, such as the acceptance of Christ as Savior; other choices carry heavy weight, such as the choice of our spouse; but even simple, daily choices can be the hinges of destiny!

> I shall be telling this with a sigh
> Somewhere ages and ages hence:
> Two roads diverged in a wood, and I—
> I took the one less traveled by,
> And that has made all the difference.
>
> Robert Frost
> "The Road Not Taken"

If we make choices that keep our behavior pleasing to God, our feelings under control, and our thinking positive, we are ensuring our destiny—a life of peace and joy, of true happiness. *Choices are the hinges of destiny!*

Appendixes

Some diseases are incurable, but not because there are no drugs or other forms of treatment to stop their course. Some diseases are incurable because the patient refuses to get cured.

Paul Lee Tan

A ll scientific information will double every five years," the professor said to me when I was a resident in psychiatry in 1972. The explosion of knowledge has even exceeded his expectations. The following scientific information is for the inquisitive mind. It plunges deep into the medical, the spiritual, and the concept of choice. It reviews the past, explores the present, and looks into the future.

Appendix A

Scriptures for Encouragement

How long will you falter between two opinions? If the LORD is God, follow Him.

Elijah

Perhaps the most powerful tool I ever learned for helping to live the Christian life, I learned as a youth in church at an RA group (Royal Ambassadors for Christ). I learned to memorize Scriptures. In college, through the encouragement of friends, I became addicted to Scripture memorization. It is the most powerful tool I know, surpassing any of my psychiatric or medical training. Memorizing Scripture, through the power of the Holy Spirit, enables the power of choice. It reveals God's choices. I commend it highly. I commend it above all other advice.

Our Problem and God's Choice	More of God's Choices
Assurance of Salvation But as many as received Him, to them He gave the right to become children of God, to those who believe in His name (John 1:12).	My sheep hear My voice, and I know them, and they follow Me. And I give them eternal life, and they shall never perish; neither shall anyone snatch them out of My hand. My Father, who has given them to Me, is greater than all; and no one is able to snatch them out of My Father's hand. I and My Father are one (John 10:27–30). And Jesus said to them, "I am the bread of life. He who comes to Me shall never hunger, and he who believes in Me shall never thirst. But I said to you that you have seen Me and yet do not believe. All that the Father gives Me will come to Me, and the one who comes to Me I will by no means cast out" (John 6:35–37). And this is the testimony: that God has given us eternal life, and this life is in His Son. He who has the Son has life; he who does not have the Son of God does not have life. These things I have written to you who believe in the name of the Son of God, that you may know that you have eternal life, and that you may continue to believe in the name of the Son of God (1 John 5:11–13). For God so loved the world that He gave His only begotten Son, that whoever believes in Him should not perish but have everlasting life. For God did not send His Son into the world to condemn the world, but that the world through Him might be saved. He who believes in Him is not condemned; but he who does not believe is condemned already, because he has not believed in the name of the only begotten Son of God (John 3:16–18).

Assurance of God's Forgiveness

If we confess our sins, He is faithful and just to forgive us our sins and to cleanse us from all unrighteousness (1 John 1:9).

As far as the east is from the west, so far has He removed our transgressions from us. As a father pities his children, so the LORD pities those who fear Him. For He knows our frame; He remembers that we are dust (Ps. 103:12–14).

Assurance of Answered Prayer

Until now you have asked nothing in My name. Ask, and you will receive, that your joy may be full (John 16:24).

Now this is the confidence that we have in Him, that if we ask anything according to His will, He hears us (1 John 5:14).

And whatever you ask in My name, that I will do, that the Father may be glorified in the Son (John 14:13).

Call to Me, and I will answer you, and show you great and mighty things, which you do not know (Jer. 33:3).

Ask, and it will be given to you; seek, and you will find; knock, and it will be opened to you. For everyone who asks receives, and he who seeks finds, and to him who knocks it will be opened (Matt. 7:7–8).

Marriage Conflicts

Submitting to one another in the fear of God. Wives, submit to your own husbands, as to the Lord. For the husband is head of the wife, as also Christ is head of the church; and He is the Savior of the body. Therefore, just as the church is subject to Christ, so let the wives be to their own husbands in everything. Husbands, love your wives, just as Christ also loved the church and gave Himself for it (Eph. 5:21–25).

Wives, submit to your own husbands, as is fitting in the Lord. Husbands, love your wives and do not be bitter toward them (Col. 3:18–19).

Likewise you wives, be submissive to your own husbands, that even if some do not obey the word, they, without a word, may be won by the conduct of their wives, when they observe your chaste conduct accompanied by fear. Do not let your beauty be that outward adorning of arranging the hair, of wearing gold, or of putting on fine apparel; but let it be the hidden person of the heart, with the incorruptible ornament of a gentle and quiet spirit, which is very precious in the sight of God. For in this manner, in former times, the holy women who trusted in God also adorned themselves, being submissive to their own husbands, as Sarah obeyed Abraham, calling him lord, whose daughters you are if you do good and are not afraid with any terror. Likewise you husbands, dwell with them with understanding, giving honor to the wife, as to the weaker vessel, and as being heirs together of the grace of life, that your prayers may not be hindered (1 Peter 3:1–7).

Now concerning the things of which you wrote to me: It is good for a man not to touch a woman. Nevertheless, because of sexual immorality, let each man have his own wife, and let each woman have her own husband. Let the husband render to his wife the affection due her, and likewise also the wife to her husband. The wife does not have authority over her own body, but the husband does. And likewise the husband does not have authority over his own body, but the wife does. Do not deprive one another except with consent for a time, that you may give yourselves to fasting and prayer; and come together again so that Satan does not tempt you because of your lack of self-control (1 Cor. 7:1–5).

Parent-Child Conflicts

Children, obey your parents in the Lord, for this is right. "Honor your father and mother," which is the first commandment with promise: "that it may be well with you and you may live long on the earth." And you, fathers, do not provoke your children to wrath, but bring them up in the training and admonition of the Lord (Eph. 6:1–4)

Children, obey your parents in all things, for this is well pleasing to the Lord. Fathers, do not provoke your children, lest they become discouraged (Col. 3:20–21).

He who spares his rod hates his son, but he who loves him disciplines him promptly (Prov. 13:24).

The rod and reproof give wisdom, but a child left to himself brings shame to his mother (Prov. 29:15).

Loneliness

O LORD, You have searched me and known me. You know my sitting down and my rising up; You understand my thought afar off. You comprehend my path and my lying down, and are acquainted with all my ways. For there is not a word on my tongue, but behold, O LORD, You know it altogether. You have hedged me behind and before, and laid Your hand upon me. Such knowledge is too wonderful for me; it is high, I cannot attain it (Ps. 139:1–6).

Let your conduct be without covetousness, and be content with such things as you have. For He Himself has said, "I will never leave you nor forsake you" (Heb. 13:5).

"Go therefore and make disciples of all the nations, baptizing them in the name of the Father and of the Son and of the Holy Spirit, teaching them to observe all things that I have commanded you; and lo, I am with you always, even to the end of the age." Amen (Matt. 28:19–20).

Moses took his tent and pitched it outside the camp, far from the camp, and called it the tabernacle of meeting. And it came to pass that everyone who sought the LORD went out to the tabernacle of meeting which was outside the camp (Exod. 33:7).

Anger

"Be angry, and do not sin": do not let the sun go down on your wrath (Eph. 4:26).

You shall not hate your brother in your heart. You shall surely rebuke your neighbor, and not bear sin because of him. You shall not take vengeance, nor bear any grudge against the children of your people, but you shall love your neighbor as yourself: I am the LORD (Lev. 19:17–18).

A soft answer turns away wrath, but a harsh word stirs up anger (Prov. 15:1).

The discretion of a man makes him slow to anger, and it is to his glory to overlook a transgression (Prov. 19:11).

Do not hasten in your spirit to be angry, for anger rests in the bosom of fools (Eccles. 7:9).

But now you must also put off all these: anger, wrath, malice, blasphemy, filthy language out of your mouth (Col. 3:8).

You have heard that it was said to those of old, "You shall not murder," and whoever murders will be in danger of the judgment. But I say to you that whoever

	is angry with his brother without a cause shall be in danger of the judgment. And whoever says to his brother, "Raca!" shall be in danger of the council. But whoever says, "You fool!" shall be in danger of hell fire. Therefore if you bring your gift to the altar, and there remember that your brother has something against you, leave your gift there before the altar, and go your way. First be reconciled to your brother, and then come and offer your gift (Matt. 5:21–24).
Bitterness Let all bitterness, wrath, anger, clamor, and evil speaking be put away from you, with all malice (Eph. 4:31).	Looking diligently lest anyone fall short of the grace of God; lest any root of bitterness springing up cause trouble, and by this many become defiled (Heb. 12:15). For I see that you are poisoned by bitterness and bound by iniquity (Acts 8:23). The heart knows its own bitterness, and a stranger does not share its joy (Prov. 14:10).
Forgiving Others And be kind to one another, tender-hearted, forgiving one another, just as God in Christ also forgave you (Eph. 4:32).	Let all bitterness, wrath, anger, clamor, and evil speaking be put away from you, with all malice (Eph. 4:31). On the contrary, you ought rather to forgive and comfort him, lest perhaps such a one be swallowed up with too much sorrow (2 Cor. 2:7). For if you forgive men their trespasses, your heavenly Father will also forgive you (Matt. 6:14). And whenever you stand praying, if you have anything against anyone, forgive him, that your Father in heaven may also forgive you your trespasses (Mark 11:25).

Overcoming Depression

Why are you cast down, O my soul? And why are you disquieted within me? Hope in God, for I shall yet praise Him for the help of His countenance (Ps. 42:5).

So the LORD said to Cain, "Why are you angry? And why has your countenance fallen? If you do well, will you not be accepted? And if you do not do well, sin lies at the door. And its desire is for you, but you should rule over it" (Gen. 4:6–7).

Let not your heart be troubled; you believe in God, believe also in Me (John 14:1).

Trials

My brethren, count it all joy when you fall into various trials, knowing that the testing of your faith produces patience. But let patience have its perfect work, that you may be perfect and complete, lacking nothing. If any of you lacks wisdom, let him ask of God, who gives to all liberally and without reproach, and it will be given to him (James 1:2–5).

In this you greatly rejoice, though now for a little while, if need be, you have been grieved by various trials, that the genuineness of your faith, being much more precious than gold that perishes, though it is tested by fire, may be found to praise, honor, and glory at the revelation of Jesus Christ (1 Peter 1:6–7).

But He knows the way that I take; when He has tested me, I shall come forth as gold (Job 23:10).

Therefore, having been justified by faith, we have peace with God through our Lord Jesus Christ, through whom also we have access by faith into this grace in which we stand, and rejoice in hope of the glory of God. And not only that, but we also glory in tribulations, knowing that tribulation produces perseverance; and perseverance, character; and character, hope. Now hope does not disappoint, because the love of God has been poured out in our hearts by the Holy Spirit who was given to us (Rom. 5:1–5).

Only let your conduct be worthy of the gospel of Christ, so that whether I come and see you or am absent, I may hear of your affairs, that you stand fast in one spirit, with one mind striving together for the faith of the gospel (Phil. 1:27).

Beloved, do not think it strange concerning the fiery trial which is to try you, as though some strange thing happened to you; but rejoice to the extent that you partake of Christ's sufferings, that when His glory is revealed, you may also be glad with exceeding joy. If you are reproached for the name of Christ, blessed are you, for the Spirit of glory and of God rests upon you. On their part He is blasphemed, but on your part He is glorified. But let none of you suffer as a murderer, a thief, an evildoer, or as a busybody in other people's matters. Yet if anyone suffers as a Christian, let him not be ashamed, but let him glorify God in this matter. For the time has come for judgment to begin at the house of God; and if it begins with us first, what will be the end of those who do not obey the gospel of God? Now "If the righteous one is scarcely saved, where will the ungodly and the sinner appear?" Therefore let those who suffer according to the will of God commit their souls to Him in doing good, as to a faithful Creator (1 Peter 4:12–19).

Suffering

And we know that all things work together for good to those who love God, to those who are the called according to His purpose (Rom. 8:28).

For our light affliction, which is but for a moment, is working for us a far more exceeding and eternal weight of glory, while we do not look at the things which are seen, but at the things which are not seen. For the things which are seen are temporary, but the things which are not seen are eternal (2 Cor. 4:17–18).

Blessed be the God and Father of our Lord Jesus Christ, the Father of mercies and God of all comfort, who comforts us in all our tribulation, that we may be able to comfort those who are in any trouble, with the comfort with which we ourselves are comforted by God (2 Cor. 1:3–4).

And lest I should be exalted above measure by the abundance of the revelations, a thorn in the flesh was given to me, a messenger of Satan to buffet me, lest I be exalted above measure. Concerning this thing I pleaded with the Lord three times that it might depart from me. And He said to me, "My grace is sufficient for you, for My strength is made perfect in weakness."

Therefore most gladly I will rather boast in my infirmities, that the power of Christ may rest upon me. Therefore I take pleasure in infirmities, in reproaches, in needs, in persecutions, in distresses, for Christ's sake. For when I am weak, then I am strong (2 Cor. 12:7–10).

And you have forgotten the exhortation which speaks to you as to sons: "My son, do not despise the chastening of the Lord, nor be discouraged when you are rebuked by Him; for whom the Lord loves He chastens, and scourges every son whom He receives." If you endure chastening, God deals with you as with sons; for what son is there whom a father does not chasten? But if you are without chastening, of which all have become partakers, then you are illegitimate and not sons. Furthermore, we have had human fathers who corrected us, and we paid them respect. Shall we not much more readily be in subjection to the Father of spirits and live? For they indeed for a few days chastened us as seemed best to them, but He for our profit, that we may be partakers of His holiness. Now no chastening seems to be joyful for the present, but grievous; nevertheless, afterward it yields the peaceable fruit of righteousness to those who have been trained by it (Heb. 12:5–11).

But the free gift is not like the offense. For if by the one man's offense many died, much more the grace of God and the gift by the grace of the one Man, Jesus Christ, abounded to many (Rom. 5:15).

Now as Jesus passed by, He saw a man who was blind from birth. And His disciples asked Him, saying, "Rabbi, who sinned, this man or his parents, that he was born blind?" Jesus answered, "Neither this man nor his parents sinned, but that the works of God should be revealed in him" (John 9:1–3).

Now when Jesus had crossed over again
by boat to the other side, a great multitude
gathered to Him; and He was by the sea.
And behold, one of the rulers of the synagogue came, Jairus by name. And when
he saw Him, he fell at His feet and begged
Him earnestly, saying, "My little daughter
lies at the point of death. Come and lay
Your hands on her, that she may be healed,
and she will live." So Jesus went with him,
and a great multitude followed Him and
thronged Him. Now a certain woman had a
flow of blood for twelve years, and had suffered many things from many physicians.
She had spent all that she had and was no
better, but rather grew worse. When she
heard about Jesus, she came behind Him
in the crowd and touched His garment; for
she said, "If only I may touch His clothes,
I shall be made well." Immediately the
fountain of her blood was dried up, and
she felt in her body that she was healed
of the affliction. And Jesus, immediately
knowing in Himself that power had gone
out of Him, turned around in the crowd
and said, "Who touched My clothes?" But
His disciples said to Him, "You see the
multitude thronging You, and You say, 'Who
touched Me?'" And He looked around to
see her who had done this thing. But the
woman, fearing and trembling, knowing
what had happened to her, came and fell
down before Him and told Him the whole
truth. And He said to her, "Daughter, your
faith has made you well. Go in peace, and
be healed of your affliction." While He was
still speaking, some came from the ruler
of the synagogue's house who said, "Your
daughter is dead. Why trouble the Teacher
any further?" As soon as Jesus heard the
word that was spoken, He said to the ruler
of the synagogue, "Do not be afraid; only
believe." And He permitted no one to follow Him except Peter, James, and John
the brother of James. Then He came to
the house of the ruler of the synagogue,
and saw a tumult and those who wept and
wailed loudly. When He came in, He said
to them, "Why make this commotion and
weep? The child is not dead, but sleeping."

And they laughed Him to scorn. But when He had put them all out, He took the father and the mother of the child, and those who were with Him, and entered where the child was lying. Then He took the child by the hand, and said to her, "Talitha, cumi," which is translated, "Little girl, I say to you, arise." Immediately the girl arose and walked, for she was twelve years of age. And they were overcome with great amazement (Mark 5:21–42).

Temptation

No temptation has overtaken you except such as is common to man; but God is faithful, who will not allow you to be tempted beyond what you are able, but with the temptation will also make the way of escape, that you may be able to bear it (1 Cor. 10:13).

For we do not have a High Priest who cannot sympathize with our weaknesses, but was in all points tempted as we are, yet without sin. Let us therefore come boldly to the throne of grace, that we may obtain mercy and find grace to help in time of need (Heb. 4:15–16).

For to be carnally minded is death, but to be spiritually minded is life and peace (Rom. 8:6).

When you walk, your steps will not be hindered, and when you run, you will not stumble (Prov. 4:12).

Therefore submit to God. Resist the devil and he will flee from you. Draw near to God and He will draw near to you. Cleanse your hands, you sinners; and purify your hearts, you double-minded (James 4:7–8).

Now therefore, listen to me, my children, for blessed are those who keep my ways (Prov. 8:32).

I have made a covenant with my eyes; why then should I look upon a young woman? (Job 31:1).

Anxiety

Peace I leave with you, My peace I give to you; not as the world gives do I give to you. Let not your heart be troubled, neither let it be afraid (John 14:27).

Be anxious for nothing, but in everything by prayer and supplication, with thanksgiving, let your requests be made known to God; and the peace of God, which surpasses all understanding, will guard your hearts and minds through Christ Jesus.

Finally, brethren, whatever things are true, whatever things are noble, whatever things are just, whatever things are pure, whatever things are lovely, whatever things are of good report, if there is any virtue and if there is anything praiseworthy—meditate on these things (Phil. 4:6–8).

Therefore I say to you, do not worry about your life, what you will eat or what you will drink; nor about your body, what you will put on. Is not life more than food and the body more than clothing? Look at the birds of the air, for they neither sow nor reap nor gather into barns; yet your heavenly Father feeds them. Are you not of more value than they? Which of you by worrying can add one cubit to his stature? So why do you worry about clothing? Consider the lilies of the field, how they grow: they neither toil nor spin; and yet I say to you that even Solomon in all his glory was not arrayed like one of these. Now if God so clothes the grass of the field, which today is, and tomorrow is thrown into the oven, will He not much more clothe you, O you of little faith? Therefore do not worry, saying, "What shall we eat?" or "What shall we drink?" or "What shall we wear?" For after all these things the Gentiles seek. For your heavenly Father knows that you need all these things. But seek first the kingdom of God and His righteousness, and all these things shall be added to you. Therefore do not worry about tomorrow, for tomorrow will worry about its own things. Sufficient for the day is its own trouble (Matt. 6:25–34).

	The LORD is my light and my salvation; whom shall I fear? The LORD is the strength of my life; of whom shall I be afraid? (Ps. 27:1).
	Wait on the LORD; be of good courage, and He shall strengthen your heart; wait, I say, on the LORD! (Ps. 27:14).
	I sought the LORD, and He heard me, and delivered me from all my fears (Ps. 34:4).
	Whenever I am afraid, I will trust in You (Ps. 56:3).
Lust of the Flesh Flee also youthful lusts; but pursue righteousness, faith, love, peace with those who call on the Lord out of a pure heart (2 Tim. 2:22).	You have heard that it was said to those of old, "You shall not commit adultery." But I say to you that whoever looks at a woman to lust for her has already committed adultery with her in his heart (Matt. 5:27–28). Do not love the world or the things in the world. If anyone loves the world, the love of the Father is not in him. For all that is in the world—the lust of the flesh, the lust of the eyes, and the pride of life—is not of the Father but is of the world. And the world is passing away, and the lust of it; but he who does the will of God abides forever (1 John 2:15–17).
Lust of the Eyes (Materialism) Do not love the world or the things in the world. If anyone loves the world, the love of the Father is not in him. For all that is in the world—the lust of the flesh, the lust of the eyes, and the pride of life—is not of the Father but is of the world. And the world is passing away, and the lust of it; but he who does the will of God abides forever (1 John 2:15–17).	Now godliness with contentment is great gain. For we brought nothing into this world, and it is certain we can carry nothing out. And having food and clothing, with these we shall be content. But those who desire to be rich fall into temptation and a snare, and into many foolish and harmful lusts which drown men in destruction and perdition. For the love of money is a root of all kinds of evil, for which some have strayed from the faith in their greediness, and pierced themselves through with many sorrows. But you, O man of God, flee these things and pursue righteousness, godliness, faith, love, patience, gentleness (1 Tim. 6:6–11).

	Command those who are rich in this present age not to be haughty, nor to trust in uncertain riches but in the living God, who gives us richly all things to enjoy. Let them do good, that they be rich in good works, ready to give, willing to share, storing up for themselves a good foundation for the time to come, that they may lay hold on eternal life (1 Tim. 6:17–19).
	But I rejoiced in the Lord greatly that now at last your care for me has flourished again; though you surely did care, but you lacked opportunity. Not that I speak in regard to need, for I have learned in whatever state I am, to be content: I know how to be abased, and I know how to abound. Everywhere and in all things I have learned both to be full and to be hungry, both to abound and to suffer need. I can do all things through Christ who strengthens me (Phil. 4:10–13).
Pride of Life The fear of the LORD is to hate evil; pride and arrogance and the evil way and the perverse mouth I hate (Prov. 8:13).	By pride comes only contention, but with the well-advised is wisdom (Prov. 13:10). A proud and haughty man—"Scoffer" is his name; he acts with arrogant pride (Prov. 21:24). He who is of a proud heart stirs up strife, but he who trusts in the LORD will be prospered (Prov. 28:25). Do not love the world or the things in the world. If anyone loves the world, the love of the Father is not in him. For all that is in the world—the lust of the flesh, the lust of the eyes, and the pride of life—is not of the Father but is of the world. And the world is passing away, and the lust of it; but he who does the will of God abides forever (1 John 2:15–17). But Jesus called them to Himself and said, "You know that the rulers of the Gentiles lord it over them, and those who are great exercise authority over them. Yet it shall not be so among you; but whoever desires to become great among you, let

him be your servant. And whoever desires to be first among you, let him be your slave—just as the Son of Man did not come to be served, but to serve, and to give His life a ransom for many (Matt. 20:25–28).

Low Self-Concept

For I say, through the grace given to me, to everyone who is among you, not to think of himself more highly than he ought to think, but to think soberly, as God has dealt to each one a measure of faith (Rom. 12:3).

O LORD, You have searched me and known me. You know my sitting down and my rising up; You understand my thought afar off. You comprehend my path and my lying down, and are acquainted with all my ways. For there is not a word on my tongue, but behold, O LORD, You know it altogether. You have hedged me behind and before, and laid Your hand upon me. Such knowledge is too wonderful for me; it is high, I cannot attain it. Where can I go from Your Spirit? Or where can I flee from Your presence? If I ascend into heaven, You are there; if I make my bed in hell, behold, You are there. If I take the wings of the morning, and dwell in the uttermost parts of the sea, even there Your hand shall lead me, and Your right hand shall hold me. If I say, "Surely the darkness shall fall on me," even the night shall be light about me; indeed, the darkness shall not hide from You, but the night shines as the day; the darkness and the light are both alike to You. For You have formed my inward parts; You have covered me in my mother's womb. I will praise You, for I am fearfully and wonderfully made; marvelous are Your works, and that my soul knows very well. My frame was not hidden from You, when I was made in secret, and skillfully wrought in the low-est parts of the earth. Your eyes saw my substance, being yet unformed. And in Your book they all were written, the days fashioned for me, when as yet there were none of them. How precious also are Your thoughts to me, O God! How great is the sum of them! If I should count them, they would be more in number than the sand; when I awake, I am still with You. Oh, that You would slay the wicked, O God! Depart from me, therefore, you blood-thirsty men. For they speak against You wickedly; Your enemies take Your name in vain. Do I not hate them, O LORD, who hate You? And do I not loathe those who rise up against You? I hate them with perfect hatred; I count them my enemies. Search me, O God, and know my heart; try me, and know my anxieties; and see if there is any wicked way in me, and lead me in the way everlasting (Psalm 139).

Blessed be the God and Father of our Lord Jesus Christ, who has blessed us with every spiritual blessing in the heavenly places in Christ, just as He chose us in Him before the foundation of the world, that we should be holy and without blame before Him in love, having predestined us to adoption as sons by Jesus Christ to Himself, according to the good pleasure of His will, to the praise of the glory of His grace, by which He has made us accepted in the Beloved. In Him we have redemption through His blood, the forgiveness of sins, according to the riches of His grace (Eph. 1:3–7).

What then shall we say to these things? If God is for us, who can be against us? He who did not spare His own Son, but delivered Him up for us all, how shall He not with Him also freely give us all things? Who shall bring a charge against God's elect? It is God who justifies. Who is he who condemns? It is Christ who died, and furthermore is also risen, who is even at the right hand of God, who also makes intercession for us. Who shall separate us from the love of Christ? Shall tribulation, or distress, or persecution, or famine, or nakedness, or peril, or sword? As it is written: "For Your sake we are killed all day long; we are accounted as sheep for the slaughter." Yet in all these things we are more than conquerors through Him who loved us. For I am persuaded that neither death nor life, nor angels nor principalities nor powers, nor things present nor things to come, nor height nor depth, nor any other created thing, shall be able to separate us from the love of God which is in Christ Jesus our Lord (Rom. 8:31–39).

But now indeed there are many members, yet one body. And the eye cannot say to the hand, "I have no need of you"; nor again the head to the feet, "I have no need of you." No, much rather, those members of the body which seem to be weaker are necessary. And those members of the body which we think to be less honorable, on these we bestow greater honor; and our unpresentable parts have greater modesty, but our presentable parts have no need. But God composed the body, having given greater honor to that part which lacks it, that there should be no schism in the body, but that the members should have the same care for one another (1 Cor. 12:20–25).

Growth in Christ

I have been crucified with Christ; it is no longer I who live, but Christ lives in me; and the life which I now live in the flesh I live by faith in the Son of God, who loved me and gave Himself for me (Gal. 2:20).

General Growth in Christ

But grow in the grace and knowledge of our Lord and Savior Jesus Christ. To Him be the glory both now and forever. Amen (2 Peter 3:18).

Growth through the Word of God

Blessed is the man who walks not in the counsel of the ungodly, nor stands in the path of sinners, nor sits in the seat of the scornful; but his delight is in the law of the LORD, and in His law he meditates day and night. He shall be like a tree planted by the rivers of water, that brings forth its fruit in its season, whose leaf also shall not wither; and whatever he does shall prosper. The ungodly are not so, but are like the chaff which the wind drives away. Therefore the ungodly shall not stand in the judgment, nor sinners in the congregation of the righteous. For the LORD knows the way of the righteous, but the way of the ungodly shall perish (Psalm 1).

Therefore, laying aside all malice, all guile, hypocrisy, envy, and all evil speaking, as newborn babes, desire the pure milk of the word, that you may grow thereby (1 Peter 2:1–2).

All Scripture is given by inspiration of God, and is profitable for doctrine, for reproof, for correction, for instruction in righteousness, that the man of God may be complete, thoroughly equipped for every good work (2 Tim. 3:16–17).

Your words were found, and I ate them, and Your word was to me the joy and rejoicing of my heart; for I am called by Your name, O LORD God of hosts (Jer. 15:16).

For the word of God is living and powerful, and sharper than any two-edged sword, piercing even to the division of soul and spirit, and of joints and marrow, and is a discerner of the thoughts and intents of the heart (Heb. 4:12).

Prayer
Then He spoke a parable to them, that men always ought to pray and not lose heart (Luke 18:1).

Ask, and it will be given to you; seek, and you will find; knock, and it will be opened to you. For everyone who asks receives, and he who seeks finds, and to him who knocks it will be opened (Matt. 7:7–8).

Now this is the confidence that we have in Him, that if we ask anything according to His will, He hears us. And if we know that He hears us, whatever we ask, we know that we have the petitions that we have asked of Him (1 John 5:14–15).

Confess your trespasses to one another, and pray for one another, that you may be healed. The effective, fervent prayer of a righteous man avails much (James 5:16).

Witnessing
For I am not ashamed of the gospel of Christ, for it is the power of God to salvation for everyone who believes, for the Jew first and also for the Greek (Rom. 1:16).

But sanctify the Lord God in your hearts, and always be ready to give a defense to everyone who asks you a reason for the hope that is in you, with meekness and fear (1 Peter 3:15).

Fellowship

That which was from the beginning, which we have heard, which we have seen with our eyes, which we have looked upon, and our hands have handled, concerning the Word of life—the life was manifested, and we have seen, and bear witness, and declare to you that eternal life which was with the Father and was manifested to us—that which we have seen and heard we declare to you, that you also may have fellowship with us; and truly our fellowship is with the Father and with His Son Jesus Christ. And these things we write to you that your joy may be full.

This is the message which we have heard from Him and declare to you, that God is light and in Him is no darkness at all (1 John 1:1–5).

And let us consider one another in order to stir up love and good works, not forsaking the assembling of ourselves together, as is the manner of some, but exhorting one another, and so much the more as you see the Day approaching (Heb. 10:24–25).

Now we exhort you, brethren, warn those who are unruly, comfort the fainthearted, uphold the weak, be patient with all (1 Thess. 5:14).

Christ the Center

As you have therefore received Christ Jesus the Lord, so walk in Him, rooted and built up in Him and established in the faith, as you have been taught, abounding in it with thanksgiving (Col. 2:6–7).

Appendix B

Depression and Grace

Amazing grace! how sweet the sound,
That saved a wretch like me!
I once was lost, but now am found,
Was blind, but now I see.

John Newton's words have encouraged many a depressed soul. His words have introduced many people to the concept of grace. No book on happiness, or its deeper cousin joy, would be complete without a few words on grace.

Grace in the Greek New Testament is *charis*. It has various uses in the New Testament. It is often used to stress divine favor and contrasts with debt (Rom. 4:4, 16), works (Rom. 2:6), and law (Rom. 6:14–15). It expresses God's mercy and favor and cannot be earned. The apostle Paul is the one who so avidly developed this concept for us today. In Ephesians 2:8–9 he states, "For by grace you have been saved through faith, and that not of yourselves; it is the gift of God, not of works, lest anyone should boast." Salvation is by grace through faith. It is a gift—the one who will receive it can have it. It cannot be given for merit or withheld because of demerit. How wonderful that is for everyone, especially a depressed person!

Related terms include *justification, redemption, and propitiation.* We are justified by the blood of Christ; we are justified because he died in our place. He is the propitiation for our sins. That means he paid the price for us. Those who have trusted Christ are redeemed and will spend an eternity in heaven because of grace through faith.

Appendix C

Should a Christian Use Psychiatric Medications?

There are several answers to the question of whether Christians should take psychiatric medications. Let me offer some of them.

The Bible does not ignore the physical, referring often to our need for medical care: "Is there no balm in Gilead, is there no physician there?" (Jer. 8:22); "A cheerful heart is good medicine" (Prov. 17:22 NIV); "Their fruit will be for food, and their leaves for medicine" (Ezek. 47:12); "He went to him and bandaged his wounds, pouring on oil and wine" (Luke 10:34 NIV). Luke, who wrote one of the Gospels, was called "the beloved physician" (Col. 4:14). And Christ said, "Those who are well have no need of a physician, but those who are sick" (Matt. 9:12).

It would be inconsistent medical practice to ignore psychiatric issues, which research and genetic studies have shown to have a physical dimension, while treating other medical conditions, such as heart disease, which we know often have a psychological dimension. We will all need medication of some kind someday. For some it may be heart medications, for some chemotherapy, and for others antidepressants.

If the position against psychiatric medications is that a person would not need them if, as a Christian, he is indeed perfect, then I agree. However, none of us is yet perfect. We are imperfect, sinful, immature individuals. That is why Christ died for us. Our minds and bodies won't be perfect until we arrive in heaven. But for now

187

it's important for us to honor God by maintaining physical, psychological, and spiritual health.

Psychiatric medications are used to return body chemicals to normal, in the same way medications are used to treat heart disease, hypertension, and cancer. They are often best used in a comprehensive approach along with counseling and a program of growth in Christ.

Whether to use psychiatric medications depends to some degree on the individual's attitude. Some individuals who are strongly against any psychiatric medications and have mild and even moderate symptoms would probably do better with a more natural approach. But when symptoms are significant or functioning is impaired, psychiatric medications are warranted. Psychiatric medications should be used when appropriate, because it may be a question of life or death, sanity or insanity, being functional or dysfunctional, experiencing tormenting symptoms or being effective for Christ.

It may be that in some cases, the longer a psychiatric condition is left untreated, the more resistant it becomes to treatment. This is known as kindling. Stress can permanently damage the brain, so when there are symptoms of a psychiatric disorder, treatment should be started early.

The Bible speaks of "spirit, soul, and body" in 1 Thessalonians 5:23. It would be naive to think the three do not interact. The real issue for Christians is not whether we take psychiatric medications but whether we are effective for Christ. Is our life lived "to know Christ and make him known" (The Navigators mission statement)? Let me be clear: Medical attention in no way nullifies the spiritual emphasis on Christ.

Appendix D

The Brain under Stress

Neuroimaging of the Brain

Through PET scans, glucose metabolism and thus cerebral functioning can be seen in the brain. PET scans allow us to actually see the damaging effects of stress and genetic factors. Below some common patterns are simulated.

Bipolar Disorder

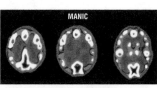

Depression

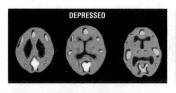

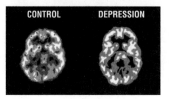

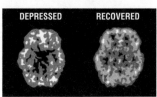

ADHD

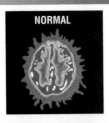

Schizophrenia

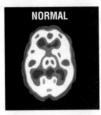

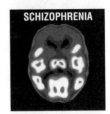

Alzheimer's Disease

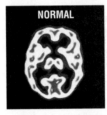

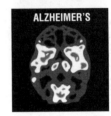

OCD

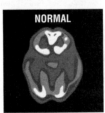

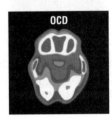

The Limbic System

Simulated PET scans reveal the effects of acute stress on the brain.

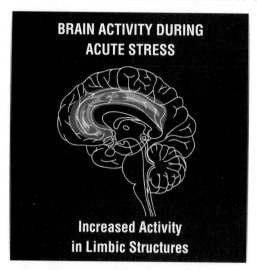

As indicated above, with acute stress there may be transient changes in brain chemistry. Under chronic stress, as indicated in the next diagram, these changes become more permanent and even anatomical.

The Hippocampus

Simulated PET scans reveal smaller hippocampus in people under chronic stress.

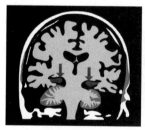 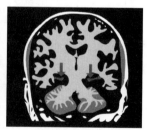

Normal   **PTSD (Post-traumatic Stress Disorder)**
Note atrophy of hippocampus

Under stress the brain changes. See below and on the following pages the specific parts of the brain affected by stress.

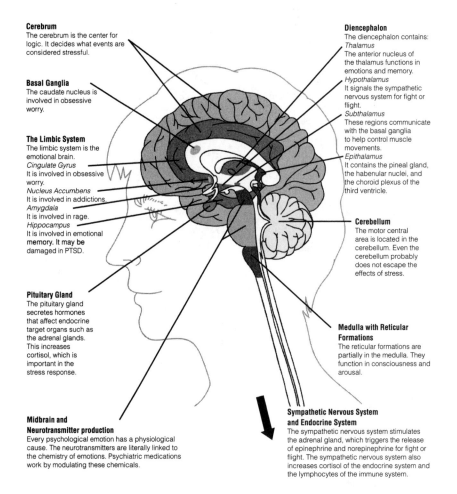

Cerebrum
The cerebrum is the center for logic. It decides what events are considered stressful.

Basal Ganglia
The caudate nucleus is involved in obsessive worry.

The Limbic System
The limbic system is the emotional brain.
Cingulate Gyrus
It is involved in obsessive worry.
Nucleus Accumbens
It is involved in addictions.
Amygdala
It is involved in rage.
Hippocampus
It is involved in emotional memory. It may be damaged in PTSD.

Pituitary Gland
The pituitary gland secretes hormones that affect endocrine target organs such as the adrenal glands. This increases cortisol, which is important in the stress response.

Midbrain and Neurotransmitter production
Every psychological emotion has a physiological cause. The neurotransmitters are literally linked to the chemistry of emotions. Psychiatric medications work by modulating these chemicals.

Diencephalon
The diencephalon contains:
Thalamus
The anterior nucleus of the thalamus functions in emotions and memory.
Hypothalamus
It signals the sympathetic nervous system for fight or flight.
Subthalamus
These regions communicate with the basal ganglia to help control muscle movements.
Epithalamus
It contains the pineal gland, the habenular nuclei, and the choroid plexus of the third ventricle.

Cerebellum
The motor central area is located in the cerebellum. Even the cerebellum probably does not escape the effects of stress.

Medulla with Reticular Formations
The reticular formations are partially in the medulla. They function in consciousness and arousal.

Sympathetic Nervous System and Endocrine System
The sympathetic nervous system stimulates the adrenal gland, which triggers the release of epinephrine and norepinephrine for fight or flight. The sympathetic nervous system also increases cortisol of the endocrine system and the lymphocytes of the immune system.

The Diencephalon

The diencephalon consists of several parts, which are extremely important in stress and emotions: the thalamus, the hypothalamus, the pineal gland, and the pituitary gland.

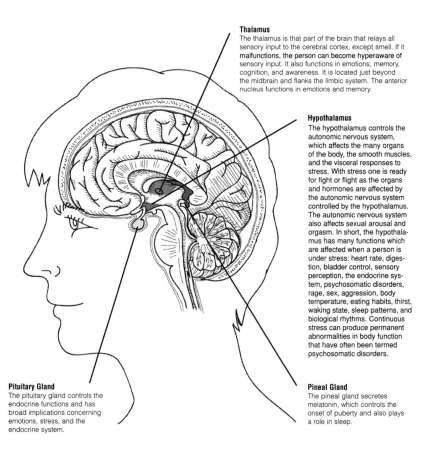

Thalamus
The thalamus is that part of the brain that relays all sensory input to the cerebral cortex, except smell. If it malfunctions, the person can become hyperaware of sensory input. It also functions in emotions, memory, cognition, and awareness. It is located just beyond the midbrain and flanks the limbic system. The anterior nucleus functions in emotions and memory.

Hypothalamus
The hypothalamus controls the autonomic nervous system, which affects the many organs of the body, the smooth muscles, and the visceral responses to stress. With stress one is ready for fight or flight as the organs and hormones are affected by the autonomic nervous system controlled by the hypothalamus. The autonomic nervous system also affects sexual arousal and orgasm. In short, the hypothalamus has many functions which are affected when a person is under stress: heart rate, digestion, bladder control, sensory perception, the endocrine system, psychosomatic disorders, rage, sex, aggression, body temperature, eating habits, thirst, waking state, sleep patterns, and biological rhythms. Continuous stress can produce permanent abnormalities in body function that have often been termed psychosomatic disorders.

Pituitary Gland
The pituitary gland controls the endocrine functions and has broad implications concerning emotions, stress, and the endocrine system.

Pineal Gland
The pineal gland secretes melatonin, which controls the onset of puberty and also plays a role in sleep.

The Limbic System

The limbic brain is the emotional brain. Pain, pleasure, anger, depression, affection, and sexuality all originate in the limbic brain. Stimulation in animals of the amygdala results in rage. Stimulation of the nucleus accumbens results in pleasure. Malfunction of the cingulate gyrus results in obsessive worry. Malfunction of the hippocampus results in painful memories that will not go away.

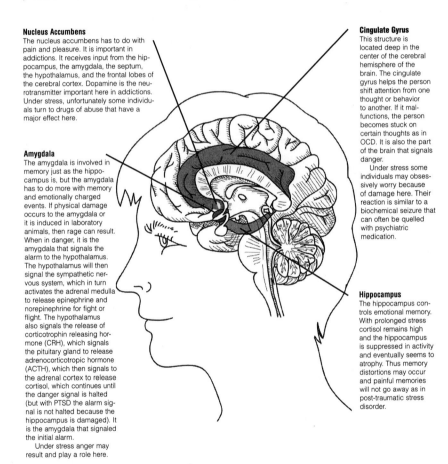

Nucleus Accumbens
The nucleus accumbens has to do with pain and pleasure. It is important in addictions. It receives input from the hippocampus, the amygdala, the septum, the hypothalamus, and the frontal lobes of the cerebral cortex. Dopamine is the neurotransmitter important here in addictions. Under stress, unfortunately some individuals turn to drugs of abuse that have a major effect here.

Amygdala
The amygdala is involved in memory just as the hippocampus is, but the amygdala has to do more with memory and emotionally charged events. If physical damage occurs to the amygdala or it is induced in laboratory animals, then rage can result. When in danger, it is the amygdala that signals the alarm to the hypothalamus. The hypothalamus will then signal the sympathetic nervous system, which in turn activates the adrenal medulla to release epinephrine and norepinephrine for fight or flight. The hypothalamus also signals the release of corticotrophin releasing hormone (CRH), which signals the pituitary gland to release adrenocorticotropic hormone (ACTH), which then signals to the adrenal cortex to release cortisol, which continues until the danger signal is halted (but with PTSD the alarm signal is not halted because the hippocampus is damaged). It is the amygdala that signaled the initial alarm.
    Under stress anger may result and play a role here.

Cingulate Gyrus
This structure is located deep in the center of the cerebral hemisphere of the brain. The cingulate gyrus helps the person shift attention from one thought or behavior to another. If it malfunctions, the person becomes stuck on certain thoughts as in OCD. It is also the part of the brain that signals danger.
    Under stress some individuals may obsessively worry because of damage here. Their reaction is similar to a biochemical seizure that can often be quelled with psychiatric medication.

Hippocampus
The hippocampus controls emotional memory. With prolonged stress cortisol remains high and the hippocampus is suppressed in activity and eventually seems to atrophy. Thus memory distortions may occur and painful memories will not go away as in post-traumatic stress disorder.

The Diencephalon (Hypothalamus), the Sympathetic Nervous System, the Pituitary Gland, the Endocrine System, and the Immune System

The sympathetic nervous system prepares the body for emergency situations. It is primarily concerned with processes involving the expenditure of energy. When the body is in homeostasis, the main function of the sympathetic division is to counteract the parasympathetic effects just enough to carry out normal processes requiring energy. During physical or emotional stress, however, the sympathetic dominates the parasympathetic. Physical exertion stimulates the sympathetic division as do a variety of emotions, such as fear, embarrassment, or rage. Emergency, excitement, exercise or embarrassment will set off sympathetic responses. Activation of the sympathetic division and release of hormones by the adrenal medulla set in motion a series of physiological responses collectively called the alarm reaction or fight-or-flight response. When in danger, it is the amygdala that signals the alarm to the hypothalamus. The hypothalamus will then signal the sympathetic nervous system, which in turn activates the adrenal medulla to release epinephrine and norepinephrine for fight or flight. The hypothalamus also signals the release of corticotrophin releasing hormone (CRH), which signals the pituitary gland to release adrenocorticotropic hormone (ACTH), which then signals to the adrenal cortex to release cortisol, which continues until the danger signal is halted (but with PTSD the alarm signal is not halted because the hippocampus is damaged).

The release of cortisol produces more glucose and more fatty acids for energy needs. Cortisol also enhances epinephrine's vasoconstrictive effects to deliver nutrients quickly. With continued stress the sympathetic nervous system overrides the normal inhibiting feedback system of high cortisol and the cortisol remains high. Sustained high cortisol can lead to hypergylcemia, hypertension, osteoporosis, bruising, poor wound healing, and a continued state of high alert. Under high cortisol and continued stress, a gene for brain derived neurotrophic factor (BDNF), a chemical that sustains the brain neurons, is repressed leading to atrophy of the neurons in the hippocampus. Thus individuals under prolonged stress may have trouble realizing that the stress is over even when the stressor is gone, because the emotional memory cells are atrophied. Furthermore, in mature animals intense stimulation of the amygdala even one time can produce lasting changes in neuronal excitability in the direction of either fight or flight. In other words, prolonged stress is not good. Under stress the sympathetic nervous system is affected and can result in traumatic memories that continue to occur. Finally, since hormones such as cortisol and epinephrine provide chemical links between the endocrine and immune systems, under stress T lymphocytes are depressed, increasing the susceptibility to physical disease (perhaps even cancer).

The Sympathetic Nervous System

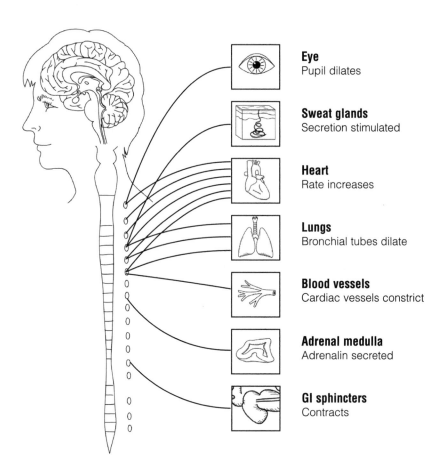

Eye
Pupil dilates

Sweat glands
Secretion stimulated

Heart
Rate increases

Lungs
Bronchial tubes dilate

Blood vessels
Cardiac vessels constrict

Adrenal medulla
Adrenalin secreted

GI sphincters
Contracts

Appendix E

Data on Major Depressive Disorder (MDD)

In 5 to 10 percent of afflicted individuals, MDD is a lifetime disorder. More than 50 percent of cases are less severe depressive disorder.

Seventeen million Americans have MDD annually.

The disease is usually recurrent.

It costs $43 billion annually.

There is high comorbidity (coexistence) with other medical diseases.

Fifteen percent of sufferers commit suicide.

Suicide is the ninth leading cause of death in America.

MDD is associated with high death rate.

MDD is very treatable.

Fewer than 50 percent of people with MDD are treated medically.

Fewer than 25 percent are adequately treated medically.

Appendix F

Major Depressive Disorder Differential

MDD (Major Depressive Disorder): low mood for two weeks, low interest, weight loss, loss of sleep, low energy, high agitation/ retardation, high sense of guilt, low concentration, suicidal

Bipolar Disorder: mood swings—high or angry to low, high mood, grandiosity, loss of sleep, rapid speech, rapid thoughts, distractibility, high activity, low judgment

GAD (General Anxiety Disorder): high worry for six months, restlessness, high fatigue, low concentration, high irritability, high muscle tension, loss of sleep

Other Anxiety Disorders: OCD, PTSD, panic disorder, phobic disorder; many develop MDD

ADHD (Attention-Deficit/Hyperactivity Disorder): inattention/ hyperactivity/ impulsivity; some develop MDD

Schizoaffective Disorder: characteristics of both schizophrenia and affective disorder

Dementia: poor memory and often euthymic or normal mood
  Dysthymia: chronic depression
  Cyclothymia: mild mood swings
  Drug Induced Mood Disorder
  Dual Diagnoses of MDD and Dysthymia

Medical Disorders and Depression: hypothyroidism, malignancies, autoimmune disorders, menopause, medications such as psychostimulants

■ Major Depressive Disorder Differential Acronyms

Major Depressive Disorder: MAAPP
- M = Mood low
- A = Affect sad
- A = Anxiety
- P = Physical symptoms
- P = Painful thinking

Bipolar Disorder: MANIC
- M = Mood swings
- A = Anger, activity, affect—all increased
- N = No insight, no judgment
- I = Insomnia, increased thoughts
- C = Concentration impaired

Generalized Anxiety Disorder: ANXIETY
- A = Anxiety
- N = No sleep
- X = Extreme worry
- I = Irritability
- E = Energy low
- T = Tension in muscles
- Y = Yearning for relief from restlessness

Schizoaffective Disorder: AAAAAAA
- A = Affect flat
- A = Alogia (without speech)
- A = Autistic
- A = Amotivational
- A = Auditory hallucinations
- A = Affective component
- A = Asocial

Dementia: IMAJO
  I = Impaired intellect
  M = Memory impaired, mood okay
  A = Affect lability
  J = Judgment impaired
  O = Orientation impaired

Appendix G

The Synapses, Neurotransmitters, and Chemicals within the Nerve Cell

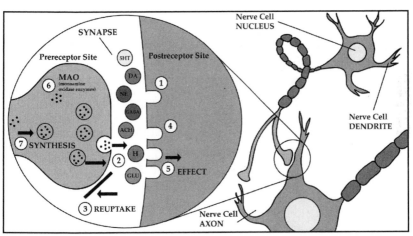

© 2002 Frank Minirth, M.D.
Illustrations by Felix Flores

Neurotransmitters are chemicals (made from amino acids) that transmit nerve impulses from one cell to the next. There are perhaps 200 of these and many more if one considers the many kinds of even one neurotransmitter such as serotonin. Every psychological emotion has a physiological component and certainly neurotransmitters are a part of that component.

Neuropeptides (endorphines, enkephalins, dynorphins) are also neuro-transmitters, and they are the body's natural painkillers. Important issues regarding neurotransmitters include:

1. Neurotransmitters are extremely important in brain functioning. We could not think or feel without neurotransmitters.
2. Neurotransmitters are very important in emotions. Every psychological emotion has a physiological cause, and neurotransmitters are part of the cause.
3. Psychiatric medications often begin to work by initially altering neurotransmitters, which results in changes at postreceptor sites, ion transport, secondary messenger systems, brain-derived neurotrophic factor, and eventually the DNA within the nucleus of the cell.

For example, antidepressants that prevent the reuptake of serotonin (5HT) may result in improved mood in depressed individuals, less worry in obsessive-compulsive individuals, and less anger. Increasing norepin-ephrine (NE) and dopamine (DA) also may lift mood. Dopamine also plays a role in sexual activity. Acetylcholine (ACH) plays a role in memory. GABA plays a role in calmness. Blocking histamine receptors could help sleep but increase weight. Glutamate, an excitatory neurotransmitter, may play a role in degenerative disease, Alzheimer's dementia, and schizophrenia. Herbs alter neurotransmitters but usually with a much less dramatic, selective, and specific effect than do psychiatric medications.

5HT	=	serotonin—important in mood, worry, and anger
DA	=	dopamine—important in energy and motivation
NE	=	norepinephrine—important in mood and energy
ACH	=	acetylcholine—important in memory
GABA	=	gamma-aminobutyric acid
H	=	histamine
GLU	=	glutamate

■ Where Psychiatric Medications and Natural Products Work

Site 1

Some psychiatric medications and natural products work on the postreceptor sites by being an agonist, as the antianxiety medication Buspar, at a specific serotonin site (5HT1). Other medications work as antagonists at the postreceptor site, as the antidepressant Serzone does. Serzone works as an antagonist at the serotonin postreceptor site, 5HT2, and by doing so may lift mood. In addition, it may also decrease anxiety by antagonizing the 5HT2 site in the frontal cortex. Furthermore, by antagonizing 5HT2 receptor sites in the spinal cord, it may lead to less sexual dysfunction.

The antipsychotics such as Haldol, Thorazine, Stelazine, and Prolixin largely work on the postreceptor of dopamine (DA). Some antipsychotics have not only DA antagonism on the postregular site but also block 5HT2, which could have a mood-lifting effect and might decrease the negative symptoms of schizophrenia, such as flat affect alogia, social withdrawal, and so on. Some antipsychotics work at DA antagonism on the postregular site but also work at site 3 to block the reuptake of serotonin and norepinephrine.

An antianxiety agent, such as Xanax, Serax, Ativan, essentially works as an agonist for the neurotransmitter GABA on the postreceptor site.

Certain herbs such as valerian and possibly kava work as GABA agonists against evoking GABA and therefore have calming effects. Side effects and impurities, however, have limited their use.

Site 2

Some psychiatric medications work by stimulating the release of neurotransmitters at the prereceptor site, as Adderall for ADHD does by causing the release of more dopamine and norepinephrine, which would increase attention span. It also works at site 3 described below with a blockage of the reuptake of dopamine and norepinephrine.

Some psychiatric medications work by causing the release of neurotransmitters at the prereceptor site. Psychostimulants like Adderall work in this manner by causing the release of dopamine, which increases the ability to pay attention. In contrast, a similar natural product, ephedra, probably works by a nonselective alpha and beta receptor agonist.

Site 3

Antidepressants such as tricyclics (Tofranil, Sinequan, Elvil), tetracyclics (Ludiomil), selective serotonin reuptake inhibitors (Prozac, Paxil, Zoloft, Luvox, and Celexa), Effexor, Serzone, to some degree, and Wellbutrin all work at site 3. They work by blocking the reuptake of different neurotransmitters. The selective serotonin reuptake inhibitors (SSRIs) block the reuptake and degradation of serotonin, so mood lifts, anger decreases, and obsessive worry decreases. Wellbutrin blocks the reuptake and degradation of dopamine so that mood lifts and energy and motivation increase. Tricyclics and tetracyclics block the reuptake of many neurotransmitters and may have many side effects. Effexor blocks the reuptake of neurotransmitters (serotonin, norepinephrine, and dopamine). St. Johns Wort works partially at least at this site.

Site 4

Psychiatric medications also work by decreasing or increasing the number of receptor sites at the postreceptor site. There is not enough research to know if St. Johns Wort works here.

Site 5

Some psychiatric medications, possibly lithium, may effect changes through a second messenger system. In fact, many psychiatric medications may ultimately work through secondary messenger systems.

Site 6

Some psychiatric medications (MAO Inhibitors) alter the metabolism of neurotransmitters and thus increase the amount available for release at the prereceptor site. St. Johns Wort may work at least partially at this site.

Site 7

The amount of neurotransmitter available could theoretically be altered by providing more or less of the precursor ingredients.

For example, L-tryptophane, a naturally occurring amino acid, is a precursor of serotonin and was given more in the past than now to help relieve depression. However, problems arose. First, the response usually seemed mild at best, and then, possibly due to impurities, several deaths caused by eosinophilia occurred in those using L-tryptophane.

Consider the natural synthesis of some of the monoamines (tyrosine→hydroxylation→DOPH→decarboxylation→dopamine→hydroxylation→norepinephrine→methylation→epinephrine). Tyrosine has been tried in depression but usually has poor results.

Controlled studies are lacking for these precursors. It may be that the digestive juices weaken effects. It may be that the blood-brain barrier weakens effects. It may very well be that a happy mood is a very complex chemical reaction, and one precursor simply will not be effective.

The same question could be asked about 5HTP (5-hydroxytryptophane). As with giving L-tryptophane directly, the benefit usually seems mild and dangers such as eosinophilia always harm.

Giving the neurotransmitter directly, as GABA, which is sold as a supplement, could be considered. The possible dangers and ineffectiveness, for the reasons mentioned above, argue for caution.

■ Selectivity

Not only do the psychiatric medications affect certain neurotransmitters and subneurotransmitters, they also may work selectively in specific brain regions in some cases. For example, the new neuroleptics, such as Risperdal, Seroquel, Zyprexa, and Geodon, are antagonists on the postreceptor side of dopamine 2 (DA2) and serotonin 2 (5HT2), but they selectively work in the limbic brain to produce the desired effects and do not work as much in the basal ganglia of the brain. Consequently, fewer undesirable side effects, such as parkinsonism, are produced. Also, the antidepressant Serzone not only blocks the prereceptor serotonin reuptake, which might cause sexual side effects, but also is an antagonist at the postreceptor site of serotonin 2 (5HT2), and this selective action in the spinal cord could block the sexual side effects as serotonin increases.

The new neuroleptic Abilify (aripipezole) is especially interesting since it works as an antagonist of DA2 in the limbic brain so that hallucinations go away, but it may work as an agonist at DA2 in the basal ganglia, so movement disorders are often avoided.

Appendix H

Stress, Genetics, and Choice

C hoice can be of major help in overcoming depression, and psychiatric medications can work like miracles for some when the depression has become medical. They can be very specific and effective and are often low in side effects. Herbs have also been used but are not specific in how they work and are often not nearly as effective.

Under stress some individuals develop symptoms of major medical depression, such as decreased mood, decrease in interests, decreased displeasure, changes in appetite, increased anxiety, decreased energy, decreased self-image, decreased concentration, and increased wishes not to live. Why? Stress and genetics are causative features in these individuals.

■ Genetic Factors

From genetic studies we know that depression runs in families. Fifty percent of individuals with major depression have a family member with major depression. If a nonidentical twin has a major depression, 10 percent of the time his or her twin will also have it, but if an identical twin has major depression, 76 percent of the time the other twin will have it. We do inherit the chemistry in neurons and in the synapses and the stability thereof. In general, people do not inherit a psychiatric disorder but a vulnerability that is triggered by stress.

■ Stress

Under stress, chemical changes, such as increased cortisol, begin to occur within the nervous system. Chemicals such as BDNF (brain-derived neurotrophic factor), which nourishes the neuron, decrease, and damage to the nerve cell may occur.

Antidepressants block the reuptake and degradation of neurotransmitters (serotonin, dopamine, norepinephrine) between synapses of nerve cells. They increase the neurotransmitters, which ultimately result in a down regulation on postreceptor sites that have been up regulated. They also ultimately alter other chemicals within the nerve cell and nervous system.

With PET scans (see appendix D) we can see how the depressed brain is not taking up glucose and therefore not functioning well. We can see unipolar and bipolar depression. With antidepressant medication we can see an altered brain with normal glucose uptake and normal functioning and a decrease in depressive symptoms.

Not only can antidepressants alter brain chemicals for the better, but behavior and cognitive techniques along with choice can as well. The cerebral cortex is so powerful that at least to a degree it may overrule the limbic (emotional) brain and cause mood and brain chemistry to improve. In fact, PET scans reveal increased glucose uptake in the frontal cortex with placebo alone, which merely offers hope. Twenty-five to 35 percent of depressed patients will respond to placebo. This is not as impressive as the improved glucose uptake with a standard antidepressant and a 70 percent response rate or the perhaps 90 percent response rate with a combination of antidepressants, but it is nonetheless very significant.

The future treatments of depression should prove impressive indeed. In general, they will be more and more specific, more effective, with fewer and fewer side effects. In appendix J, I discuss antidepressants from past to present to future and their benefits.

Appendix I

The Chemistry of Depression

The chemistry of depression involves complex genetic, environmental, and choice factors. How the antidepressants work is equally complex with changes in neurotransmitters, receptor sites, secondary messengers, ions, and the DNA in the nucleus of the cell. Below are just a few of the more salient features of the chemistry of depression.

In some depressions, there is a significant medical or biochemical component. Neurotransmitters in the brain have tremendous power from a physiological standpoint because they trigger a cascade of chemical reactions. They have major impact on sadness, happiness, worry, anger, logic, sleep, memory, anxiety, thinking, and even facial expression. These neurotransmitters are chemicals in the synapses between the nerve cells. We now know from research that by altering these neurotransmitters we can cause a cascade of chemical reactions that ultimately lift mood.

Today we know not only about specific neurotransmitters but also about the various postreceptor sites of the various neurotransmitters. For example, there are several postreceptors for serotonin alone, and we have medications that will work at these various postreceptor sites. The biochemistry of depression has become a science in and of itself. The midbrain with the raphe nucleus produces serotonin, the locus ceruleus produces norepinephrine, and the substantia nigra produces dopamine. The limbic system with the hippocampus is important in memory, the amygdala is important in anger, the nucleus accumbens is important in addictions, and the hypothalamus is important in eating and endocrine issues. The frontal lobe of the cerebral cortex is the center for higher thoughts and actions.

The old tricyclic antidepressants, such as Elavil, Tofranil, Sinequan, Pamelor, and Vivactil, blocked many neurotransmitters and tended to have many side effects. The same was true of the old MAO inhibitors. In the mid-1980s, a new series of antidepressants started to be produced—the SSRIs, or selective serotonin reuptake inhibitors such as Prozac, Paxil, Zoloft, Luvox, Celexa, and Lexapro. They are more specific in that they mostly block one neurotransmitter, serotonin. Other antidepressants have been developed also such as Wellbutrin, Effexor, Serzone, Remeron, and Cymbalta. With some of these the specificity has increased so that even subtype receptors of serotonin may now be modulated.

Three major factors act on the brain chemistry with all of its power on emotions. One is stress, another is genetics, and the third is choice. The medications above can be extremely helpful when the brain has become damaged, just as heart medications can be helpful after the heart has been damaged from stress, genetics, and choice.

Appendix J

The Antidepressants

Studies have indicated that when depression is treated with medication, there is a 70 percent effectiveness rate of lessening depression. The old tricyclics (TCAs), such as Elavil (amitriptyline), Pamelor (nortriptyline), Sinequan (doxepin), and Tofranil (imipramine), were effective in blocking many neurotransmitters, but there were many possible side effects. The monoamine oxidase inhibitors (MAOIs), such as Nardil (phenelzine) and Parnate (tranylcypromine), were also effective but had many possible side effects. In the mid-1980s, doctors began administering a new antidepressant series known as selective serotonin reuptake inhibitors (SSRIs). They would prove to be among the best of the antidepressants. They now include Lexapro (escitalopram), Celexa (citalopram), Paxil (paroxetine), Luvox (fluvoxamine), Prozac (fluoxetine), and Zoloft (sertraline). They mostly target one neurotransmitter and produce fewer side effects. The SSRIs have been used to treat a broad array of disorders, including depression, panic attacks, social phobias, PMS, eating disorders, anger, and OCD.

More antidepressants have come along in recent years such as Wellbutrin, Serzone, Effexor, and Remeron. Wellbutrin (bupropion) is a dopamine reuptake blocker and has few if any sexual side effects. It usually causes no increase in weight and may increase energy, increase sex drive, decrease smoking addiction, and increase focus in ADHD. Effexor (venlafaxine) is a 5HT NE reuptake inhibitor that is used in treating not only regular depression but also resistant depression.

Cymbalta (duloxetine) is another dual neurotransmitter inhibitor of both serotonin (5HT) and norepinephrine (NE). Remeron (mirtazapine) has proven effective for depression with anxiety and insomnia. It may provide a fast onset and lead to an increase in NE and 5HT at the presynaptic terminal. It also works by antagonism of the 5HT2 and 5HT3 at the postsynaptic terminal and in so doing may avoid sexual and gastrointestinal side effects. Desyrel (trazodone) and Serzone (nefazadone) are two more compounds that may be beneficial to depressives who also have insomnia and anxiety. Serzone is a 5HT2 antagonist and also blocks the reuptake of NE and serotonin. Because of the 5HT2 antagonism, sexual side effects are avoided.

Vestra (reboxetine), a norepinephrine reuptake inhibitor, may never be introduced because of side effects. Xanax (alprazolam), a minor tranquilizer, may help in depression. Augmentations with Buspar (a 5HT1A agonist), beta blockers (such as Visken), lithium, and thyroid may produce added results in depression.

Numerous drugs, some new to the market, may be effective for mania. Lithium has been the gold standard, but the anticonvulsant medications including Depakote (valporic acid), Tegretol (carbamazepine), Neurontin (gabapentin), Lamictal (lamotrigine), Gabitril (tiagabine), Trileptal (oxcarbazepine), Topamax (topiramate), and Zonegran (zonisamide) have also been used. Zonegran and Topamax may even have the side effect of weight loss.

The older antipsychotic drugs, such as Haldol (haloperidol), Mellaril (thioridazine), Moban (molindone), Navane (thiothixene), and Thorazine (chlorpromazine), may still be effective in depression with a possible psychotic element but may have undesirable side effects.

In recent years, there has been a wave of new antipsychotic drugs, such as Zyprexa (olanzapine), Risperdal (risperidone), Seroquel (quetiapine), Geodon (ziprasidone), and Abilify (aripiprazole), which are more specific at their sites of action and have fewer undesirable side effects and a potential for more desirable results, although any drug can potentially have almost any side effect. Paul Ehrlich, a German scientist in the early 1900s, made a prediction that is coming close to reality. He stated that in the future there would be "a drug [that] would be aimed precisely at a disease site and wouldn't harm healthy tissue."

Appendix K

Medications and Herbs

Past, Present, Future

This appendix may be of interest to those who are more medically inclined. It gives the history of the antidepressants, a more detailed discussion of how they work, and what the plans are for the future. For those who have had side effects or drug interactions, you may gain an indication why and gain insight into how your doctor may help. Finally, the medical doctors who read this book may enjoy it the most. It is the latest of the latest in the biochemistry of the brain and medications used to treat it when appropriate.

■ *Class:* TCAs (Tricyclic Antidepressants)

History: The initial TCA (imipramine) was synthesized in 1954 and tested as a major tranquilizer. It was accidentally found to have antidepressant effects.

Examples: Tofranil (imipramine), Elavil (amitriptyline), Sinequan (doxepin), Vivactil (protriptyline), Pamelor (nortriptyline), Norpramin (desipramine), Surmontil (trimipramine), Asendin (amoxapine)

Actions: They block the reuptake at the prereceptor site. Effects and side effects include:

Serotonin. As serotonin is increased, mood may be lifted and obsessive worry may decrease. As serotonin increases and as it affects various postreceptor serotonin sites, such as 5HT2, side effects may result, including anxiety, restlessness, muscle jerks, awakening during the night, inorgasmia, and apathy. As another postreceptor site of serotonin, 5HT3, increases, nausea and gastrointestinal upset may occur. Increased serotonin often eventually decreases anxiety but initially may increase anxiety.

Norepinephrine. Benefits of increased norepinephrine may include increased attention span, increased focus, increased motivation, and increased energy. A possible side effect of increased norepinephrine is increased anxiety. Also, it is believed that norepinephrine may be increased in manic.

Histamine. Side effects of increased histamine include weight gain and drowsiness.

Acetylcholine. As acetylcholine is increased, side effects may include dry mouth, drowsiness, blurred vision, and constipation. Acetylcholine seems to play an important role in memory.

Alpha Adrenergic. Side effects include decreased blood pressure, dizziness, and sedation.

Results: Because of the many potential side effects, TCAs are used less today. They are used for some pain disorders.

Drug Interactions: Many possible through the P450 liver enzyme system.

▪ *Class:* MAOIs (Monoamine Oxidase Inhibitors)

History: In the 1950s the first MAOI (iproniazid) was used in treating tuberculosis and accidentally found to have an antidepressant effect.

Examples: Nardil, Parnate

Actions: They inhibit the enzyme (MAO) that metabolizes the monoamines (dopamine, serotonin, norepinephrine), thereby increasing the monoamines that are so important in antidepressant actions.

MAO in nerve cell inhibited—increased serotonin

Norepinephrine, dopamine—antidepressant action

MAOIs—increased norepinephrine

If tyramine is added through foods that contain it, then more norepinephrine is released and dangerous elevations of blood pressure can occur.

Results: Because of the potential side effects, they are used less and less in recent years. Not only were they powerful antidepressants, they were powerful in treating panic disorder and social phobia.

Drug Interactions: Examples (not exclusive) of drugs that may interact with MAOI: tricyclic antidepressants, SSRI antidepressants, Effexor. Fatal reactions have occurred with serotoninergic agents. Other examples of drug or food interactions with MAOI include cold and cough preparations with dextromethorphan, nasal decongestants, hay fever medications, asthma inhalant medications, sinus medications, antiappetite medications, ephedra preparations, L-tryptophane preparations, caffeine, chocolate, yeast, meat extract, reduced alcohol products, beer, wine, yogurt, cheese, cream cheese, sauerkraut, fava beans, dry sausage, and pickled herring.

■ *Class:* SSRIs (Selective Serotonin Reuptake Inhibitors)

History: In the mid-1980s Prozac, an SSRI, was introduced and took America by storm. It focused on blocking the reuptake of mainly one neurotransmitter (serotonin) and therefore had fewer side effects in general. SSRIs were introduced as a class in the 1980s, but new SSRIs (Zoloft, Luvox, Celexa) were introduced in America in the 1990s. Lexapro (escitalopram) was introduced in late 2002.

Examples: Prozac, Paxil, Zoloft, Luvox, Celexa, Lexapro

Actions: They block the reuptake and degradation mainly of serotonin, resulting in more serotonin and an antidepressant effect. However, some were less pure than others and some side effects still continue. Plus, even serotonin can have undesirable side effects.

Prozac (fluoxetine)

- Blocks serotonin reuptake and therefore degradation, resulting in more serotonin and antidepressant action. More serotonin at various serotonin postreceptor sites (5HT2A or 5HT2C) may result in some unlikely but possible side effects:

  5HT2A and 5HT2C in limbic cortex may cause mental agitation or anxiety.

  5HT2A in basal ganglia may cause restlessness, retardation, mild parkinsonism, odd movements.

  5HT2A in spinal cord may cause sexual dysfunction (trouble with orgasm).

  5HT2A in cerebral cortex may cause apathy (a numbing of emotions and decreased sex drive).

  5HT3 may cause nausea or gastrointestinal upset.
- Blocks some norepinephrine reuptake and therefore degradation, resulting in some possible mild antidepressant action.
- Agonist action at a postreceptor site of serotonin (5HT2C).
- Drug interactions: Many possible drug interactions through the P450 metabolic enzyme system of the liver. Refer to Physician's Desk Reference (PDR).

Paxil (paroxetine)

- Blocks serotonin reuptake and therefore degradation, resulting in antidepressant action. See above for possible side effects of serotonin.
- Blocks some norepinephrine reuptake and therefore degradation, resulting in possible mild antidepressant action.
- Blocks some muscarinic cholinergic receptors, possibly causing some sedation, dry mouth, and blurred vision.
- Drug interactions: Many possible drug interactions through the P450 metabolic enzyme system of the liver. Refer to PDR.

Zoloft (sertraline)

- Blocks serotonin reuptake and therefore degradation, resulting in more serotonin and antidepressant action. See above for possible side effects of serotonin.

- Blocks some dopamine reuptake and therefore degradation, resulting in possible antidepressant action and motivating and energizing effects of dopamine.
- Drug interactions: Many possible drug interactions through the P450 metabolic enzyme system of the liver. Refer to PDR.

Luvox (fluvoxamine)

- Blocks serotonin reuptake and therefore degradation, resulting in more serotonin and antidepressant action. See above for possible side effects of serotonin.
- Drug interactions: Many possible drug interactions through the P450 metabolic enzyme system of the liver. Two examples are theophyllin (for asthma) and caffeine.

Celexa (citalopram)

- Blocks serotonin reuptake and therefore degradation, resulting in more serotonin and antidepressant action. See above for possible side effects of serotonin.
- Celexa is the most serotonin specific blocker we have. It can affect other neurotransmitters but does so less than any other SSRI.
- Drug interactions: Drug interactions are possible (see PDR) but perhaps fewer overall.

Lexapro (escitalopram)

- Lexapro is an isomer of Celexa. It is more effective at a lower dose and has even fewer side effects overall than Celexa.

Other Uses: The SSRIs have been used for several disorders other than depression, including panic disorder, phobias, obsessive-compulsive disorder, posttraumatic stress disorder, and eating disorders.

■ Parlodel (bromocriptine)

History: In the 1980s Parlodel, an agonist-antagonist, was tried experimentally for depression but never proved a major force.

■ Serzone (nefazadone)

History: In the 1990s several new antidepressants that were more specific in their actions were introduced. Serzone is one that blocks a postreceptor site of serotonin, 5HT2, with fewer sexual side effects. It also causes less insomnia than the SSRIs.

Class: Serotonin 2A antagonist/reuptake inhibitor, less potent serotonin reuptake inhibitor, weak norepinephrine reuptake inhibitor, weak alphal adrenergic blocking properties.

Action: See above. Since this drug blocks the reuptake of both serotonin and norepinephrine, it is an antidepressant. Since it blocks the uptake of serotonin on the postreceptor site at 5HT2 in the spinal cord and in the frontal lobes, it may have fewer sexual side effects. The 5HT2 antagonism in the frontal lobes of the cerebral cortex may also account for less apathy. The 5HT2 antagonism in the limbic system may account for fewer anxiety side effects.

■ Remeron (mirtazapine)

History: In the 1990s the antidepressants became more and more specific. Remeron lifts mood, and because of the antagonism post-synaptically at 5HT2A, it may not have sexual side effects; because of the 5HT3 antagonism, it may not have gastrointestinal side effects; and because of the H1 antagonistic postsynaptic effects, it may be a good sleeping pill without being addicting. Because of the 5HT2C effects, it may cause weight gain.

Class: Dual serotonin and norepinephrine actions via alpha 2 antagonism; serotonin postreceptor antagonism at 2A, 2C, and 3; and histamine 1 antagonism.

■ Effexor (venlafaxine)

History: The old tricyclic antidepressants were very effective since they affected several neurotransmitters without antidepressant effect, but they had too many side effects because of affecting too many neurotransmitters. What if an antidepressant could be developed that could increase all three neurotransmitters that lift mood but would not affect other neurotransmitters? Effexor filled the need.

Class: Dual serotonin and norepinephrine reuptake inhibitor (and even dopamine).

■ Cymbalta (duloxetine)

History: Cymbalta is another dual reuptake inhibitor of serotonin and norepinephrine. It is being released in early 2003.

■ Secondary Messenger Systems

Antidepressants of the future may target secondary messenger systems (6 proteins or CAMP) within the neuron on the postreceptor site. Even today it may be that lithium (an inhibitor of inositol monophatase) and some of the anticonvulsants work that way.

■ Dual Dopamine/Serotonin Reuptake Antagonist (Minaprine and Bazinaprine)

Antidepressants that strongly target both dopamine and serotonin are being tested.

■ Serotonin 1D Antagonist

Antidepressants (CP–448, 187) that are serotonin 1D antagonists that rapidly inhibit the serotonin neuron are being tested.

■ 5HT1A Agonist

An antidepressant, Gepirane ER, which is a 5HT1A agonist, is being tested. Even today Visken (pindolol), a partial agonist at 5HT1A as well as antagonist at 5HT1A, has been tested to speed the antidepressant action of SSRIs.

■ Substance P

Substance P antagonists are also being tested for antidepressant effects.

■ The Anticonvulsants

Anticonvulsants are being used more and more off-label as anti-manic as well as antidepressant drugs. The term *anticonvulsant* is unfortunate since these are really neuromodulators, neurostabilizers, and mood stabilizers. They tend to calm the brain whether a person has a seizure, a manic high, aggression, or even in some cases depression. They act as ion channels (sodium, potassium, calcium) in the cell membrane to either augment the action of GABA (a calming or inhibitory neurotransmitter) or inhibit the action of glutamate (an excitatory neurotransmitter). Depakote (valproic acid), Tegretol (carbamazepine), Lamictal (lamotrigine), Neurontin (gabapentin), Topamax (topiramate), Trileptal (oxcarbazepine), and Keppra (levetiracetam) for the most part work to either augment the actions of GABA or inhibit the actions of glutamate. Lamictal in particular is interesting since it may have the most antidepressant action. Topamax (topiramate) and Zonegran (zonisamide) in particular are interesting since they often cause mood stabilization with weight loss.

■ The Antipsychotics

The newest atypical neuroleptics or antipsychotics (poor nomenclature since they are broad in their actions) may have some antidepressant actions. We have long known that even the old antipsychotics (Haldol, Thorazine) helped in manic highs. Of the new atypical antipsychotics, Zyprexa (olanzapine) has been approved specifically for bipolar manic depressive disorder. What is new is that some of the new atypical neuroleptics have been used off-label for their antidepressant effects. For example, Geodon (ziprasidone) has a specific mechanism of action that at least theoretically should give some antidepressant action. In a manner similar to the antidepressants, it blocks the reuptake and degradation of both serotonin and norepinephrine, which theoretically should give some antidepressant action. Like the traditional antipsychotics, Geodon blocks D2 at the postreceptor site. And like the other newer atypical antipsychotics, it is antagonistic at 5HT2 on the postreceptor site, which results in less dopamine in some parts of the brain (more D2 reuptake blockage in the limbic system so the antipsychotic action on the positive symptoms of psychosis such as hallucinations results) but more dopamine in other parts of the brain (as the cortex, so there are fewer negative symptoms of psychosis, such as apathy; the basal ganglia, so there are fewer extrapyraminal symptoms; and the pituitary pathway, so there is less hyperprolactinemia and thus fewer hormonal effects). However, Geodon goes even further in being specific and blocks the reuptake of serotonin and norepinephrine at the prereceptor site and thus could conceivably have some antidepressant effects along with its antipsychotic effects. It illustrates how specific drugs of the future will work.

Another new antipsychotic, Abilify (aripiprazole), works as a partial agonist at 5HT1A postreceptor site and thus conceivably could have some antidepressant effects.

■ More Specific MAO Inhibitors

Monoamine oxidase enzymes metabolize the monoamine neurotransmitters (dopamine, norepinephrine, and serotonin) that play a role in mood. Increased monoamines result in improved mood in depressed individuals. The monoamine oxidase inhibitors (MAOIs) thus are antidepressants. They were first discovered to be antidepressants by accident in the 1950s when used in TB patients. There are actually two types of MAOIs (types A and B). The A form is the antidepressant. The B form has antiparkinsonian effects. Both of these original forms of MAOI were irreversible, resulting in more monoamines (norepinephrine, for example), and when tyramine foods and certain medications were taken, elevation of blood pressure and stroke could occur. In recent years more specific forms of A and B have been developed that are reversible and less likely to cause the dangerous elevations of blood pressure and stroke. Aurorix (moclobemide), broforamine, befloxatone, and RS–8359 are reversible MAOIs under investigation as antidepressants.

■ Hormones

Thyroid hormones (T3 and T4) have long been used to augment the antidepressant action of antidepressants. T3 has probably been used more in unipolar depression and T4 more in bipolar depression.

Estrogen replacement therapy has also long been reported to help some perimenopausal and postmenopausal women who are depressed.

■ Provigil (modafinil)

Provigil is a relatively new cognitive enhancing type drug. It is marked for narcolepsy and people who have difficulty staying awake during the day (idiopathic hypersomnolence). It seems to have some great side effects—increased focus, increased energy, and increased motivation, as well as the effect of an antidepressant. It works mainly in the hypothalamus and works through excipatory histimine projection.

■ Buspar (buspirone)

Buspar is in the minor tranquilizer (antianxiety) category but seems unique for several reasons. It has demonstrated antidepressant properties in double-blind studies. It is not addicting. It works by being an agonist at a postreceptor site of serotonin, 5HT1, rather than augmenting GABA effectiveness at the postreceptor site as the other minor tranquilizers do.

■ Other Minor Tranquilizers

In general, most of the benzodiazepine antianxiety agents seem to be lacking in antidepressant effects, except for Xanax, a possible exception. While Xanax (alprazolam) can be addicting, it seems to have an antidepressant effect. Since Xanax works by allosteric modulation of the fast-acting neurotransmitter GABA, its benefits are almost immediate and not delayed as are those of the true antidepressants.

■ Desyrel (trazodone)

Desyrel is often listed as an atypical antidepressant. It is a dual serotonin antagonist/serotonin reuptake inhibitor just as Serzone (nefazadone) is. In addition, Desyrel has antihistamine properties and thus is a great sleeping medication for many. In fact, it has never proved to be as good an antidepressant as it is a sleeping aid. Because of an unlikely but undesirable side effect (priapism), this drug is often not used in men.

■ Psychostimulants

In the past Ritalin (methylphenidate) and Dexadrine (dextro-amphetamine) were used more than currently to treat the elderly depressed. Adderall XR is the new drug (for amphetamine) that is used for ADHD.

■ Ultram (tramadol)

Ultram is an analgesic that binds to u-opioid receptors but is also a weak inhibitor of the reuptake of norepinephrine and serotonin and therefore theoretically might have some antidepressant benefits in those who are being treated for pain.

■ Sigma/5HT1A Agonist/5HT Reuptake Inhibitor

The physiology of the sigma receptor remains poorly understood, while the serotonin reuptake inhibitor action is well understood. A sigma 5HT1A agonist/5HT reuptake inhibitor is being tested as an antidepressant.

■ Calcium Channel Blockers

Calcium channel blockers such as Norvasc (amlodipine), Dyna Circ (isradipine), and Nimotop (nimodipine) have been tried in bipolar and unipolar disorders but with only limited success so far.

■ Strattera (atomoxetine)

Strattera, a selective reuptake inhibitor of norepinephrine, approved for ADHD in late 2002, could conceivably have antidepressant effects.

■ Herbs

St. Johns Wort (hypericum) dates back to antiquity and is the most studied herb for depression in the world. It is by far the most used herb for depression or any other mental issue. Recent studies reveal it is not effective for major depression. Perhaps it helps in more minor depressions. It probably works rather nonspecifically on a variety of neurotransmitters. It acts by blocking the reuptake of serotonin, norepinephrine, and dopamine. It also may inhibit monoamine oxidase to some degree.

It is conceivable that it could interact with other medications of the P450 liver enzyme system. It may have toxic effects on reproductive functioning, may negatively affect fertility in both sexes, and may cause mutation of the gene in sperm cells.

SAMe, a natural substance found in every cell of the body, has also been touted for depression. It probably increases neurotransmitters, such as dopamine, norepinephrine, and serotonin. One problem with SAMe is that a significant percentage of those using it are found to have increased levels of formaldehyde in their blood.

Fish oil with omega-3 fatty acids seems to have a mood lifting and mood stabilizing effect in some people. In fact, a few people on fish oil go too high and become manic.

L-tryptophane and 5HTP are precursors of serotonin and as such have been used in mild depression. However, cases of eosinophilia and death have raised great concern.

B_{12} and folic acid seem to have an added antidepressant benefit for some women who are on SSRIs.

■ The Future

Drugs of the future may include CRF (coricotropin-releasing factor) antagonists. CRF triggers the pituitary gland to release ACTH (adrenocorticotropic hormone), which then triggers the adrenal cortex to release cortisol, which will decrease BDNF (brain-derived neurotrophil factor), which nourishes brain cells. Thus an antagonist of CRF would increase BDNF, which would nourish brain cells and lift mood. Another antidepressant drug of the future that also may increase BDNF is a CREB antidepressant. C stands for a secondary messenger cAMP; REB stands for response element-binding protein.

Another drug of the future for depression may be a transdermal system of Eldepryl (selegiline) that is an MAO–type B inhibitor currently used only in parkinsonism. The MAO-B inhibitor blocks the degradation of dopamine and the increased dopamine helps in parkinsonism. It may also have some MAO-A inhibitory effects when used in a transdermal delivery system. The MAO-A inhibition blocks the degradation of serotonin and norepinephrine and thus lifts mood. Also, MAO–type A reversible inhibitors may be coming. Moclobemide (Aurorix) is one such drug already approved in Canada. The irreversible MAO inhibitors of the 1950s, such as Nardil and Parnate, are difficult to use because norepinephrine increases if foods with tyramine are eaten. This often causes blood pressure to rise, and stroke could occur.

Substance P antagonists are in preclinical studies as antidepressants. Substance P has long been associated with pain. It is also associated with pleasure or a lack of it.

Agonists or partial agonists of serotonin (5HT1), a postreceptor site, are surely to come. Gepirone ER is in clinical development.

Dual reuptake inhibitors of serotonin and dopamine are in clinical testing.

Serotonin 1D agonists, such as CP–448, 187 are entering clinical development as possible antidepressants of the future.

Finally, a beta 3 agonist, SR5861, is in preliminary clinical testing.

Appendix L

Common Medications and Herbs for Anxiety

■ Benzodiazepines

Benzodiazepines such as Librium (chlordiazepoxide), Paxipam (halazepam), Valium (diazepam), Klonopin (clonazepam), Xanax (alprazolam), Serax (oxazepam), and Ativan (lorazepam) are perhaps the best-known group of drugs for stress and anxiety relief. This group of drugs has also been used for anxiety associated with seizures, withdrawal syndromes, insomnia, restless legs, agitation, bipolar disorder, panic, and PMS. Tolerance can be a concern. These drugs are often effective within minutes for anxiety since they act on the GABA system. GABA is a fast-acting neurotransmitter as opposed to serotonin, norepinephrine, and dopamine, which are slow neurotransmitters that are affected by the antidepressants.

■ Antidepressants

Some of the antidepressants that have been used in depression with anxiety include Remeron (mirtazapine); Effexor (venlafaxine); Serzone (nefazadone); the SSRI drugs, such as Paxil (paroxetine), Celexa (citalopan), Lexapro, Zoloft, and Prozac; and the old tricyclic drugs, such as Elavil (amitriptyline). In general, the newer drugs have fewer potential side effects and may have a quicker onset of action—within two weeks as opposed to four to six weeks. These drugs work on various neurotransmitters (serotonin and norepinephrine especially) in the brain.

Many times anxiety and worry are considered synonymous. For obsessive anxiety or worry, the SSRIs (Prozac, Zoloft, Paxil, Luvux, Celexa, and Lexapro) often have a great track record.

■ Buspar (Buspirone)

This drug is especially interesting in that, unlike the benzodiazepines that work on a neurotransmitter called GABA, it is an agonist at a postreceptor site of serotonin (5HT1). Also, it produces no tolerance. It may take a month to be effective.

■ Antihistamines

Antihistamines have been used for years for mild anxieties. Vistaril (hydroxyzine) and Benadryl (diphenhydramine) may be the best known. However, they have long half lives and tend to be sedating.

■ Beta Blockers

β-adrenergic receptor antagonists, such as Inderol (propranolol), Visken (pindolol), Tenormin (atenolol), Lopressor (metoprolol), and Corgard (nadolol), have been used for the somatic (physical) symptoms of anxiety and stress. They have been used primarily for hypertension but have also been used for aggressive behaviors and phobias. Pindolol in particular may help boost antidepressant response.

■ Major Tranquilizers (Neuroleptics)— the Antipsychotics

This group of drugs has often been used when anxiety and stress are severe enough to begin to cause a disorganization of thoughts, hallucinations, delusions, or bizarre behaviors with social withdrawal. They affect various neurotransmitters (dopamine, hista-mine, norepinephrine, and acetylcholine) but seem to have their most benefit by an antagonism on a postreceptor site of dopamine (DA2). This class of medication includes some newer drugs that, in general, may have fewer side effects and may be more effective overall, such as Zyprexa (olanzapine), Risperdal (risperidone), Se-roquel (quetiapine), and Abilify (aripiprazole). These newer drugs block dopamine reuptake like the old major tranquilizers, such as Thorazine (chlorpromazine), Mellaril (thioridazine), Navane (thiothixene), Moban (molindone), Haldol (haloperidol), Prolixin (fluphenazine), and Stelazinew (trifluoperazine). However, the newer ones also affect a specific serotonin receptor (5HT2 antagonist) on the postsynaptic side. The newer antipsychotics with their dual 5HT2 and DA2 effects antagonism are able to affect the limbic brain responsible for hallucinations and yet spare the basal ganglia so that parkinsonism side effects are avoided.

The newer tranquilizers not only help what are referred to as the positive symptoms of schizophrenia, such as hallucinations and delusions, but also decrease the negative symptoms, such as social withdrawal, poverty of thoughts, lack of facial expression, and an-hedonia. Thus most major tranquilizers help special kinds of severe anxieties, but the newer ones, as a class, may have added benefits with fewer overall side effects. The agent Clozaril (clozapine) was the first of the newer dopamine agents, but it can have troublesome side effects and is not used in pure anxiety disorders. Abilify (aripip-razole), which came out in late 2002, may prove especially helpful not only with psychosis but possibly with anxiety and depression as well. Abilify's key to success may be its ability to act not only as an antagonist at DA2 but also as agonist at DA2 at times. This balance may hold the key. Since it has some serotonin reuptake blocking effect, antidepressant effects are conceivable, and since it is an agonist at 5HT1A, antianxiety effects are conceivable.

■ Other Agents for Anxiety and Sedation

Neurontin (gabapentin) and Gabitril (tiagabine), antiseizure medications, are often used in individuals who have seizures and, because they affect GABA, may produce a calming effect on those with anxiety. In the past, bromide-containing compounds, such as

Miles Nervine, were sold over the counter and also were touted to decrease anxiety. Several agents may be used to help one's sleep when associated with anxiety. Included in this category are Doral (quazepam), ProSom (estazolam), Restoril (temazepam), and others. It may be that quazepam is more specific in the benzodiazepine receptor side and associated with less amnesia and fewer cognitive impairments. The same may be true for Paxipam (halazepam). Other agents (barbiturates and nonbarbiturate sedatives such as Quaalude, Miltown, Equanil, Doriden, Placidyl, and chloral hydrate) are rarely used today because of fear of addiction.

◼ Herbs

The use of herbs has taken America and the world by storm. Perhaps more than 70 percent of the world's population uses herbs and more than 40 percent of the American population may be using herbs. Billions of dollars are spent annually. These are used for everything from boosting the immune system to calming stress. The ones that have become best known for use during times of stress are St. Johns Wort, kava, inositol, melatonin, SAMe, valerian, and GABA. The reality is that these chemicals are extremely popular and are being used extensively. They do help at times, but several words of caution should be given.

While these substances may benefit some, they can also be dangerous, because, first of all, they may prevent someone from seeking conventional medical help that has a proven track record. Second, these chemicals are dangerous because in and of themselves they may produce harm. For example, kava has caused liver failure and valarian has caused hepatitis. Third, these chemicals may be dangerous because of adulteration. For example, heavy metals have appeared in some of the various herbal populations. Fourth, these chemicals can be dangerous because of potential interactions with other chemicals or medications. Kava, in particular, has proven dangerous at times with Xanax, which is used for anxiety. Fifth, the lack of education in regard to the use of these chemicals can be dangerous. There is often no FDA control.

Appendix M

Troubled Teens and Medication

ADHD medications, such as Adderall (dextroamphetamine), Focalin (dexmethylphenidate-hydrochloride), Metadate (methylphenidate), Concerta (methylphenidate), and the new Strattera (atomoxetine), work almost like miracles. Sometimes the antidepressants, such as Wellbutrin (bupropion) and Effexor (venlafaxine), are helpful, as is the antihypertensive medication Tenex (guanfacine).

Medications that have been used in bipolar disorder, such as Depakote (valporic acid), Trileptal (oxcarbazepine), Tegretol (carbamazepine), Lamictal (lamotrigine), Topamax (topiramate), Zonegran (zonisamide), and Zyprexa (olanzapine), may turn a life around as they abate anger and stabilize mood.

For depression disorder, medications such as Lexapro (escitalopram), Celexa (citalopram), Wellbutrin (bupropion), Prozac (fluoxetine), Paxil (paroxetine), Zoloft (sertraline), Luvox (fluvoxamine), Effexor (venlafaxine), Serzone (nefazadone), Cymbalta (duloxetine), and Remeron (mirtazapine) may mean the difference between a good life and suffering or death.

For OCD, medications such as Prozac (fluoxetine), Paxil (paroxetine), Celexa (citalopram), Lexapro (escitalopram), Zoloft (sertraline), Anafranil (clomipramine), and Luvox (fluvoxamine) can abate tormenting worries.

For Asperger's disorder, medications such as the new neuroleptics and selective serotonin reuptake inhibitors may dispel much trouble.

For schizophrenia, the new neuroleptics, such as Geodon (ziprasidone), Abilify (aripiprazole), Risperdal (risperidone), Seroquel (quetiapine), and Zyprexa (olanzapine), can eliminate tormenting voices.

Appendix N

Medications and Herbs
for Dementia

Medications such as Aricept (donepezil), Exelon (rivastigmine), and Reminyl (galantamine) and herbs such as hyperzine and huprine X have been used in Alzheimer's disease. They are acetylcholinesterase inhibitors and work by enhancing ACh neurotransmission. These medications have been demonstrated to reduce the decline in cognitive and overall functioning. The result of this is that patients may be able to live independently or at home longer, requiring nursing home care only later in the disease course. Other medications that have been tried in Alzheimer's dementia include Memantine, which acts on postsynaptic NMDA receptors; estrogen; anti-inflammatories; statins; antioxidants, such as vitamin E; and antiamyloid medications.

The extract from the plant ginkgo biloba has recently been approved for use in Germany for patients with mild to moderate dementia. In the United States it is currently undergoing scientific study to validate its use in dementia patients. However, as yet, no well-designed studies have been conducted. It is available over the counter currently and may prove to be useful.

Aggression, psychosis, sleep disturbance, anxiety, and depression are common findings in dementia patients. They are managed with the usual psychotropic medications that are used in the new antidepressants. The new antipsychotics may prove especially helpful.

232

However, dementia patients are far more sensitive to medication dosage and choice of medication than nondemented patients, and often have in addition multiple medical conditions for which they are taking several other medications. Because of these and other factors, treating the dementia patient is often complicated. If a specific cause or exacerbating medical condition is discovered, treatment of the medical condition is important (for example, thyroid hormone replacement in hypothyroid-induced dementia, vitamin replacement, and so on). However, it is fairly common that, despite correction of the medical condition, there is little, if any, gain in function. Often dementia is an irreversible late finding of many illnesses. Comorbid psychosis, insomnia, depression, and anxiety should be treated.

Appendix O

Medications for Seniors

■ Medications for Dementia

See appendix N.

■ Medications for Depression

Perhaps the most common disorder in the elderly is depression, and it does not have to be so. There are new and often wonderful antidepressants, such as Duloxetine, Lexapro, Celexa, Paxil, Prozac, Zoloft, Serzone, Effexor, Remeron, and Wellbutrin.

■ Medications for Anxiety

Anxiety is also common as individuals grow older. Not only are the traditional antianxiety and sleep medicines available, such as Xanax, Ativan, Serax, and Ambien, which are often used short-term, but now there are ones that produce no tolerance, such as Buspar. When anxiety is pushing an individual to the point of near breaking with reality, new major tranquilizers, such as Zyprexa, Risperdal, Seroquel, and Geodon, often tend to be highly effective and have fewer side effects in general.

■ Medications for Osteoporosis

New medicines are now available, such as Evista and Actonel, that do not have the cancer concerns that hormone replacement

234

might have at times; and yet these medications seem to help in the vital area of osteoporosis, which is a major concern as many individuals age.

■ Medications for Circulatory Problems

Aspirin that is coated (such as Ecotrin) is used by many individuals as they age to help thin the blood and decrease pain. Of course, any kind of aspirin can cause ulcers, so consult your doctor. Ticlid is another medication that is also being used for some circulatory problems.

■ Medications for Pain

Nonsteroidal anti-inflammatory drugs have been used for several years now for pain. There is always the concern of ulcers as a side effect, but newer NSAIDs are less dangerous.

Various new pain medications continue to be developed, such as Ultram, a narcotic-like drug, but with serotonin effects. There are also new triptan pain medications for migraines, such as Frova, Imitrex, Zomig, Maxalt, and Amerge.

■ Medications for Infections

Recent years have seen the explosion of new antibiotics. They are becoming more and more user-friendly with less frequent dosing. They range from Z-Pack for some upper respiratory, bacterial infections (two tablets on day one, followed by one tab per day for the next four days) to Monurol (a one-time dose) for some urinary tract infections. Many other new and improved antibiotics continue to be developed.

■ Medications for Heartburn

Not only do we have the H_2 receptor antagonists, such as Zantac, Axid, Pepcid, and Tagamet, but now we also have new proton pump inhibitors, such as Prevacid, Prilosec, Nexium, and Aciphex.

◼ Medications for Impotence

Viagra may help certain individuals. Of course, side effects are possible and potentially dangerous interactions with other medications can be a concern, but a doctor can alert you to the possible side effects.

◼ Medications for Diabetes Mellitus

As individuals age, some will develop Type II Diabetes. New medications continue to come out. New blood sugar monitoring devices continue to be developed.

◼ Medications for High Blood Lipids

New drugs such as Lipitor may reduce both cholesterol and triglycerides. Supplements such as fish oil and CLA may decrease cholesterol and triglycerides to a minor degree.

◼ Medications for High Blood Pressure

High blood pressure remains a major killer in the United States. New blood pressure medications, such as beta blockers; ACE inhibitors, such as Zestril; angiotension inhibitors, such as Atacand; and calcium channel blockers continue to be developed.

◼ Medications for Cancer

Great strides are being made in this area. This may be the most exciting area of research yet.

◼ Anti-Aging Medications

In the near future it may even be possible to stop the hand of time; so hold on, and don't give up yet.

Appendix P

Drugs with Possible Antidepressant Effects

TCAs

MAOIs

Tetracyclic antidepressants
  amoxapine (Asendin)
  maprotiline (Ludiomil)

SSRIs

Atypical antidepressants
  bupropion (Wellbutrin)
  nefazadone (Serzone)
  venlafaxine (Effexor)
  mirtazapine (Remeron)
  duloxetine (Cymbalta)
  roboxetine (Vestra)

Antipsychotics
  ziprasidone (Geodon)
  aripiprazole (Abilify)

Anxiolytic benzodiazepines

alprazolam (Xanax)

Non-benzodiazepine anxiolytics

buspirone (Buspar)

Mood stabilizers and anticonvulsants

lithium carbonate

lamotrigine (Lamictal)

zonisamide (Zonegran)

topiramate (Topamax)

Psychostimulants

atomoxetine (Strattera) for ADHD

thyroid-augmenting effect of T_3 *(Cytomel)*

modafinil (Provigil) for Narcolepsy

Calcium channel inhibitors

amlodipine (Norvasc)

isradipine (Dyna Circ)

nimodipine (Nimotop)

β-adrenergic receptor antagonist

pindolol (Visken)

Estrogen and testosterone

Reversible MAO-A inhibitors

moclobemide (Aurorix) in Canada

Herbs and natural products

St. Johns Wort

omega-3 fatty acids

B_6 and folic acid

L-tryptophane and 5HTP

SAMe

DHEA

Placebo

■ Points of Interest

Geodon (ziprasidone)—an antipsychotic:

D_2 antagonism ➜ positive symptoms efficacy in schizophrenia

5HT1A agonist ➜ antianxiety activity conceivable

5HT1D antagonism ➜ antidepressant activity conceivable

5HT2A antagonism ➜ reduced EPS

5HT2C antagonism ➜ antidepressant activity conceivable

Mixed 5HT/NE reuptake inhibition ➜ antidepressant activity conceivable

Abilify (aripiprazole)—an antipsychotic:

D_2 partial agonist

possible D_2 antagonist in areas of the brain with high dopamine

5HT2A antagonism ➜ reduced EPS

5HT1A partial agonist ➜ antidepressant activity conceivable ➜ antianxiety activity conceivable

Zonegran (zonisamide)—an anticonvulsant:

increased GABA ➜ antimanic activity

decreased glutamate ➜ antimanic activity

S D reuptake inhibitor ➜ antidepressant activity conceivable

Appendix Q

Possible Antidepressants of the Future

Beta 3 agonist
  SR5861 (preliminary clinical testing)
Secondary messenger systems
  CREB antidepressants with increased BDNF (camp-response element-binding protein)
5HT1A agonist and partial agonist
  Gepirone ER (in clinical development)
Dual reuptake blockers of serotonin and dopamine (in clinical testing)
Serotonin 1D antagonists
  CP–448, 187 (entering clinical development)
Substance P antagonists
  MK–869 (preclinical studies)
MAO-B inhibitor + MAO-A inhibitor in transdermal system selegiline (Eldepryl)
CRF (corticotropin-releasing factor) antagonists
Non-drug methods
  electroconvulsive therapy (ECT)
  transmagnetic stimulation (TMS)
  vagus nerve stimulation (VNS)

Appendix R

Genetic Factors in Psychiatric Disorders

Genetic factors may make certain individuals more vulnerable to certain mental problems. The second factor that is required is some kind of environmental factor, such as life events, medical disease, a drop in hormones, a virus, or low social support.

Bipolar disorder occurs in about .5 to 1 percent of the general population. In 90 percent of the cases of bipolar psychosis, there is a first-degree relative with the disorder.

- A parent or sibling—10 percent
- Fraternal twin raised in the same home—26 percent
- Identical twin raised in the same home—66 to 96 percent
- Identical twin raised separately—75 percent

Major depressive disorder occurs relatively often in certain families. In at least 30 percent of the cases of depression, there is a family history. As in other disorders, if one twin suffers, the risk to the other twin is high:

- Fraternal twin—7 to 29 percent
- Identical twin raised in the same home—60 to 76 percent
- Identical twin raised separately—44 to 67 percent

Schizophrenia occurs in only about 1 percent of the general population, but Kallman and Kety have discovered that the risk is much higher if one has a close relative who has suffered from the disorder:

- One parent—10 percent risk
- Both parents—50 percent
- Sibling—10 percent
- Fraternal twin—10 percent
- Identical twin—80 to 90 percent

OCD (obsessive-compulsive disorder). Individuals will have a first-degree relative with OCD 40 percent of the time.

ADHD (attention-deficit/hyperactivity disorder). Individuals will have a first-degree relative with ADHD 35 percent of the time.

Appendix S

Psychiatric Medications by Categories of Use

The following is a list of psychiatric medications by category of use. Some are used on-label; others are used off-label, such as some of the anticonvulsants that are used for pain relief and mood stabilization.

■ Anxiolytics (Antianxiety Agents)

Anxiolytic Benzodiazepines

Alprazolam (Xanax)
Chlordiazepoxide (Librium, Libritabs)
Clonazepam (Klonopin)
Clorazepate (Tranxene)
Diazepam (Valium)
Halazepam (Paxipam)
Lorazepam (Ativan)
Oxazepam (Serax)

Non-Benzodiazepine Anxiolytics

Buspirone (Buspar)
Hydroxyzine (Atarax, Vistaril)

Benzodiazepine Hypnotics (Medications for Insomnia)
Estazolam (ProSom)
Flurazepam (Dalmane)
Quazepam (Doral)
Temazepam (Restoril)
Triazolam (Halcion)

Non-Benzodiazepine Hypnotics (Medications for Insomnia)
Chloral Hydrate (Somnote)
Diphenhydramine (Benadryl)
Zaleplon (Sonata)
Zolpidem (Ambien)

Barbiturates
Amobarbital (Amytal)
Pentobarbital (Nembutal)

■ Antidepressants

Selective Serotonin Reuptake Inhibitors
Citalopram (Celexa)
Escitalopram (Lexapro)
Fluoxetine (Prozac, Sarafem)
Fluvoxamine (Luvox)
Paroxetine (Paxil)
Sertraline (Zoloft)

Tertiary Amine Tricyclic Antidepressants
Amitriptyline (Elavil, Endep)
Clomipramine (Anafranil)
Doxepin (Adapin, Sinequan)
Imipramine (Tofranil)
Trimipramine (Surmontil)

Secondary Amine Tricyclic Antidepressants
Desipramine (Norpramin)
Nortriptyline (Pamelor, Aventyl)

Protriptyline (Vivactil)

Tetracyclic Antidepressants
Amoxapine (Asendin)
Maprotiline (Ludiomil)
Mirtazapine (Remeron)

Monoamine Oxidase Inhibitors
Phenelzine (Nardil)
Tranylcypromine (Parnate)

Atypical Antidepressants
Bupropion (Wellbutrin and Wellbutrin SR)
Duloxetine (Cymbalta)
Nefazadone (Serzone)
Trazodone (Desyrel)
Venlafaxine (Effexor and Effexor XR)

■ Mood Stabilizers

Lithium Carbonate (Eskalith, Lithonate, Eskalith CR)

Anticonvulsants
Carbamazepine (Tegretol)
Gabapentin (Neurontin)
Levetiracetam (Keppra)
Oxcarbazepine (Trileptal)
Topiramate (Topamax)
Zonisamide (Zonegran)

Benzodiazepines
Alprazolam (Xanax)
Clonazepam (Klonopin)
Lorazepam (Ativan)

■ Antipsychotics

High-Potency Antipsychotics
Fluphenazine (Prolixin)
Haloperidol (Haldol)
Pimozide (Orap)
Thiothixene (Navane)
Trifluoperazine (Stelazine)

Mid-Potency Antipsychotics
Loxapine (Loxitane)
Molindone (Moban)
Perphenazine (Trilafon)

Low-Potency Antipsychotics
Chlorpromazine (Thorazine)
Mesoridazine (Serentil)
Thioridazine (Mellaril)

Atypical Antipsychotics
Aripiprazole (Abilify)
Clozapine (Clozaril)
Olanzapine (Zyprexa, Zydis)
Quetiapine (Seroquel)
Risperidone (Risperdal)
Ziprasidone (Geodon)

■ Attention-Deficit/Hyperactivity Disorder (ADHD)

Psychostimulants
Atomoxetine (Strattera)
Dextroamphetamine (Dexadrine)
Dextroamphetamine plus amphetamine (Adderall)
Methylphenidate (Concerta, Metadate, Methylin, Ritalin)
Dexmethylphenidate-hydrochloride (Focalin)
Pemoline (Cylert)

Alpha Agonists
Clonidine (Catapress)
Guanfacine (Tenex)

Antidepressants
Bupropion (Wellbutrin)
Venlafaxine (Effexor)

Narcolepsy Medication
Modafinil (Provigil)

■ Dementia (Alzheimer's Type)

Donepezil (Aricept)
Galantamine (Reminyl)
Rivastigmine (Exelon)
Tacrine (Cognex)

■ Substance Dependence

Management of Substance Dependence
Bupropion (Zyban)
Clonidine (Catapres, Catapres-TTS)
Disulfiram (Antabuse)
Methadone (Dolophine)
Naltrexone (ReVia)

■ Medications for Pain

Medications for Acute Migraine Headache Pain
Almotriptan (Axert)
Butalbitol, acetaminophen, caffeine combination (Esgic)
Butorphanol nasal spray (Stadol)
Dihydruergotamine Mesylate nasal spray (Migranal)
Ergotamine (Wygesic)
Frovatriptan (Frova)

Isomethopetene (Midrin)
Naratriptan (Amerge)
Rizatriptan (Maxalt)
Sumatriptan (Imitrex)
Sumatriptan nasal spray (Imitrex)
Zolmitriptan (Zomig)

Medications for the Prophylactic Treatment of Migraines
Acetylsalicylic acid (Aspirin)
Amitriptyline (Elavil)
Clonidine (Catapress)
Cyproheptadine (Periactin)
Ergonovine (Maleate)
Fluoxetine (Prozac)
Imipramine (Tofranil)
Methysergide (Sansert)
Propranolol (Inderol)
Sertraline (Zoloft)
Verapamil (Calan)

Nonsteroidal Anti-Inflammatory Pain Medications
Acetaminophen (Tylenol, Datril)
Acetylsalicylic acid (Aspirin)
Celecoxib (Celebrex)
Choline magnesium salicylate (Trilisate)
Choline salicylate (Arthropan)
Diclofenac (Voltaren, Cataflam)
Diclofenac sustained release (Voltaren-XR)
Diflunisal (Dolobid)
Etodolac (Lodine)
Fenoprofen calcium (Nalfon)
Flurbiprofen (Ansaid)
Ibuprofen (Motrin, Advil, Rufen)
Indomethacin (Indocin, Indometh)
Ketoprofen (Orudis, Oruvail)
Ketorolac tromethamine (Toradol)
Magnesium salicylate

Meclofenamate sodium (Meclomen)
Mefenamic acid (Ponstel)
Nabumetone (Relafen)
Naproxen (Naprosyn, Anaprox, Aleve [OTC])
Oxaprozin (Daypro)
Piroxicam (Feldene)
Rofecoxib (Vioxx)
Sodium salicylate
Sulindac (Clinoril)
Tolmetin (Tolectin)
Valdecoxib (Bextra)

Opioid Pain Medications
Codeine
Hydrocodone (in Lorcet, Lortab, Vicodin)
Hydromorphone (Dilaudid)
Levorphanol (Levo-Dromoran)
Meperidine (Demerol)
Methadone (Dolophine)
Morphine
Morphine controlled release (MS Contin, Roxanol, Oramorph)
Oxycodone (Roxicodone, Percocet, Percodan, Tylox)
Oxymorphone (Numorphan)
Tramadol (Ultram)

Neuropathic Pain Medications

Tricyclic Antidepressants
Amitriptyline (Elavil)
Desipramine (Norpramin)
Nortriptyline (Pamalor)

Nontricylic Antidepressants
Sustained-release bupropion (Wellbutrin SR)

Anticonvulsants
Carbamazepine (Tegretol)
Clonazepam (Klonopin)

Gabapentin (Neurontin)
Levetiracetam (Keppra)
Oxycabazepine (Trileptal)
Topiramate (Topamax)
Zonisamide (Zonegran)

■ Antiparkinsonian Drugs

Dopamine Precursors
Carbidopa (Lodosyn)
Levadopa (Larodopa)
Levadopa-carbidopa (Sinemet)

Dopamine Agonists
Bromocriptine (Parlodel)
Pergolide (Permax)
Pramipexole (Mirapex)
Ropinirole (Requip)

Entacapone (Comtan)

Anticholinergic Medications

Benztropine (Cogentin)
Biperiden (Akineton)
Ethopropazine (Parsidol)
Orphenadrine (Norflex)
Procyclidine (Kemadrin)
Trihexyphenidyl (Artane)

Amantadine (Symmetrel)

MAO-B Inhibitor
Selegiline (Eldepry)

Antihistamine Medication
Diphenhydramine (Benadryl)

◼ Anorexiants (Weight-Loss Medication)

Fat Blocker
Orlistat (Xenical)

Serotonin, Norepinephrine Reuptake Inhibitor
Sibutramine (Meridia)

Sympathomimetics
Amphetamine (Biphetamine)
Benzephetamine (Didrex)
Diethylpropion (Tenuate)
Mazindol (Mazanor, Sanorex)
Methamphetamine (Desoxyn)
Phendimetrazine (Adipost, Bontril)
Phenmetrazine (Preludin)
Phentermine (Adipex, Fastin, Ionamin)

Notes

Introduction *Choices—the Hinges of Destiny*

1. George F. Root, "Why Do You Wait"; T. Calvin Bushey, "O Why Not Tonight?"; and Philip P. Bliss, "Almost Persuaded."

Chapter 1 *Discouragement*

1. Basil Miller, *The Gold under the Grass* (Nashville: Cokesbury, 1930).

Chapter 2 *Depression*

1. See Chris Thurman, *The Lies We Believe* (Nashville: Nelson, 2003).

Chapter 4 *Anxiety*

1. Gary Collins, *Overcoming Anxiety* (Vision House, 1973).

Chapter 6 *Stress*

1. *Prevention's Giant Book of Health Facts* (Emmaus, Penn.: Rodale, 1991), 442.
2. *New England Journal of Medicine* 338 (Jan. 1998): 176.
3. *Prevention's Giant Book of Health Facts,* 440.
4. Ibid., 430.

Chapter 8 *Trials*

1. Frank Minirth, *Beating the Odds* (Grand Rapids: Baker, 1987).
2. Philip P. Bliss (1838–1876), "Dare to Be a Daniel."

Glossary

The following is a glossary of theological, physiological, and psychological terms. The aim is to aid the reader in understanding the discussions within this book.

Abuse. Abuse refers to a maladaptive pattern of substance use; a recurrent substance use that results in failure to fulfill duties at work and home, resulting in significant impairment socially and in interpersonal relationships; and a substance use that is physically dangerous, such as driving when intoxicated. Substance abuse may cause recurring legal problems.

Acetylcholine (ACh). Acetylcholine is a neurotransmitter of the nervous system involved in memory. Antagonists of acetylcholine are used in the treatment of Parkinson's disease. Drugs that block an enzyme (acetylcholinesterase) that metabolizes acetylcholine are used in the treatment of Alzheimer's dementia. Acetylcholine is important in both the central and peripheral nervous systems. Acetylcholine receptors are divided into two types—muscarinic and nicotinic.

Acting-out. Acting-out is a defense mechanism whereby one deals with internal stress, external stress, or emotional conflicts with unhealthy behavior. For example, a depressed adolescent may act-out and have trouble with his parents and the law.

Acute Stress Disorder. Acute stress disorder is an anxiety disorder that is similar to posttraumatic stress disorder (PTSD), caused by a traumatic event that threatened life. It involves a sense of numbness and detachment, a decrease in awareness of one's surroundings, feelings of de-realization, feelings of depersonalization, a reexperiencing of the event, avoidance of related stimuli, and marked symptoms of anxiety. One major difference is that in PTSD the symptoms must be present for more than one month, whereas with acute stress disorder the symptoms are present for less than one month.

254

Addiction. Addiction refers to the maladaptive behavioral pattern of drug abuse. It refers to a compulsive use of a drug and to the unhealthy obtaining of the drug.

Adjustment Disorders. Adjustment disorders are a group of disorders with either a disturbance of mood, anxiety, or conduct secondary to an identifiable stressor(s), occurring within three months of the onset of the stressor(s). The symptoms are significant and cause impaired social or occupational functioning. The symptoms do not persist for more than six months after the stressor(s) has terminated.

Adolescence. Adolescence is a period of time in life characterized by physical and emotional changes that lead to sexual, physical, and emotional maturity. The time period is not well defined. It is often considered to exist during the teen years, but some authors, myself included, think it may last until the age of thirty.

Adrenal Glands. The adrenal glands are part of the endocrine system. They are located on the superior borders of the kidneys and consist of an outer cortex layer and inner medulla layer. The cortex secretes cortisol, androgen, and alderstone. The medulla secretes epinephrine and norepinephrine.

Aggression. Aggression is specific, directed, physical or verbal hostile action. Aggression may be seen in bipolar or unipolar depression.

Agitation. Agitation is anger, restlessness, and emotional tension.

Agonist. Agonists are drugs that alter the physiology of a cell or neuron by binding to a receptor, producing an effect in the brain and therefore the body.

Alcohol. Alcohol is the most common drug of abuse. One hundred thousand Americans die each year from complications of alcohol abuse. Alcohol dependency is characterized by a need for increased amounts. Withdrawal symptoms include a lack of control and significant physical, psychological, and social consequences.

Alpha Adrenergic Receptor (Alpha). Drugs that have an alpha adrenergic receptor antagonism, such as the old TCIs, can have bothersome side effects, including dizziness, decreased blood pressure, and drowsiness.

Alzheimer's Dementia. See Dementia.

Amphetamines. Amphetamines are drugs that can be used appropriately for certain medical conditions, such as ADHD, or inappropriately as psychostimulant drugs of abuse.

Amygdala. The amygdala is that part of the limbic system of the brain that has to do with memory and emotionally charged events. Stimulation of the amygdala in animals can result in rage.

Anabolic Steroids. Anabolic steroids are drugs that are used and often abused for muscle building. Anabolic steroids can cause irritability, aggression, depression, psychosis, and mania.

Anger. Anger is an emotion of hostility resulting from opposition.

Anhedonia. Anhedonia is a loss of interest in things that are normally pleasurable.

Antagonist. An antagonist blocks the response of an agonist.

Anticipation. Anticipation is a defense mechanism whereby one deals with emotions in a healthy way by looking forward to a future event.

Anticonvulsant Medications. Anticonvulsant medications are drugs that are used to treat seizures or convulsions. They are often used off-label in bipolar and other mood disorders.

Antidepressants. Antidepressants are a group of heterogeneous drugs in structure and action that act on the neurotransmitters of the central nervous system to relieve depression. They are not addicting. They are also used in PTSD, panic disorder, social phobia, and OCD.

Anxiety. Anxiety refers to uneasiness, worry, and apprehension over an unknown danger. Technically, in anxiety the cause is not known, whereas in fear the cause is known. Anxiety is a symptom, not a diagnosis, of many emotional disorders; is a broader term than *worry;* and is mental but often has physical symptoms.

Anxiety Disorders. Anxiety disorders are a group of disorders with anxiety as the underlying symptom, manifested in different ways. The anxiety disorders include generalized anxiety disorder, panic disorder, specific phobia, social phobia, obsessive-compulsive disorder, posttraumatic stress disorder, acute stress disorder, and anxiety due to a general medical condition.

Apathy. Apathy is an emotional tone of indifference or detachment, often seen in depression and schizophrenia.

Arteriosclerosis. Arteriosclerosis is a hardening of the arteries and is responsible for some cases of dementia and organic brain syndrome in the elderly. It is responsible for some cases of heart disease (arteriosclerotic heart disease).

Asperger's Disorder. Asperger's disorder is a mental disorder starting in childhood and is characterized by impairment in social interaction, possibly including impairment in eye gaze, facial expression, body posture, and gestures. It may include a failure to develop peer relationships, a lack of spontaneous sharing, and a lack of social reciprocity.

Attention. Attention is the ability to concentrate on an activity or task. The lack of attention is often seen in ADHD.

Autistic Thinking. Autistic thinking is egocentric and often seen in schizophrenia.

Autonomic Nervous System. The autonomic nervous system is one of two divisions of the peripheral nervous system; the other being the somatic nervous system. It regulates important functions of the body such as heart rate, blood pressure, intestinal activity, and gland activity. It has two divisions—the sympathetic and parasympathetic nervous systems.

Their actions are often antagonistic. For example, the sympathetic nervous system raises heart rate and blood pressure, whereas the parasympathetic nervous system lowers heart rate and blood pressure.

Barbiturates. See Sedative-Hypnotics.

Basal Ganglia. The basal ganglia is that part of the brain that influences muscle movement. When impaired, a disturbance of posture and muscle tone, involuntary movement, a tremor, and abnormal slowness may occur.

Behavior Therapy. Behavior therapy is a treatment approach that focuses on changing a client's behavior directly, which is then felt to decrease emotional symptoms. It is different from insight-oriented psychotherapy, which focuses on dynamics in the patient's past.

Bipolar Disorder. A bipolar disorder is a physiological mood disorder characterized by severe mood swings, going from high, elated, or irritable to sad, depressed, and even suicidal. In the manic phase, symptoms may include elevated mood, irritability, grandiosity, rapid thinking, pressured speech, little sleep, hypersexuality, distractibility, and poor judgment. In the depressive phase, symptoms may include a sad mood, not enjoying life, altered sleep, altered appetite, low energy, agitation, guilt, and not wanting to live.

Blood-Brain Barrier (BBB). The BBB is a structure of capillaries that surround connective tissue and the vascular processes of astrocytes. The BBB controls what substances can move from the blood plasma to the extracellular fluid of the brain. Some substances, such as fat-soluble compounds, water, oxygen, carbon dioxide, glucose, alcohol, nicotine, and anesthetics, pass easily.

Body Language. Body language refers to the messages transmitted by a person's body posture and motion. A depressed person may have a downcast facial appearance, stooped posture, and slow walk or a defensive, angry stance.

Borderline Personality Disorder. Borderline personality disorder is a maladaptive, long-existing pattern of behavior, thinking, feeling, and functioning characterized by at least a couple of the following: recurrent suicidal ideations; mood instability or depression, anxiety, or anger; feelings of emptiness; paranoid feelings; feelings of abandonment; a pattern of unstable relationships; unstable self-image; and impulsivity in areas such as sex, spending, drug abuse, binge eating, or reckless driving. They often present with the chief complaint of depression.

Brain. The brain is the portion of the central nervous system that is located within the skull. The receiver, organizer, and distributor of information for the body, the brain has several parts—the cerebrum, limbic system, and basal ganglia; the diencephalon with the thalamus, hypothalamus, pituitary gland, and pineal gland; the midbrain; the pons and medulla; and the cerebellum. The brain weighs approximately three pounds, is

composed of more than two hundred billion neurons, consists of right
and left halves, and operates twenty-four hours a day. The brain directs
all thinking, feeling, moving, talking, and activity and makes us human.

Caffeine. Caffeine, the alkaloid present in coffee, tea, and cola, is a stimulating
drug and can be a psychostimulant drug of abuse. Side effects can include
anxiety, insomnia, irritability, and headaches.

Catacholamines. Catacholamines are the biogenic amines of epinephrine,
norepinephrine, and dopamine that are so important to the nervous
system.

Caudal Nucleus. The caudal nucleus is a part of the basal ganglia of the brain
and may be involved in obsessive-compulsive disorder.

Central Nervous System (CNS). The central nervous system consists of
the brain and spinal cord. The other part of the nervous system, the
peripheral nervous system (PNS), is that part of the nervous system
outside the CNS. The PNS connects the CNS to the sensory organs and
organs of the body, glands, blood vessels, and muscles.

Cerebellum. The cerebellum, located dorsal to the pons and medulla, is that
part of the brain that coordinates movements.

Cerebrum. The cerebrum is that part of the brain responsible for thought,
memory, reasoning, voluntary movement, perception of sensory impulse,
and higher functions in general. It consists of five lobes—frontal, parietal,
temporal, occipital, and insular.

Choice. Choice is the action of selecting and involves examining options and
alternatives and, with an act of the will, selecting. Thus happiness is often
a choice.

Cingulate Gyrus. The cingulate gyrus is that part of the limbic system of the
brain that has to do with shifting attention from one thought or behavior
to another. It malfunctions in obsessive-compulsive disorder, resulting in
obsessive worry. It is also a part of the brain that signals danger.

Circumstantial Conversation. Circumstantial conversation is a disturbance in
speech so that a person goes into unnecessary details, some of which
may be inappropriate. It may be observed in bipolar disorder, OCD, and
schizophrenia.

Codeine. See Opioids.

Cognitive Therapy. Cognitive therapy is a form of therapy or counseling that
focuses on the correction of inaccurate beliefs that may be producing
emotional symptoms by offering more accurate beliefs.

Computerized Tomography (CT Scan). A CT scan is a brain-imaging device,
using X rays, that produces radiographic images of the brain or spinal
cord. An iodinated radio-opaque substance is injected intravenously
before obtaining the CT scan. Tumors, abscesses, and sometimes
subacute cerebral infarcts can be seen on CT scans.

Conduct Disorder. A conduct disorder is a repetitive pattern of behavior in children that violates the rights of others. It may involve aggression to people and animals, destruction of property, deceitfulness, or theft.

Confession. Confession is the acknowledgment of a fault or wrongdoing and is a wonderful defense against guilt.

Conflict. A conflict is an emotional struggle that arises from opposing issues, such as drives, environmental stimuli, impulses, and other internal and external opposing forces.

Confusion. Confusion is a disturbance in orientation and may involve thinking, beliefs, time, place, self, or others.

Controlling. Controlling is a defense mechanism whereby one deals with insecurities by becoming overly controlling of others.

Cyclothymic Disorder. A cyclothymic disorder is a mood disorder characterized by mild mood swings. The mood swings are not severe enough to meet the criteria for major depressive disorder or the manic phase of bipolar disorder.

Cytochrome P450 Enzymes (P450). P450 is an enzyme system in the liver that metabolizes most psychiatric and other medical drugs. It is so named because it strongly absorbs light at a wavelength of 450nm. The system is composed of families and subfamilies—the family is noted by a numeral, the subfamily by a capital letter, and the individual member of the subfamily by a second numeral. Thus a drug might be metabolized by 1A2, 2C9/10, 2C19, 2D6, 3A4, or 3A3/4.

Defense Mechanisms. Defense mechanisms are mental mechanisms used to adjust to environmental stressors and emotional conflicts. Some are conscious, while others are unconscious. In depression, common defense mechanisms include denial, displacement, introjection, and projection. For example, depressed individuals sometimes deny that they are depressed or angry; they may displace anxiety and emotions to their body and have fatigue, poor sleep, headaches, and weight changes; they may assume responsibility beyond what is realistic; and they may project that others do not want to be close to them when in reality they are the ones who stay apart.

Delirium. Delirium is an acute and fluctuating disturbance of consciousness, inability to focus, inability to shift attention, and perceptual disturbances. The disturbance is secondary to a medical disturbance.

Delirium Tremens. Delirium tremens is a severe and sometimes fatal brain disorder that commonly occurs four to five days after cessation of heavy consumption of alcohol.

Delusion. A delusion is a false belief held in spite of objective evidence to the contrary.

Dementia. Dementia is a combination of several possible cognitive deficits, such as impaired memory; disturbance in planning, organizing, sequencing, and of abstracting; impairment of ability to carry out motor activities; and language disturbance. It can be mild initially and severe as it progresses and is caused by Alzheimer's dementia 66 percent of the time. Other causes include multi-infarct dementia from arteriolosclerosis, substance-induced dementia, and dementia due to HIV, parkinsonism, and head trauma. Dementia is chronic, whereas delirium is acute. Alzheimer's dementia is more common in women and involves diffuse atrophy of the brain cells, increased senile plaques, increased neurofibrillary tangles, increased amyloid proteins, and enlarged cerebral ventricles. The cause is not known. Acetylcholine is the neurotransmitter of the brain most affected.

Denial. Denial is a defense mechanism whereby one refuses to acknowledge what is present and often obvious to others. For example, a depressed, angry-appearing individual may deny he is depressed and angry.

Dependency. Dependency refers to a person's need for something, such as a drug or substance, to function normally. It is characterized by withdrawal symptoms when the substance is missed. The dependency can be physical, as with alcohol, minor tranquilizers, and even some laxatives, and it can also be psychological.

Dependency Needs. Dependency needs are the needs for love, affection, security, protection, food, and warmth that all people have.

Depersonalization. Depersonalization is a sensation of unreality that occurs under stress.

Depression. Depression refers to a low or sad mood. It is a symptom, not a diagnosis.

***Diagnostic and Statistical Manual of Mental Disorders* (DSM-IV).** DSM-IV is the official manual of mental disorders, detailing symptoms, not causes or cures. It has five axes—axis I is for the clinical disorder, axis II is for personality disorders or personality traits, axis III is for the general medical conditions, axis IV is for psychosocial and environmental stressors, and axis V is for global assessment of functioning.

Diencephalon. The diencephalon is a part of the brain that consists of the hypothalamus, pineal gland, pituitary gland, and thalamus, which are extremely important in stress and emotions.

Discouragement. Discouragement is a lay term that refers to a loss of enthusiasm, a loss of courage, and a loss of confidence.

Displacement. Displacement is a defense mechanism whereby one deals with emotional conflict by transferring feelings from the person who engendered the feelings to another, less threatening person. For example, a depressed employee who has a harsh boss may be hostile toward his wife.

Diurnal. Diurnal refers to the daytime. Depressed individuals may have diurnal mood changes. Some feel worse in the early morning.

Dominance. Dominance in personality refers to the playing of a controlling role in interactions with others. Dominance in genetics refers to the ability of a gene to express itself over a recessive gene.

Dopamine (DA). Dopamine is a neurotransmitter of the nervous system involved in pleasure, sexual functioning, interest, and apathy. There are several dopamine receptors. Most of the antipsychotic drugs work by blocking D2. Many antiparkinson's drugs work by increasing dopamine transmission. Drugs used for ADHD work in part by releasing and blocking the reuptake of dopamine at the presynaptic terminal. Some drugs that are used in narcolepsy have a dopamine augmenting effect also. Thus dopamine can be involved in psychosis, parkinsonism, ADHD, and narcolepsy.

Drug. By definition a drug is any agent, whether a pharmaceutical, herb, vitamin, mineral, hormone, supplement, beverage, amino acid, or any substance, that is administered to the body to mediate or produce a biologic response.

Dysthymic Disorder. Dysthymic disorder is a disorder of chronic depression—a depressed mood that lasts for at least two years. It is characterized by a sad mood, changes in appetite, changes in sleep, fatigue, low self-worth, and difficulty making decisions.

Eating Disorders. Eating disorders are characterized by a disturbance in perception of body weight and shape and include anorexia nervosa and bulimia. With these conditions, there is an intense fear of becoming fat. In anorexia nervosa there is a refusal to maintain normal body weight, so that the body weight is less than 85 percent of what is optimal. Amenorrhea often accompanies anorexia nervosa, and the disorder ends in death 5 to 10 percent of the time. In bulimia there are recurrent episodes of binge eating with recurrent inappropriate compensatory behavior, such as vomiting, laxative abuse, fasting, and excessive exercise.

Ego Alien. Ego alien refers to thoughts that are repugnant, recurrent, unwanted, undesired, and not consistent with a person's usual thinking. They occur in obsessive-compulsive anxiety disorder (OCD). Most of those with OCD are depressed, and a significant percent of those with mood and anxiety disorders have OCD with ego alien thoughts. In OCD the thoughts are ego alien, whereas in obsessive-compulsive personality disorder (OCPD) the thoughts are egosyntonic, or consistent with the usual ego state.

Electroconvulsive therapy (ECT). ECT is a form of treatment in psychiatry used in some cases of severe, suicidal, resistant depressions, during which an electric current is administrated, resulting in the induction of a convulsion. While it may have the highest effectiveness rate in decreasing depression, it is rarely used today because of the great advances in psychiatric medication.

Endocrine System. The endocrine system includes adrenal glands, hypothalamus, pancreas, parathyroid, pituitary gland, thyroid, and other organs. The endocrine system coordinates complex body functions through blood-borne chemicals to distant target organs.

Euphoria. Euphoria is an exaggerated emotion of elation or sense of well-being. It occurs in the manic phase of bipolar disorder. In bipolar disorders individuals often go from euphoria to sadness.

Extrapyraminal Symptoms (EPS). The extrapyraminal nervous system is a system of nerve tracks connecting the cerebral cortex, basal ganglia, thalamus, cerebellum, reticular formation, and spinal nerves in complex pathways. Some psychiatric medications, especially the old antipsychotic medications, can cause disease with resulting symptoms in this system. These symptoms include movement disorders, such as tardive dyskinesia, parkinsonism, dystonias, and akathisia.

Faith. Faith is trust and confidence in God and can be a very healthy way to deal with stress.

Fear. Fear is an apprehension or a concern regarding a known danger.

Flat Affect. A flat affect is an absence of facial expression. It is often seen in schizophrenia.

Flight of Ideas. Flight of ideas refers to an abnormal speech pattern of rapid thoughts and speech that changes abruptly. It may be seen in bipolar disorder—manic type.

Forgiveness. Forgiveness is giving up resentment of or a claim to requital for a wrongdoing. It can be a healthy defense mechanism for dealing with anger.

Gamma-Aminobutyric Acid (GABA). GABA is an inhibitory neurotransmitter of the nervous system. Many antianxiety drugs work by augmenting the actions of GABA. Some anticonvulsant medications work in part by augmenting GABA.

Generalized Anxiety Disorder. Generalized anxiety disorder is a professional diagnosis from the *Diagnostic and Statistical Manual of Mental Disorders*. It pertains to a specific set of symptoms that have gone on for at least six months. The symptoms may include worry, restlessness, fatigue, irritability, muscle tension, sleep disturbance, and difficulty concentrating.

Generic Drugs. The generic name of a drug is the name given to the drug by the U.S. Food and Drug Administration (FDA). The brand name is the name given by the pharmacy company. A generic drug is often a less expensive alternative to a brand-name drug, but it is important to realize that the concept of generic equivalent does not necessarily mean exact clinical equivalent. Also, one could have an allergic reaction to one form and not the other because of differences in other substances present, such as dye.

Genes. Genes composed of DNA are the fundamental units of heredity. It is believed that genetic factors, as well as environmental factors and a person's choices, are factors of depression.

Grace. Grace is God's unmerited favor.

Grief. Grief is a feeling of intense sadness resulting from a loss.

Hallucination. Hallucinations are false sensory perceptions. They can be auditory, visual, or tactile and occur in schizophrenia but can also occur in major depressive disorder with psychosis or in some bipolar disorders.

Hallucinogens. Hallucinogens are drugs of abuse, such as LSD (lysergic acid diethylphetamine), mushrooms (psilocybin), STP (dimethoxymethylamph-etamine), peyote (mescaline), and MDMA or ecstasy (methylenedioxymet-hamphatime). Intoxication symptoms include rapid heartbeat, high blood pressure, dilated pupils, sadness, and other perceptual distortions.

Happiness. Happiness is an emotion characterized by feelings of good fortune, well-being, pleasure, satisfaction, and prosperity. Choices often play a major role in happiness.

Heroin. See Opioids.

Hippocampus. The hippocampus is that part of the limbic system of the brain that controls emotional memory. With prolonged stress, cortisol remains high, and a chemical that nourishes brain cells known as brain-derived neutrophilic factor decreases. As a result, the hippocampus atrophies, and painful memories will not go away.

Histamine (H). Histamine is a neurotransmitter of the nervous system. Some psychiatric medications, such as some antidepressants, have an antihistamine effect, which can cause sedation and weight gain.

Histrionic Personality Disorder. A histrionic personality disorder is characterized by a long existing maladaptive pattern of behavior, feelings, thinking, and functioning characterized by at least five of the following: a rapid shifting of emotions, seductive behavior, a need to be the center of attention, the use of physical appearance to draw attention to self, impressionistic speech, exaggerated emotions, suggestibility, and the considering of relationships to be more intense than they are. The one with histrionic personality disorder often presents with depression.

Hormones. Hormones are chemical messengers secreted by the endocrine gland or organs. They affect specific receptors on target cells, resulting in biochemical reactions and specific responses. Hormones fall into four chemical structure groups: aminos, peptides, proteins, and steroids.

Humor. Humor can be a healthy defense mechanism for dealing with tension.

Hypochondriasis. Hypochondriasis is a mental disorder whereby one is preoccupied with fears of having a serious medical disease, even though appropriate medical evaluations have not been remarkable. Some depressed individuals become hypochondriacal.

Hypothalamus. The hypothalamus is the part of the brain that controls the autonomic nervous system that controls the flight or fight response to stress. It also plays a role in many other body functions, including heart rate, digestion, bladder control, sensory perception, the endocrine system, psychosomatic disorders, rage, sex, aggression, body temperature, eating habits, thirst, working state, and sleep patterns.

Idealization. Idealization is a defense mechanism for dealing with internal conflicts and insecurities by overly valuing the qualities of another individual.

Impotence. Impotence refers to the inability to maintain an erection. It is common in depressive disorders.

Inhalants. Inhalants are a variety of chemicals found in glues, solvents, cleaners, gasoline, kerosene, plastics, paint thinners, paints, rubber cements, lacquers, enamels, aerosols, furniture polish, fingernail polish, cleaning fluids, removers, and nitrous oxide that are inhaled as drugs of abuse. Used more often by adolescents than by older people, these chemicals, when inhaled, can produce euphoria, ataxia, and confusion. They can also produce psychosis, seizures, coma, arrhythmias, liver damage, kidney damage, bone marrow damage, and death.

Intellectualization. Intellectualization is a defense mechanism whereby one deals with internal conflicts and insecurities by the excessive pursuit of knowledge along with the excessive use of clever words to defend against emotions.

Introjection. Introjection is a defense mechanism whereby one deals with emotional conflicts by accepting blame beyond what is realistic. For example, a depressed individual who feels worthless and unimportant may introject and feel everything that goes wrong is totally his or her fault.

Joy. Joy is an emotion characterized by feelings of delight and great pleasure. Joy is the deeper cousin of happiness. According to Galatians 5:22, it is a fruit of the Spirit. Thus while happiness implies a kind of psychological contentment, joy implies more of a spiritual contentment. Technically joy can exist even when happiness does not, because joy is a gift from God.

Kindling. Kindling is the phenomenon by which a psychiatric condition becomes more resistant to treatment the longer it is left untreated.

Learning Disability. A learning disability is a condition affecting children of normal IQ. It manifests with specific difficulties in reading (dyslexia), writing, or math. It is often present in ADHD.

Licensed Professional Counselor (L.P.C.). An L.P.C. holds a master's degree plus extra training in counseling.

Lifetime Prevalence. Lifetime prevalence refers to the chance of experiencing a condition over the course of a lifetime.

Limbic System. The limbic system has been described as the emotional brain since it is that part of the brain that controls pain, pleasure, anger, mood, and affection. It consists of the nucleus accumbens, amygdala, cingulate gyrus, and hippocampus.

Loneliness. Loneliness is the feeling of isolation.

Love. Love is a genuine caring for other individuals. It is a choice and can counter unhealthy emotions.

Magnetic Resonance Imaging (MRI). An MRI is a brain-imaging device that reveals the anatomy of the brain. As opposed to a CT scan, it uses no X rays, produces a clearer visualization of the anatomy, has minimal distortion from bone, and has the ability to obtain images through any plane. With an MRI, tissue hydrogen protons are subjected to radio frequency waves in a magnetic field.

Major Depressive Disorder. Major depressive disorder is a professional term from the DSM-IV. It refers to a specific set of criteria, including at least a two-week period of symptoms, such as depressed mood, decreased pleasure in most activities of daily living, significant appetite or weight changes, changes in sleep pattern, agitation, fatigue, guilt, feelings of worthlessness, diminished ability to think, and recurrent thoughts of death.

Mania. Mania is officially used in the definition of bipolar disorder—manic type. It refers to a mood that is characterized by elation, grandiosity, agitation, hyperactivity, and hypersexuality. The individual has rapid thinking, pressured speech, and poor judgment.

Marijuana. Marijuana is a drug of abuse. Intoxication symptoms can include euphoria, altered perceptions, rapid heartbeat, anxiety, paranoia, red conjunctiva, and incoordination.

Midbrain. The midbrain is a part of the brain located between the pons and diencephalon. It contains the nuclei that produce neurotransmitters—the chemical messengers of the brain. The substantia nigra produces dopamine, the raphe nuclei produce serotonin, and the locus coeruleus produces norepinephrine.

Migraine Headaches. Migraine headaches are characterized by being periodic, throbbing, severe, and often unilateral. They are often genetic in origin and 75 percent of the time they occur in females. Fifty percent of the time they are precipitated by stress, 25 percent by food, and 25 percent by other factors.

Milieu Therapy. Milieu therapy is a socioenvironmental approach used in inpatient and, to some degree, outpatient settings. The approach changes depending on the needs of the individual. An actively friendly, warm, and kind approach is often used with depressed individuals; a passively friendly approach is often used with paranoid individuals.

Monoamine Oxidase Inhibitor (MAOI). MAOIs are among the older antidepressants, introduced in the 1950s and used today more for niche conditions. They are so named because they work by inhibiting the enzyme monoamine oxidase that metabolizes the neurotransmitters of serotonin, norepinephrine, and dopamine. Thus, when administered, more neurotransmitters are made available. MAOI (A)s, which result in more serotonin and norepinephrine, are antidepressants, whereas MAOI (B)s are used in parkinsonism, since they result in more dopamine. The MAOIs interact with certain medications and drugs (stimulant drugs, diet pills, cocaine, cold preparations, nasal sprays) and with foods that contain tyramine (many cheeses, some wines and beer, beef liver, chicken liver, yeast preparations, fava beans, herring, canned figs, protein extracts in some soups and gravies, and certain meat products such as bologna, salami, Spam, and pepperoni).

Mood. Mood is the feeling tone of an individual. It influences thinking and actions.

Mood Disorders. Mood disorders are a group of disorders with depression as an underlying symptom, including major depressive disorder, dysthymic disorder, depressive disorder not otherwise specified (NOS), bipolar I disorder, bipolar II disorder, cyclothymic disorder, and bipolar disorder NOS. Mood disorder can also be caused by a general medical condition.

Morphine. See Opioids.

MRI. See Magnetic Resonance Imaging.

Narcolepsy. Narcolepsy is a sleep disorder characterized by irresistible attacks of sleep that occur daily for at least three months. There may also be brief episodes of loss of muscle tone, hypnagogic hallucinations, sleep paralysis, or the recurrent intrusion of elements of rapid eye movement (REM) sleep into the transition between sleep and wakefulness.

Neuron. A neuron is a nerve cell. Neurons are found in both the central nervous system (CNS) and the peripheral nervous system (PNS). Neurons are composed of a cell body, an axon, and a dendrite. Neurotransmitters or chemical messengers are located in the synapse between neurons.

Neuropathic Pain. Neuropathic pain is a type of pain that is characterized as burning or shooting and is often associated with numbness. It often responds best to tricyclic antidepressants and anticonvulsants.

Neurosis. Neurosis is an old term that is less frequently used today. It refers to emotional maladaptations that are believed to arise from unconscious conflict.

Neurotransmitters. Neurotransmitters are chemical messengers—amino acids or amines—that influence behavior and emotions. They are located in the synapses between nerve cells. There are more than two hundred different neurotransmitters. Among the most important are serotonin, norepinephrine, dopamine, acetylcholine, gamma-aminobutyric acid (GABA), and endorphins. Some of these, such as GABA, are fast acting, and drugs that affect them, such as minor tranquilizers, act quickly. Other neurotransmitters, such as serotonin, are slow acting, and drugs, such as the antidepressants, that affect them have a slower onset of action.

When an electrical impulse reaches the presynaptic axon terminal where the neurotransmitters are stored, they are released. Most drugs that act in the central nervous system do so by initially altering neurotransmitters, which then causes a cascade of chemical reactions in the brain to produce the desired results. The neurotransmitters diffuse across the synapse and are taken up at a postreceptor site. Then a secondary messenger is produced and ultimately the DNA command center of the cell is altered. The cascade of chemical reactions that follows ultimately alters emotions and behavior.

Norepinephrine (NE). Norepinephrine is a neurotransmitter of the nervous system that is involved in attention, concentration, focus, motivation, memory, and energy. Some of the drugs that are used for ADHD work in part by either the releasing and/or blocking of NE at the presynaptic terminal. Some antidepressants such as venlafaxine (Effexor) work in part by the blocking of norepinephrine at the presynaptic terminal. Other antidepressants such as reboxetine (Vestra) work by the blockage of the reuptake of norepinephrine alone at the presynaptic terminal.

Norepinephrine Reuptake Inhibitor (NRI). As the name implies, these drugs work by blocking the reuptake of norepinephrine. An NRI such as Strattera is used in ADHD. Another NRI, such as Vestra, may have an antidepressant effect.

Nucleus Accumbens. The nucleus accumbens is that part of the limbic system of the brain that has to do with pain and pleasure. It plays a role in addictions.

Object Relations. The term *object relations* refers to the emotional bond between an individual and another person. Some depressed individuals have unresolved problems with object relations of their youth.

Obsession. The term *obsession* is officially used in obsessive-compulsive anxiety disorder (OCD) and obsessive-compulsive personality disorder (OCPD). In the anxiety definition of OCD it refers to persistent, unwanted, recurrent thoughts and worries. In OCPD it refers to maladaptive patterns of behavior such that the individual is preoccupied with rules, regulations, details, and being pedantic, parsimonious, pecuniary, perfectionistic, inflexible, and overly conscious.

Obsessive-Compulsive Disorder (OCD). OCD is an anxiety disorder characterized by recurrent thoughts or repetitive actions. Although the client knows the thoughts are extreme, he or she continues with them. The thoughts may center around a fear of germs, violence, symmetry, or theological issues, for example. The compulsion may center on checking, counting, hand washing, or putting things in order. Some individuals with major depressive disorder have comorbid OCD.

Obsessive-Compulsive Personality Disorder (OCPD). Obsessive-compulsive personality disorder is characterized by maladaptive behavior patterns rather than symptoms. These patterns include recurrent thoughts and repetitive actions, which may appear as being detail oriented, perfectionistic, stubborn, rigid, and inflexible.

Off-Label. Off-label refers to the use of a drug for a purpose other than that for which it is officially approved. For example, Depakote, originally an anticonvulsant medication dating back to the 1960s, was effectively used off-label for years for its mood stabilizing effects in bipolar disorder. It was not until the 1990s that it was officially approved for use in bipolar disorder and migraine headaches.

Opioids. Opioids may come from naturally occurring substances, such as opium, morphine, or codeine; from synthetic substances, such as Darvon (propoxyphene), Demerol (meperidine), or Dolophine (methadone); or from semi-synthetic substances, such as heroin, Dilaudid (hydromorphine), or Percodan (oxycodone). They can be used appropriately by medical doctors in the treatment of pain, and they can also be abused. They may produce a lifting of mood and calming effect. With intoxication they may cause sedation, decreased respiration, slow heart rate, low body temperature, pinpoint pupils, constipation, and euphoria. Withdrawal symptoms include diarrhea, vomiting, muscle cramps, yawning, dilated pupils, achiness, and rhinorrhea. The opioids such as endorphins, enkephalins, and dynorphins are natural agonists at opioid receptors. The drug morphine and related narcotic pain-relieving drugs act at opioid receptors. During times of stress or pain, our own endogenous opioids act at opiate receptors. Narcotic pain medications can be addicting.

Oppositional Defiant Disorder. Oppositional defiant disorder is a persistent pattern of defiant behavior in children with possible issues of temper, arguing, being easily annoyed, blaming, anger, and vindictiveness.

Orgasm. Orgasm is the climax of the sexual response cycle. It is often impaired in depression.

Orthomolecular Treatment. Orthomolecular treatment is based on the belief that twisted molecules cause psychiatric disorders and that vitamins, herbs, hormones, and diets can cure the problems.

Panic Disorder. Panic disorder is an anxiety disorder characterized by extreme anxiety and such symptoms as a rapid heartbeat, trembling, sweating, shortness of breath, chest discomfort, nausea, dizziness, feelings of unreality or detachment, fear of going insane, fear of dying, hot flashes or chills, and a feeling of choking. It is more common in women, and the average age of onset is twenty-five years. It occurs more often in identical (monozygotic) versus nonidentical (dizygotic) twins. A recent stress such as marital separation may be a precipitant.

Parasympathetic Nervous System. The parasympathetic nervous system is one of two divisions of the autonomic nervous system; the other being the sympathetic nervous system. It slows the heart rate, increases gland activity, relaxes the sphincter muscle, and increases intestinal activity.

Partial Agonist. A partial agonist is a drug that does not produce maximal effects.

Peripheral Nervous System (PNS). The peripheral nervous system is that part of the nervous system outside of the central nervous system (CNS) or outside of the brain and spinal cord. It consists of the autonomic nervous system and somatic nervous system. The autonomic nervous system consists of the sympathetic and parasympathetic nervous systems, which control glandular secretions, cardiac muscle contractions, and muscle contractions. The divisions of the autonomic nervous system—sympathetic and parasympathetic—generally oppose each other. The somatic nervous system is responsible for voluntary movement of skeletal muscles and conducts sensory information. Acetylcholine and norepinephrine are the neurotransmitters of the autonomic nervous system. Acetylcholine is also the neurotransmitter of the somatic nervous system.

Personality. Personality is the outward expression of the mind, emotion, and will, which distinguish behavior.

Personality Disorder. Personality disorders are characterized by long-lasting, maladaptive patterns of behavior and may include areas of cognition, affectivity, interpersonal functioning, and impulse control. The borderline, histrionic, narcissistic, and antisocial personality disorders are emotional and dramatic and more likely to present with depression. The obsessive-compulsive, dependent, and avoidant personality disorders are more likely to present with anxiety.

PET Scan. See Positron Emission Tomography.

Pineal Gland. The pineal gland is that part of the brain that secretes melatonin, which controls the onset of puberty and plays a role in sleep.

Pituitary Gland. The pituitary gland is that part of the brain that controls endocrine functions and as such has broad implications in emotions and stress. It is located just below the hypothalamus.

Placebo. A placebo is an inert substance that is used in place of a known physiologically effective medication. What is interesting is that perhaps upward of 30 percent of people with depression may respond to a placebo. What is even more interesting is that PET scans document beneficial antidepressant effects of placebos. For an antidepressant to be approved, it must have around a 50 percent beneficial response rate; otherwise it would be no better than a placebo. Placebos demonstrate that we have our own powerful chemical messengers in the brain that are released through hope, belief, and choices.

Positron Emission Tomography (PET). A PET scan is a brain imaging device. Through injected radioactive isotope, glucose consumption can be measured in different parts of the brain. Thus it maps brain functioning and as such is proving useful in the evaluation of depression, ADHD, bipolar disorder, schizophrenia, dementia, and other psychiatric conditions.

Posttraumatic Stress Disorder (PTSD). PTSD is an anxiety disorder precipitated by experiencing or witnessing an event in which life was threatened with the result of an intense fear. It is characterized by recurrent recollections and dreams of the event, persistent avoidance of any stimuli associated with the event, diminished interest in life, feelings of detachment, a sense of a foreshortened future, and persistent symptoms of increased arousal, such as difficulty sleeping, anger, difficulty concentrating, and hypervigilance.

Pressured Speech. Pressured speech is rapid speech that is seen, for example, in the manic phase of manic-depressive disorder.

Primary Insomnia. Primary insomnia refers to difficulty initiating or maintaining sleep for at least one month. The insomnia causes significant disruption of social or occupational functioning.

Projection. Projection is a defense mechanism whereby one attributes his or her faults to another. For example, if a depressed individual fears becoming close to others, the individual may imagine that no one wants to be friends with him or her.

Psychiatric Medications. Psychiatric medications are used for various symptoms and mental disorders. See appendix S.

Psychiatrist. A psychiatrist is a medical doctor, a licensed physician, who specializes in mental issues. He or she has spent several years beyond the medical degree training in specialty training in psychiatry.

Psychologist. A psychologist usually has the doctor of philosophy or doctor of psychology degree and is trained in psychology.

Psychosis. Psychosis is a loss of touch with reality. It is a thought disorder caused by abnormalities in brain chemistry and structure in which perceptions of reality are distorted. Symptoms may include hearing or seeing things not present. Psychotic disorders can include schizophrenia, severe bipolar disorder, a brief psychotic episode, major depressive disorder with psychosis, delusional disorder, psychosis secondary to substance abuse, and psychosis secondary to a medical condition. There are new and effective medical treatments today to help individuals with psychosis.

Psychostimulants. Psychostimulants are drugs of abuse that include cocaine and crack, amphetamine, and caffeine. They can produce euphoria, restlessness, and rapid heartbeat. They can also produce heart arrhythmias, seizures, stroke, or coma. Withdrawal symptoms include fatigue, agitation, and depression.

Psychotherapy. Psychotherapy is a generic term for the treatment of emotional issues. There are different types of psychotherapy. Some are behaviorally focused; some are cognitive or thinking focused; and some are insight focused.

Rationalization. Rationalization is a defense mechanism whereby one deals with emotional conflict and pain by choosing unacceptable behavior and convincing oneself that it is reasonable. This then produces even more emotional pain. For example, an individual in conflict with his wife may choose to have an affair, convincing himself that it is the reasonable thing to do.

Reality Therapy. Developed by William Glasser in the 1960s, reality therapy focuses on encouraging responsible behavior.

Sad Affect. A sad affect, typical of depression, is a melancholic or sad facial expression. The corners of the mouth may turn down and the eyes may appear sad.

Schizoaffective Disorder. Schizoaffective disorder is a mental disorder that has symptoms characterized by both schizophrenia and affective symptoms of depression or mania.

Schizophrenia. Schizophrenia is a mental disorder characterized by such symptoms as delusions, hallucinations, disorganized speech, disorganized behavior, and marked social and occupational dysfunction.

Sedative-Hypnotics. Sedative-hypnotics can be used appropriately by medical doctors in the treatment of insomnia and anxiety or they can also become drugs of abuse. They include anxiolytic benzodiazepines, such as alprazolam (Xanax), chlordiazepoxide (Librium), clonazepam (Klonopin), clorazepate (Tranxene), diazepam (Valium), halazepam (Paxipam), and lorazepam (Ativan); benzodiazepines used for insomnia, such as flurazepam (Dalmane), estazolam (ProSom), quazepam (Doral), temazepam (Restoral), and triazolam (Halcion); and barbiturates, such as amobarbital (Amytal) and pentobarbital (Nembutal). In intoxication, symptoms include sedation, slurred speech, ataxia, confusion, and coma. Withdrawal symptoms include anxiety, tremor, rapid heartbeat, high blood pressure, nausea, vomiting, and headache.

Selective Serotonin Reuptake Inhibitors—(SSRI). SSRIs are a type of antidepressant so named because mainly they selectively block the reuptake of one neurotransmitter, serotonin.

Serotonin (5HT). Serotonin is a neurotransmitter involved in mood regulation, obsessive worry, migraine headaches, pain perception, and hunger. There are several different serotonin receptors. Selective serotonin reuptake inhibitor antidepressants work initially by blocking the reuptake and therefore degradation of serotonin at the presynaptic terminal. Thus more serotonin is made available. Also, some of the medications for migraines work by being selective agonists at serotonin receptor sites on the postreceptor side (5HT1B and 5HT1D).

Serotonin/Norepinephrine Reuptake Inhibitor (SNRI). An SNRI, Effexor, works as an antidepressant by blocking the reuptake of both serotonin and norepinephrine as the dose is increased. It also has some blocking of dopamine as the dose is increased even higher.

Sleep. Sleep is the recurring rest for the body during which there is little conscious thought. Sleep consists of REM (rapid eye movement or dream) sleep and NREM (non-rapid eye movement) sleep. In depression one often has more early morning awakening (EMA); whereas in anxiety there is more difficulty falling asleep (DFA). However, since depression and anxiety often coexist, both EMA and DFA may be present in depressed individuals. Also, depressed individuals often have a shortened REM latency and begin to dream more quickly.

Sleeping Pills. See Sedative-Hypnotics.

Social Phobia. Social phobia is an anxiety disorder characterized by an excessive, persistent, and recognizably unreasonable fear of social or performance situations.

Soma. Soma refers to the body. Depression may have somatic or physical symptoms.

Somatic Nervous System. The somatic nervous system is one of two divisions of the peripheral nervous system; the other being the autonomic nervous system. It contains the nerves that enervate the skeletal muscles of the body and is responsible for voluntary movement.

Somatization. Somatization is a defense mechanism whereby one deals with emotional conflicts by displacing the tension to the body and developing numerous physical symptoms. For example, depressed individuals may develop an increase in body aches and pains.

Specific Phobia. Specific phobia is an anxiety disorder characterized by an excessive, persistent, and recognizably unreasonable fear of a specific object or situation such as flying, animals, needles, or heights.

Stress. Stress refers to a mental tension caused by a known environmental event. Stress points more to the external stressors, whereas worry points more to the internal uneasiness.

Substance P. Substance P is a neurotransmitter or chemical messenger in the synapses of the nervous system. Substance P was originally thought to be mainly involved in the pain response. Now it is considered to be involved in mood regulation. Substance P antagonists may improve mood as well as relieve pain. Substance P belongs to a new class of peptide neurotransmitters known as neurokinins.

Sympathetic Nervous System. The sympathetic nervous system is one part of the autonomic nervous system; the other being the parasympathetic nervous system, which generally opposes the sympathetic nervous system. The sympathetic nervous system prepares the body for emergency situations. Emergency, excitement, exercise, embarrassment, stress, fear, and worry all set off sympathetic responses. Activation of the sympathetic nervous system with subsequent release of adrenaline from the adrenal medulla sets in motion a series of physiological responses collectively called the alarm reaction or fight-or-flight response. With stress, the amygdala signals the hypothalamus, which signals the sympathetic nervous system.

Synapse. Synapses are the junctions between nerve cells. Neurotransmitters or chemical messages are released at the presynaptical terminal secondary to an electrical impulse. The neurotransmitter then diffuses across the gap or synapse and attaches to a postsynaptic receptor site in another neuron.

Tension Headaches. Tension headaches are headaches that are characterized by being tension induced, chronic, bilateral, diffuse, steady, often located in the front or back of the head, and producing a bandlike pressure. More than 90 percent of people have tension headaches at some time. They occur more frequently in those with mood and anxiety disorders.

Thalamus. The thalamus is the part of the brain that relays sensory input to the cerebral cortex. It also plays a role in emotions, memory, cognition, awareness, and pain.

Thyroid (T3 and T4). Thyroid is a hormone. T3 (Cytomel) is a thyroid hormone that has been used off-label in unipolar, resistant depression. T4 (Synthroid) has been used off-label in bipolar disorder.

Tic. A tic is an involuntary, stereotyped movement of a group of muscles that occurs during times of stress or organic disease such as Tourette's syndrome.

Tolerance. Tolerance refers to a decreased response to a drug so that an ever-increasing dose of the drug must be given to achieve the same effect. Alcohol can produce a tolerance. Some minor tranquilizers at times can produce a tolerance.

Transference. Transference refers to the automatic assignment to an individual today of feelings that were held toward an individual in the past. For example, a depressed individual automatically and without apparent reason may feel anger toward an authority figure today if an authority figure in his or her past was harsh.

Tricyclic Antidepressant (TCA). TCAs are a type of antidepressants so named because of their tricyclic structure. They are older antidepressants, introduced in the 1950s, and are used less today.

Unconscious. The unconscious is that part of the mind that is present but ordinarily not subject to awareness. Many details of things we learned or experienced in the past are in the unconscious.

Withdrawal. Withdrawal is a defense mechanism whereby one deals with tension or emotional conflict by withdrawing socially. Depressed

individuals often withdraw as they become more depressed, and the more
they withdraw the more depressed they become. Withdrawal also refers
to the state and symptoms that occur when a person no longer takes a
substance of dependency.

Worry. Worry is to be troubled, bothered, and uneasy in one's mind.

▧ Key to Abbreviations

ACh acetylcholine

Alpha adrenergic

DA dopamine

EPS extrapyraminal symptoms

H histamine

MAOI monoamine oxidase inhibitor

N norepinephrine

NDRI norepinephrine/dopamine reuptake inhibitor

NE norepinephrine

NRI norepinephrine reuptake inhibitor

P450 enzyme system in liver responsible for metabolizing most
drugs

S serotonin

SNRI serotonin/norepinephrine reuptake inhibitor

SSRI selective serotonin reuptake inhibitor

TCA tricyclic antidepressant

T_3/T_4 thyroid

5HT serotonin

5HT2 postreceptor serotonin site

5HT1A postreceptor serotonin site

Bibliography

■ Medical Sources

Abramowicz, Mark, ed. "Ginkgo Biloba for Dementia." *The Medical Letter* 40, no. 1029 (19 June 1998): 63–64.

———, ed. "St. John's Wort." *The Medical Letter* 39, no. 1014 (21 Nov. 1997): 107–8.

Albers, Lawrence J., Rhoda K. Hahn, and Christopher Reist. *Current Clinical Strategies: Handbook of Psychiatric Drugs.* Laguna Hills, Calif.: Current Clinical Strategies Publishing, 2001.

Allen, James R., and Barbara Ann Allen. *Guide to Psychiatry.* New York: Medical Examination Publishing, 1978.

"Alzheimer's Disease: The Search for Causes and Treatments: Part II." *Harvard Mental Health Letter* 17: 4–5.

American Psychiatric Association. *Quick Reference to the Diagnostic Criteria from DSM-IV.* Washington, D.C.: American Psychiatric Association, 1994.

American Psychiatric Association 2001 Annual Meeting New Research Abstracts. Washington, D.C.: American Psychiatric Association, 2001.

Anderson, Lynn G. "University Researchers Confirm Three Most Important Factors in Weight Loss." *Journal of Longevity* 6 (2000).

Andreasen, Nancy D., and Donald W. Black. *Introductory Textbook of Psychiatry.* 2d ed. Washington, D.C.: American Psychiatric Press, 1995.

Arky, Ronald, medical consultant. *2001 Physician's Desk Reference.* Montvale: Medical Economics, 1997.

Ayd, Frank J., Jr. "Expanding Clinical Indications and Treatment Strategies for Psychopharmacology in the New Millennium." *International Drug Therapy Newsletter* 35, no. 10 (Oct. 2000): 73.

———. "Omega-3 Fatty Acids–Induced Hypomania/Mania." *International Drug Therapy Newsletter* 35, no. 10 (Oct. 2000): 73–74.

Bannister, Roger. *Brain's Clinical Neurology*. 5th ed. Oxford: Oxford University Press, 1978.

Beers, Mark H., and Robert Berkow, eds. *The Merck Manual of Diagnosis and Therapy*. 17th ed. Whitehouse Station: Merck Research Laboratories, 1999.

Benjamin, Ludy T., Jr., J. Roy Hopkins, and Jack R. Nation. *Psychology*. 3d ed. New York: McMillan, 1994.

Bergin, James D. *Medicine Recall*. Baltimore: Lippincott Williams and Wilkins, 1997.

Bernstein, Carol A., Brian J. Ladds, Ann S. Maloney, and Elyse D. Weiner. *On Call Psychiatry*. 1997. Reprint, Philadelphia: W. B. Saunders, 2001.

Braunwald, Eugene, Kurt J. Isselbacher, Jean D. Wilson et al., eds. *Harrison's Principles of Internal Medicine*. 13th ed. New York: McGraw-Hill, 1994.

———, eds. *Harrison's Principles of Internal Medicine: Companion Handbook*. 14th ed. New York: McGraw-Hill, 1998.

Brett, A. S. "A Simple Treatment for Migraine Headaches . . . and Simple Prophylaxis for Migraine." *Journal Watch for Psychiatry* 4, no. 4 (April 1998): 34.

———. "More on Estrogen and Cognitive Function." *Journal Watch* 21, no. 5 (1 March 2001): 37–38.

Carey, Charles F., Hans H. Lee, and Keith F. Woeltje, eds. *The Washington Manual of Medical Therapeutics*. 29th ed. Philadelphia: Lippincott-Raven, 1998.

Carlson, Neil R. *Psychology: The Science of Behavior*. Boston: Allyn and Bacon, 1990.

Charney, Dennis S., Eric J. Nestler, and Benjamin S. Bunny, eds. *Neurobiology of Mental Illness*. Oxford: Oxford University Press, 1999.

Conners, C. Keith, and Juliet L. Jett. *Attention Deficit Hyperactivity Disorder (In Adults and Children): The Latest Assessment and Treatment Strategies*. Kansas City: Compact Clinicals, 1999.

Coppen, A. "Folic Acid Enhances Antidepressant Response." *Psychiatric Drug Alerts* 14: 1–8.

Coyle, J. "Seeing a Placebo Work in the Brain." *Journal Watch Psychiatry* 7, no. 11 (Nov. 2001): 85–86.

Criders, Andrew B., George R. Goethals, Robert D. Kavanaugh, and Paul R. Solomon. *Psychology*. 3d ed. Glenview: Scott, Foresman and Company, 1989.

DiCaprio, Nicholas S. *Personality Theories: Guides to Living*. Philadelphia: W. B. Saunders, 1974.

"The Emerging Recognition of Herb-Drug Interactions with a Focus on St. John's Wort." *Psychopharmacology Bulletin* 35: 53–64.

Ewald, Gregory A., and Clark R. McKenzie, eds. *The Washington Manual: Manual of Medical Therapeutics*. 29th ed. Boston: Little, Brown, 1995.

Fadem, Barbara, and Steven Simring. *Psychiatry Recall.* Baltimore: Williams and Wilkins, 1997.

Feldman, Robert S. *Essentials of Understanding Psychology.* New York: McGraw-Hill, 1989.

Feltman, John, ed. *Prevention's Giant Book of Health Facts.* Emmaus: Rodale, 1991.

First, Michael B., ed. *Diagnostic and Statistical Manual of Mental Disorders.* 4th ed. Washington, D.C.: American Psychiatric Association, 1994.

Flaherty, Joseph A., John M. Davis, and Philip G. Janicak, eds. *Psychiatry: Diagnosis and Treatment.* 2d ed. Norwalk: Appleton and Lange, 1993.

"Folic Acid Enhances Antidepressant Response." *Psychiatry Drug Alerts* 14, sample issue: 1.

"Ginkgo Biloba for Dementia." *Medical Letter* 40 (June 1998): 63–64.

Gitlin, Michael J. *The Psychotherapist's Guide to Psychopharmacology.* 2d ed. New York: The Free Press, 1996.

Glasser, William, *Reality Therapy: A New Approach to Psychiatry.* New York: Harper and Row, 1965.

Goldberger, Leo, and Shlomo Breznitz, eds. *Handbook of Stress: Theoretical and Clinical Aspects.* New York: The Free Press, 1982.

Goldman, H. H., ed. *Review of General Psychiatry.* 2d ed. Los Altos: Lange Medical Publications, 1988.

Gorman, Kristine. "Herbal Warning." *Time* (18 June 2001).

Grinspoon, Lester, ed. "Alzheimer's Disease: The Search for Causes and Treatments—Part II." *The Harvard Mental Health Letter* 15, no. 3 (September 1998): 1–5.

———. "How Does Melatonin Affect Sleep?" *The Harvard Mental Health Letter* 12, no. 12 (June 1996): 8.

———. "Inositol for OCD." *The Harvard Mental Health Letter* 13, no. 6 (December 1996): 7.

———. "What Is a Nocebo?" *The Harvard Mental Health Letter* 14, no. 1 (July 1997): 8.

Guyton, Arthur C. *Textbook of Medical Physiology.* Philadelphia: W. B. Saunders, 1991.

Hahn, Rhonda K., Christopher Reist, and Lawrence J. Albers. *Psychiatry: 1999–2000 Edition.* Laguna Hills: Current Clinical Strategies, 2000.

Hirsch, Michael. "What Are the Uses and Dangers of Kava?" *Harvard Mental Health Letter* 17: 8.

Hollander, Eric, and Cheryl M. Wong. *Contemporary Diagnosis and Management of Common Psychiatric Disorders.* Newton: Handbooks in Health Care, 2000.

Hyman, Steven E., George W. Arana, and Jerrold F. Rosenbaum. *Handbook of Psychiatric Drug Therapy*. 3d ed. Boston: Little, Brown, 1995.

Jacob, Leonard S. *Pharmacology*. 4th ed. Baltimore: Williams and Wilkins, 1996.

Janicak, Philip G. *Handbook of Psychopharmacotherapy*. Baltimore: Lippincott Williams and Wilkins, 1999.

Kaplan, Harold I., and Benjamin J. Sadock. *Comprehensive Textbook of Psychiatry*. 7th ed. Vols. 1 and 2. Baltimore: Lippincott Williams and Wilkins, 2000.

———. *Pocket Handbook of Primary Care Psychiatry*. Baltimore: Williams and Wilkins, 1996.

———. *Pocket Handbook of Psychiatric Treatment*. 2d ed. Baltimore: Williams and Wilkins, 1996.

———. *Synopsis of Psychiatry, Behavioral Sciences, Clinical Psychiatry*. 7th ed. Baltimore: Williams and Wilkins, 1994.

Kaufman, David Myland. *Clinical Neurology for Psychiatrists*. 3d ed. Philadelphia: W. B. Saunders, 1990.

Keck, Paul, and Susan McElroy. *Overview of CNS Disorders 2001*. New York: McMahon, 2000.

Kleinmuntz, Benjamin. *Essentials of Abnormal Psychology*. New York: Harper and Row, 1974.

Leonard, Brian E. *Fundamentals of Psychopharmacology*. 2d ed. Chichester: Wiley, 1997.

Lewis, Melvin, ed. *Child and Adolescent Psychiatry: A Comprehensive Textbook*. Baltimore: Williams and Wilkins, 1991.

Lezak, Muriel Deutsch. *Neuropsychological Assessment*. 3d ed. Oxford: Oxford University Press, 1995.

Long, Donlin M. *Contemporary Diagnosis and Management of Pain*. 2d ed. Newtown: Handbooks in Health Care, 2000.

Lullmann, Heinz, Klaus Mohr, Albrecht Ziegler, and Detlef Bieger. *Color Atlas of Pharmacology*. New York: Thieme Medical Publishers, 1993.

Marangell, Lauren B., James M. Martinez, Jonathan M. Silver, and Stuart C. Yudofsky. *Concise Guide to Psychopharmacology*. Washington, D.C.: American Psychiatric Publishing, 2002.

Marieb, Elaine N. *Human Anatomy and Physiology*. 2d ed. Redwood City: Benjamin Cummings Publishing, 1992.

McCarthy, Malia, Mary B. O'Malley, and Sanjay Saint. *Saint-Frances Guide to Psychiatry*. Baltimore: Lippincott Williams and Wilkins, 2001.

McNeil, Elton B., and Zick Rubin. *The Psychology of Being Human*. San Francisco: Canfield Press, 1977.

Miller, James, and Nathan Fountain. *Neurology Recall*. Baltimore: Williams and Wilkins, 1997.

Minirth, Frank B., and Paul D. Meier. *Happiness Is a Choice: A Manual on the Symptoms, Causes, and Cures of Depression*. Grand Rapids: Baker, 1978.

Morelli, Vincent, and Roger J. Zoorob. "Alternative Therapies, Part I: Depression, Diabetes, Obesity." *American Family Physician* 62, no. 5 (1 Sept. 2000): 1051–58.

"Natural Medicines in Clinical Management." *Pharmacist's Letter/Prescriber's Letter Education Booklet* (Spring 2001): 1–36.

Nemeroff, Charles B., and Thomas W. Uhde, eds. *Depression and Anxiety*. Vol. 12. New York: Wiley-Liss, 2000.

Nicoli, Armand M., Jr., ed. *The New Harvard Guide to Psychiatry*. Cambridge: Belknap Press, 1988.

Olson, William H., Roger A. Brumback, Iyer Vasudeva, and Generso Gascon. *Handbook of Symptom-Oriented Neurology*. St. Louis: Mosby, 1994.

Psychopharmacology Update 1997. Houston: Department of Psychiatry, Baylor College of Medicine, 1997.

Psychopharmacology Update 1998. Houston: Department of Psychiatry, Baylor College of Medicine, 1998.

Psychopharmacology Update 1999. Houston: Department of Psychiatry, Baylor College of Medicine, 1999.

Psychopharmacology Update 2000. Houston: Department of Psychiatry, Baylor College of Medicine, 2000.

Psychopharmacology Update 2001. Houston: Department of Psychiatry, Baylor College of Medicine, 2001.

Psychopharmacology Update 2002. Houston: Department of Psychiatry, Baylor College of Medicine, 2002.

Ramachandran, Anand. *Pharmacology Recall*. Baltimore: Lippincott Williams and Wilkins, 2000.

Rassmussen, S. A., J. L. Eisen, and M. T. Pato. "Current Issues in the Pharmacological Management of Obsessive Compulsive Disorder." *Journal of Clinical Psychiatry* (1993): 4–9.

Restak, Richard M. *The Brain*. Toronto: Bantam, 1984.

———. *The Modular Brain*. New York: Scribner's, 1994.

———. *The Secret Life of the Brain*. The Dana Press and the Joseph Henry Press, 2001.

Rutter, Michael, Eric Taylor, and Lionel Hersov, eds. *Child and Adolescent Psychiatry: Modern Approaches*. Oxford: Blackwell Scientific Publications, 1994.

Sadock, Benjamin J., and Virginia A. Sadock, eds. *Kaplan and Sadock's Comprehensive Textbook of Psychiatry*. 7th ed. Vol. 1. Philadelphia: Lippincott Williams and Wilkins, 2000.

———. *Kaplan and Sadock's Comprehensive Textbook of Psychiatry.* 7th ed. Vol. 2. Philadelphia: Lippincott Williams and Wilkins, 2000.

Sahley, Billie Jay. *GABA: The Anxiety Amino Acid.* San Antonio: Pain and Stress Publications, 2001.

"St. John's Wort." *Medical Letter* 39 (Nov. 1997): 107–8.

"St. John's Wort." *Psychopharmacology Update* 12 (2001): 7.

"SAM-e: A 1950's Discovery Reappears to Treat Mild to Moderate Depression." *Psychopharmacology Update* 10, no. 6 (June 1999): 1, 6.

"SAM-e for Depression." *Harvard Mental Health Letter* 17: 4–5.

"SAMe for Depression." *Medical Letter* 41, no. 1065 (5 Nov. 1999): 107–8.

Schatzberg, Alan F., and Charles DeBattista. *The Black Book of Psychotropic Dosing and Monitoring 2002.* New York: MBL Communications, 2002.

Schillenberg, R. "Chasteberry, Vitex." *Psychopharmacology Update* 12 (2001): 4.

Scully, James H. *The National Medical Series for Independent Study: Psychiatry.* 3d ed. Baltimore: Williams and Wilkins, 1996.

Shaner, Roderick. *Psychiatry: Board Review Series.* Baltimore: Williams and Wilkins, 1997.

Smith, James, and M. Smith. "Herbal Toxicity." *Directions in Psychiatry* 19 (1999): 363–73.

Sneed, Sharon M., and Joe S. McIlhaney. *PMS: What It Is and What You Can Do about It.* Grand Rapids: Baker, 1988.

Stahl, Stephen M. *Essential Psychopharmacology: Neuroscientific Basis and Practical Applications.* 2d ed. Cambridge: Cambridge University Press, 2000.

Thies, Roger, and Robert J. Person, eds. *Physiology.* New York: Springer-Verlag, 1987.

Tierney, Lawrence M., Jr., Stephen J. McPhee, and Maxine A. Papadakis. *2003 Current Medical Diagnosis and Treatment.* 42d ed. New York: McGraw-Hill, 2003.

Tilkian, Sarko M., Mary Boudreau Conover, and Ara G. Tilkian. *Clinical Implications of Laboratory Tests.* St. Louis: C. V. Mosby, 1996.

Tomb, David A. *Psychiatry.* House Officer Series. 5th ed. Baltimore: Williams and Wilkins, 1995.

Tortora, Gerard J., and Sandra Reynolds Grabowski. *Principles of Anatomy and Physiology.* 8th ed. New York: Harper Collins, 1996.

"Troubling News on Kava—Plus a Look at Herbals in Drinks." *The Brown University Child and Adolescent Psychopharmacology Update* 4, no. 3 (March 2002): 1, 5–7.

"The Updated Therapeutic Uses of Herbs: Part 1." *Stockton: Pharmacist's Letter/ Prescriber's Letter Continuing Education Booklet* (2000).

"The Updated Therapeutic Uses of Herbs: Part 2." *Stockton: Pharmacist's Letter/ Prescriber's Letter Continuing Education Booklet* (2000).

Weber, Wim. "Gingko Not Effective for Memory Loss in Elderly." *The Lancet* 356 (Oct. 2000): 1333.

Weiner, Howard L., and Lawrence P. Levitt. *Neurology.* 5th ed. Baltimore: Williams and Wilkins, 1994.

———. *Neurology for the House Officer.* 4th ed. Baltimore: Williams and Wilkins, 1989.

Wortman, Camille, and Elizabeth F. Loftus. *Psychology.* New York: McGraw-Hill, 1992.

Yudofsky, Stuart C., and Robert E. Hales. *The American Psychiatric Press Textbook of Neuropsychiatry.* 3d ed. Washington, D.C.: American Psychiatric Association, 1997.

Zhdanova, I., R. Wurtman, and C. H. Green. "How Does Melatonin Affect Sleep?" *Harvard Mental Health Letter* 12 (1996): 8.

■ Christian/Theological Sources

Bainton, Roland H. *Here I Stand: A Life of Martin Luther.* New York: Mentor Books, 1950.

Berkhof, Louis. *Systematic Theology.* Carlisle, Pa.: Banner of Truth Trust, 1958.

Berry, George R. *The Interlinear Greek-English New Testament with Lexicon and Synonyms.* Grand Rapids: Zondervan, 1976.

Bounds, E. M. *Power through Prayer.* Grand Rapids: Baker, 1991.

Brown, Colin, ed. *The New International Dictionary of New Testament Theology.* Vols. 1–3. Grand Rapids: Zondervan, 1979.

Chafer, Lewis Sperry. *Grace, the Glorious Theme.* Grand Rapids: Academie Books/ Zondervan, 1950.

———. *Major Bible Themes.* Grand Rapids: Zondervan, 1974.

Coleman, Robert E. *The Master Plan of Evangelism.* Grand Rapids: Revell, 1964.

Collins, Gary. *Overcoming Anxiety.* Santa Ana: Vision House, 1973.

Design for Discipleship: A Bible Study Series. Colorado Springs: The Navigators, 1973.

Dillow, Linda. *Creative Counterpart.* Nashville: Thomas Nelson, 1977.

Douglas, J. D., ed. *The New Bible Dictionary.* Grand Rapids: Eerdmans, 1962.

Ellicott, Charles John, ed. *Ellicott's Commentary on the Whole Bible.* Grand Rapids: Zondervan, 1981.

Ellicott, Charles John. *Ellicott's Bible Commentary in One Volume*. Grand Rapids: Zondervan, 1971.

Erickson, Millard J. *Christian Theology*. 2d ed. Grand Rapids: Baker, 1998.

Gaebelein, Frank E., ed. *The Expositor's Bible Commentary*. Grand Rapids: Zondervan, 1981.

Grudem, Wayne. *Systematic Theology*. Grand Rapids: Zondervan, 1994.

Harrison, R. K. *Leviticus: An Introduction and Commentary*. Downers Grove: InterVarsity Press, 1980.

Henry, Matthew, and Thomas Scott. *Commentary on the Holy Bible*. Nashville: Thomas Nelson, 1979.

Ironside, H. A. *Full Assurance*. Chicago: Moody Press, 1937.

Little, Paul E. *Know What You Believe*. Wheaton: Scripture Press, 1970.

MacDonald, William. *Believer's Bible Commentary*. Nashville: Thomas Nelson, 1990.

McDowell, Josh. *Evidence That Demands a Verdict*. Vols. 1 and 2. Nashville: Thomas Nelson, 1993.

McGee, Robert S. *The Search for Significance*. Nashville: Word, 1998.

Miller, Basil W. *The Gold under the Grass*. Nashville: Cokesbury, 1930.

Minirth, Frank B., and Paul D. Meier. *Happiness Is a Choice: A Manual on the Symptoms, Causes, and Cures of Depression*. Grand Rapids: Baker, 1978.

Narramore, Bruce, and Bill Counts. *Freedom from Guilt*. Santa Ana: Vision House, 1974.

Nee, Watchman. *Christ, the Sum of All Spiritual Things*. New York: Christian Fellowship Publishers, 1973.

———. *Sit, Walk, Stand*. Wheaton: Tyndale, 1977.

Osbeck, Kenneth W. *101 Hymn Stories*. Grand Rapids: Kregel, 1982.

Pentecost, Dwight J. *Design for Discipleship*. Grand Rapids: Kregel, 1996.

Ryrie, Charles C. *Biblical Theology of the New Testament*. Chicago: Moody, 1959.

———. *So Great Salvation*. Wheaton: Victor, 1989.

———. *A Survey of Bible Doctrine*. Chicago: Moody, 1972.

Ryrie, Charles Caldwell, ed. *The Ryrie Study Bible, King James Version*. Chicago: Moody, 1978.

———. *The Ryrie Study Bible, New American Standard Version*. Chicago: Moody, 1976.

———. *The Ryrie Study Bible, New International Version.* Chicago: Moody, 1986.

Scofield, C. I., ed. *The New Scofield Study Bible.* Nashville: Thomas Nelson, 1982.

Smith, Jerome H., ed. *The New Treasury of Scripture Knowledge.* Nashville: Thomas Nelson, 1992.

Stoop, David. *Self Talk: Key to Personal Growth.* Old Tappan, N.J.: Revell, 1982.

Stoop, Jan, and David Stoop. *Saying Goodbye to Disappointments.* Nashville: Thomas Nelson, 1993.

Thieme, R. B., Jr. *The Biblical View of Sex, Love and Marriage.* Houston: Thieme, 1964.

Thomas, Ian W. *The Saving Life of Christ.* Grand Rapids: Zondervan, 1961.

Unger, Merril F. *Unger's Bible Handbook.* Chicago: Moody, 1967.

Vine, W. E. *An Expository Dictionary of New Testament Words.* Old Tappan, N.J.: Fleming H. Revell Co., 1966.

Vine, W. E., Merrill F. Unger, and William White, Jr. *Vine's Complete Expository Dictionary of Old and New Testament Words.* Nashville: Thomas Nelson, 1985.

Walvoord, John E., ed. *Christian Counseling for Contemporary Problems.* Dallas: Dallas Theological Seminary, 1968.

Walvoord, John F., and Roy B. Zuck. *The Bible Knowledge Commentary: New Testament Edition.* Wheaton: Victor, 1983.

Wheat, Ed, and Gaye Wheat. *Intended for Pleasure: Sex Technique and Sexual Fulfillment in Christian Marriage.* 3d ed. Grand Rapids: Revell, 1997.

Wheat, Ed, and Gloria Okes Perkins. *Love Life for Every Married Couple.* Grand Rapids: Zondervan, 1980.

Woodbridge, John D. *Great Leaders of the Christian Church.* Chicago: Moody, 1988.

Youngblood, Ronald F., ed. *Nelson's New Illustrated Bible Dictionary.* Nashville: Thomas Nelson, 1995.

Dr. Frank B. Minirth is a diplomate of the American Board of Psychiatry and Neurology, a diplomate of the American Board of Forensic Medicine, and certified by the American Society of Clinical Psychopharmacology. Holding doctorate degrees in medicine and theology, he has been in private practice in the Dallas area since 1975. He holds degrees from Arkansas State University, Arkansas School of Medicine, Dallas Theological Seminary, where he is an adjunct professor, and Christian Bible College.

Dr. Minirth is president of the Minirth Clinic, P.A., in Richardson, Texas; he is a consultant for the Minirth Christian Group at Green Oaks Behavioral Healthcare Services in Dallas, Texas, and the Minirth Christian Services at Millwood Hospital in Arlington, Texas; and he is heard weekly both locally and nationally on radio.

Dr. Minirth has authored or coauthored more than sixty books, many of which have been translated into foreign languages. Bestsellers include *Happiness Is a Choice, Love Is a Choice,* and *100 Ways to Overcome Depression.* He has more than four million books in print.

He and his wife of thirty-five years, Mary Alice, have five daughters.

For more information on the Minirth Clinic, call 1-888-646-4784, or visit the web site at www.minirthclinic.com.